The Official Guide

Visio 2000

John Hedtke &
Elisabeth Knottingham

Osborne/**McGraw-Hill**

Berkeley New York St. Louis San Francisco
Auckland Bogotá Hamburg London Madrid
Mexico City Milan Montreal New Delhi
Panama City Paris São Paulo
Singapore Sydney Tokyo Toronto

Osborne/**McGraw-Hill**
2600 Tenth Street
Berkeley, California 94710
U.S.A.

For information on translations or book distributors outside the U.S.A., or to arrange bulk purchase discounts for sales promotions, premiums, or fund-raisers, please contact Osborne/McGraw-Hill at the above address.

Visio 2000: The Official Guide

1234567890 AGM AGM 019876543210

ISBN 0-07-212075-4

Publisher: Brandon A. Nordin
Associate Publisher and
Editor-in-Chief: Scott Rogers
Acquisitions Editor: Megg Bonar
Project Editor: Ron Hull
Editorial Assistant: Stephane Thomas
Technical Editor: Charlie Zaragoza
Copy Editor: Kevin Murray
Proofreader: Stefany Otis
Indexer: Irv Hershman
Computer Designers: Dick Schwartz, Gary Corrigan
Illustrators: Brian Wells, Robert Hansen

This book was composed with Corel VENTURA™ Publisher.

To Garrick and Julia Damir on the occasion of their first anniversary.
John Hedtke

To Lonnie Foster, my loving husband, the light of my life.
Elisabeth Knottingham

Contents At A Glance

Contents

Acknowledgments

A book is created not just by the authors, but by the combined talents of a team working hard together. We would like to extend our sincerest thanks to everyone who helped us create the book you hold in your hands, because without the support of these fine people this book would never have happened. Thank you to:

Charlie Zaragoza, for performance above and beyond the call of duty. Charlie, you are THE MAN! We own you so much, not only for your vigilant technical support and your consistent follow through, but also for you last minute saves (like writing Chapter 10) as well as lots of other valuable assistance, without which this book would never would have been possible.

Lonnie Foster, for supporting both of us, for last minute computer magic, and for cat wrangling.

Constance Maytum, for an unwavering commitment to our success.

Rebecca and Guy Champ, for putting all the pieces back together.

Thank you to the huge list of people from Visio including:

Stacy Dellas and Lorrin Smith-Bates, for handling the paperwork and finding ways to make time in your schedules to help us.

Nanette Eaton, for insight and without whom this book would have been much harder.

John Bove, for assistance with all the legal details.

Mitch Boss, Dail Bridges, Jan Bultmann, Kris Dinkel, Janet Williams, Brady Wildermuth, Erin Schulz, Kevin E. Forbes, John Forbes, Jennifer M. Bruner, and Richard Miyauchi (our technical team), for digging up the answers to obscure questions and for amazing technical support. All of you performed amazing feats that will continue to stun us for years to come.

James Hedrick and Bill Holt, for staying late Friday night and answering weird questions about the CAD converter so we could keep working over the weekend.

Iain Heath, for reinstalling the entire system when we had screwed it up.

Troy Cameron Phillips, for burning our Gold CD (with a smile even!) after being up all night to RTM.

Troy Sandal, for being the one and only Mr. HTML.

Barry Allyn, for handling our setup and installation issues, and even coming to our home from the ship party to fix the mess we'd made.

And to the great people at *Visio SmartPages,* Steve Biehler, Lori Zentner, and Alan White, for adding part of Chapter 8 to their magazine and for dealing with us well during the crunch time.

A special thanks to all the outstanding people at Osborne/McGraw-Hill:

Brandon A. Nordin and Scott Rogers, for their continued support.

Megg Bonar, our acquisitions editor, for editorial duties extraordinaire, even from the far reaches of Utah.

Stephane Thomas, our editorial assistant, for keeping track of all the details and making sure we got it all done.

Ron Hull, our project editor, without who's inestimable assistance this book would not be the book it is.

Kevin Murray, our copy editor, for making sure we not only dotted our I's, but crossed our T's as well.

As well as the rest of our production team—this book would never have been completed without each and every one of you.

A big thanks to Simon Fraser at Espresso Splendido (the best espresso place in Seattle), for keeping our eyes open in the morning.

And lastly, thank you to the readers, for without you there would be no need of books.

Without all these people, and many more, you would not be holding this book. Our heartfelt thanks to all who saw us through this project; we owe you more than words can say.

Introduction

Welcome to *Visio 2000: The Official Guide*. This book shows you how to use Visio 2000 to create diagrams of all shapes and sizes.

Why This Book Is for You

Visio 2000: The Official Guide is for anyone who wants to use Visio 2000 to its fullest. Readers who are unfamiliar with Visio 2000 will be able to learn about the features and options it offers to create professional-looking diagrams. Readers who are already familiar with the program will learn about the powerful new features in Visio 2000 Standard Edition as well as learn about some features and options in the other Visio products: Visio 2000 Professional Edition, Visio 2000 Technical Edition, and Visio 2000 Enterprise Edition. Everyone will able to further their productivity with Visio 2000 and be able to tailor-make Visio solutions for their own diagrams.

TIP	*If haven't yet purchased Visio 2000 but are considering buying it, you can download a trial version of the software from http://www.visio.com.*

If you already have Visio 2000 to create diagrams, the process-oriented approach of this book makes it excellent for an easy reference guide to features that you haven't used before. Experienced users will find discussions on how features can be used together to create more sophisticated Visio 2000 solutions.

How This Book Is Organized

This book is divided into eleven chapters and three appendices, as described here.

Chapter 1, "Visio 2000 Basics," introduces you to Visio 2000. It shows you how to install Visio 2000 Standard Edition and discusses its various options and basic components. You'll learn how to install and configure the program, understand the basic screen layout, and use the product's general features. You'll also learn about printing and saving your Visio 2000 drawings.

Chapter 2, "Creating Your First Diagram," introduces you to creating Visio 2000 diagrams. You'll learn how to create a drawing using the standard tools, such as stencils, connectors, and templates. You'll also learn how to print drawings using basic printing options. You'll be shown how the drag-and-drop feature works, as well as how to draw lines and add text to Visio 2000 drawings. You'll also learn how to use the text rotation, drawing, freehand, shape, view, and pointer tools.

In Chapter 3, "Going Further," you'll continue exploring Visio 2000 tools. You will learn techniques to create custom shapes, layers, backgrounds, pages, and other advanced tools. This chapter demonstrates how to create an overall look for presentations using these tools. You'll learn how to insert graphics and how to use them to make drawings look personal and meaningful.

Chapter 4, "Using Stencils and Templates," discusses the many kinds of stencils and templates that come with Visio 2000. You'll learn how to bring up a stencil, choosing it from the list of stencils that ship with Visio 2000. You'll see how to modify a stencil with either standard or custom shapes created in Chapter 3. This chapter also teaches you how to create a stencil in Visio 2000. You'll learn how a template works and how to choose one from the list of templates that come with Visio 2000. You'll understand how templates and stencils work together, and you'll learn to choose new stencils to go with your template from a list showing which stencils come with which templates. You'll see how to modify an existing template and how to create a template of your own.

In Chapter 5, "Creating Flowcharts," you'll learn how to choose the right flowchart template and how to use the special features of connectors and SmartShape symbols to make your flowcharts work beautifully. You'll learn how to create organization charts and flowcharts from databases, as well as how to create database information from flowcharts.

Chapter 6, "Using Visio 2000 with Microsoft Office," teaches you how to use Visio with Microsoft Office products. You'll learn how to place a copy of your current drawing into an Office document and how to dynamically link Visio 2000 diagrams to Office 2000, Office 97, and some Office 95 products for automatic updates when the data changes in either the drawing or the Office document. This chapter discusses linking and embedding Visio 2000 diagrams with Word for Windows, as well as going from Excel data to a Visio 2000 diagram. It also discusses how to use the PowerPoint color schemes in Visio 2000.

Chapter 7, "Linking and the Internet," discusses how Visio 2000 is completely Internet-compatible. You'll learn how to set links between pages or documents within Visio 2000 and how to link to documents outside Visio 2000. You'll learn how to use Visio 2000 with HTML and the Internet. This chapter shows you how to create hyperlinks in Visio 2000 diagrams, as well as how to create HTML documents in Visio 2000. You'll see how this can be useful for creating Web pages and for linking to Web documents and HTML Help.

Chapter 8, "Organizing Your Business with Visio 2000," shows you how to track a project with Visio 2000. You'll learn how to keep track of project status and scheduling using Visio 2000 solutions, such as special templates Visio 2000 developed for this purpose. You'll also learn how Visio 2000 works smoothly with Microsoft planning software by importing and exporting Microsoft Project information. You'll learn how to use the Office Layout template to create an office layout diagram and how to use the template to create an office inventory.

Chapter 9, "Getting Your Point Across Graphically," shows you how to use Visio 2000 to communicate graphically in meetings and on paper. You'll learn how to create charts, forms, and graphs, as well as how to add maps and geographic shapes to your diagrams. You'll also learn how to create a slide show in Visio 2000, how to add comments to shapes, and how to find all the shapes on a stencil.

Chapter 10, "Using Visio 2000 Technical Edition," discusses the differences between Visio 2000 Standard Edition and Visio 2000 Technical Edition. You'll learn how Visio 2000 Technical Edition is used by engineers to create specific drawings and precise diagrams. This chapter also includes a discussion of the added stencils and templates that come with this version.

Chapter 11, "Using Advanced Visio 2000 Features," discusses the highly technical, advanced features that come with different versions of Visio 2000 and how to take advantage of some of these features to help with specific types of diagrams.

Appendix A, "Stencils and Templates," lists all the shapes, stencils, and templates that come with Visio 2000, as well as special features of each template.

Appendix B, "Features in Visio 2000 Editions," describes the different editions of Visio 2000 and helps you identify which one has the functions you need.

Appendix C, "Resources," contains a selection of Internet, newsgroup, and other online resources for Visio 2000 users. The appendix also mentions user groups and other interesting information.

Conventions Used in This Book

This book has several standard conventions for presenting information:

Defined terns are in *italics*.

Keyboard keys appear in SMALL CAPITALS. If you're supposed to press several keys together, the keys are joined with a hyphen. For example, "Press CTRL-F1" means to hold down the Control key (CTRL) and press F1.

There are three types of special paragraphs in the text:

 A Note is simply a comment related to the material being discussed.

 A Tip is a technique for doing things faster, easier, or better in Visio 2000.

 A Caution is a warning to prevent you from doing something that could result in a loss of data or cause you problems.

Other Books of Interest

If you aren't already familiar with Windows 95 you may want to buy *Windows 95 Made Easy* by Tom Sheldon (Osborne/McGraw-Hill, 1995), a comprehensive guide for readers who aren't familiar with Windows 95. If you aren't already familiar with Windows 98 and will be using it with Visio 2000, you may want to buy *Windows 98 Answers! : Certified Tech Support* by Martin S. Matthews (Osborne/McGraw-Hill, 1998), a complete guide for Windows 98. If you're using Windows NT, you might consider buying *Windows NT 4 for Busy People* by Stephen Nelson (Osborne/McGraw-Hill, 1996), an inclusive, quick guide to Windows NT.

For More Information

For news and information about other products of interest to Visio 2000 users, check out Visio 2000's Web site at:

http://www.visio.com

There you can get demonstration versions of Visio 2000 software, as well as some troubleshooting tips.

For news and information about upcoming books and software, check out the authors' Web pages at:

http://www.hedtke.com

and

http://www.oz.net/~efk

There you'll find general information on Visio 2000 and other books the authors have written.

CHAPTER 1

Visio 2000 Basics

1

This chapter shows you how to install Visio 2000 and introduces you to its basic features and screen layout. You'll learn how to install and configure the program, and you'll get acquainted with the various options and features of Visio 2000.

What Is Visio 2000?

Visio 2000 is a drawing application that helps you easily create professional-looking business diagrams. Visio 2000 is produced by the Visio Corporation and comes in four editions: Standard, Professional, Technical, and Enterprise. This book covers all four editions, but it focuses primarily on Visio 2000 Standard Edition. The other three editions build on the Standard Edition.

Visio 2000 Standard Edition comes with dozens of templates and stencils to help you draw great diagrams easily, as well as ways to automate repetitive drawing tasks. The Enterprise Edition and Professional Edition have several extra features that aid with common business tasks. Visio 2000 Technical Edition is designed for engineering and facilities professionals to help them create detailed schematics.

 For simplicity's sake, throughout this book Visio 2000 Standard Edition will be referred to simply as Visio 2000. All other editions of the product will be referred to by their full names.

Installing Visio 2000

Visio 2000 is easy to install. It comes on a CD-ROM, and it is compatible with Microsoft Windows 95, Windows 98, and Windows NT.

Installing Visio 2000 usually takes about 20 minutes. The installation of Visio 2000 has two parts: installation of the Microsoft system files and installation of the Visio 2000 system files.

 The installation process for Visio 2000 involves restarting your system. Make sure to close all other programs before you begin installation. Otherwise, you could lose data.

Installing Microsoft System Files for Visio 2000

Visio 2000 works closely with other common products, including Microsoft Windows and Microsoft Office. The first part of the Visio 2000 installation involves registering and setting up communication with Microsoft system files.

To start the installation of Visio 2000, insert the CD-ROM into your computer's CD-ROM drive. The installation should start automatically. If the installation doesn't start automatically, select Run from the Start menu and then type **D:/setup** (where D is the drive letter of your CD-ROM drive), and click OK.

The first installation screen is shown in Figure 1-1. It is the Visio 2000 installation splash screen. There are three options in the splash screen: install Visio 2000 program files, install the Discover Visio 2000 training sampler, and take a tour of the Visio 2000 working environment.

The Discover Visio 2000 training sampler is available after you've registered the product. After you submit your registration, you receive the unlocking code

FIGURE 1-1   Installation splash screen

(a nine-digit number) to sample the Visio 2000 interactive training CD-ROM. This sample is Module 1 from Discover Visio 2000 Interactive, Volume 1.

The Visio 2000 tour gives you a brief look at the features in Visio 2000. Here are some tips for running the Visio 2000 introductory tour:

- Depending on your particular system configuration, you can improve the performance of the Visio introductory tour by installing it on your hard disk and running it from there rather than running it directly from the CD-ROM.

- The Visio introductory tour doesn't run properly on a screen resolution of 640 × 480 pixels; a screen resolution of at least 800 × 600 pixels is required to view the tour.

- Visio recommends a color palette of at least 256 colors for viewing the introductory tour.

- For instructions on how to make the introductory tour available on network servers, see the Network.txt file in the Visio folder installed on your computer.

To install Visio, select the first option, Install Visio 2000. The next installation screen appears, as shown in Figure 1-2. This is the Microsoft End User License Agreement. This is a standard agreement stating that you promise to use the product only on the computer it was purchased for. When you've finished reading the License Agreement, click the Accept button to continue.

The Visio 2000 installer then displays a dialog box telling you it needs to restart the system before it can continue installing Visio 2000. (It needs to restart the system so Visio 2000 can be properly registered with the Microsoft system files before files are added to your hard drive.) Click Update. Another dialog box appears, telling you that the installer will restart your computer. This is your last chance to close and save any files you have open. Do so now if you didn't before you started the Visio 2000 installation. When all other programs are closed, click OK. Your system will restart.

Installing Visio 2000 Program Files

After your system has restarted, installation of the Visio 2000 program file begins. You'll see the Visio Installation Manager screen, as shown in Figure 1-3. First, the Installation Manager scans your system to make sure all the files it needs have been installed. When it has done that, it displays a message telling you that it will install Visio 2000 and asks if you want to continue. To continue, click Next.

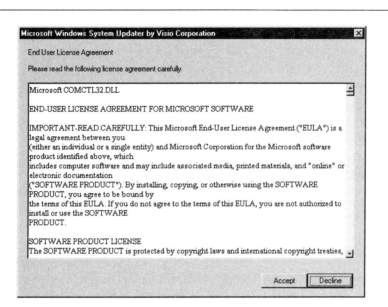

FIGURE 1-2   Microsoft End User License Agreement

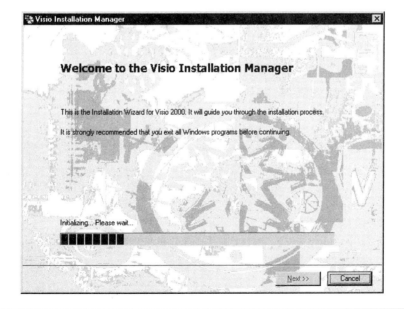

FIGURE 1-3   Visio Installation Manager

The Installation Manager then displays the Visio 2000 End User License Agreement, as shown in Figure 1-4. When you've read the Visio 2000 End User License Agreement, click "I Accept" in the lower left-hand corner, and then click Next to continue.

The next Visio 2000 installation screen asks for your personal information. The Installation Manager automatically fills in the name of the registered user of the computer and the company name (if one was provided when Windows was installed). You need to fill in the Visio product ID number, which is included in the Visio 2000 packaging. You should place the product ID sticker on the CD-ROM case. After you've filled in the personal information, click Next.

The next installation screen is the Setup Type screen, which is shown in Figure 1-5. There are three types of Visio 2000 installation:

■ **Typical** Installs the parts of Visio 2000 that are usually used most often. This includes all the system files, but no developer support, and leaves off a few macros. This installation takes about 100 megabytes (MB) of hard-drive space

■ **Compact** Installs just the Visio 2000 program files. This installation takes about 75MB of hard-drive space.

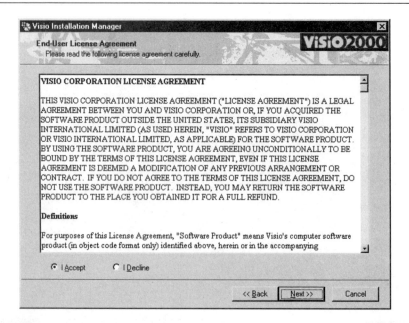

FIGURE 1-4   Visio 2000 End User License Agreement

- **Custom/Complete**   Installs everything that comes with Visio 2000. This option also gives you the ability to choose exactly which part of Visio 2000 you want on your system. This installation can take about 140MB of hard drive space.

NOTE   *It is best to perform a Complete installation of Visio 2000 if you have enough space on your hard drive.*

If you choose either of the first two options, the next screen asks if you would like to install Visio 2000 Help files. If you have the room, select to install these files and then click Next.

If you choose a Complete or Custom installation, the next screen is the Custom Setup screen, which is shown in Figure 1-6. The Custom Setup screen lists all the available components of Visio 2000. The components with the hard-drive icon next to them have been set to install, and the ones with the ×'s have been set *not* to install. You can customize the installation by right-clicking on each component and choosing either to install it or not install it. Regardless of how you decide to customize the setup, make sure you choose to install all the Visio 2000 program files. Also, make sure you click the plus signs to the left of components to see their subordinate components. The installation of subordinate components can also be customized.

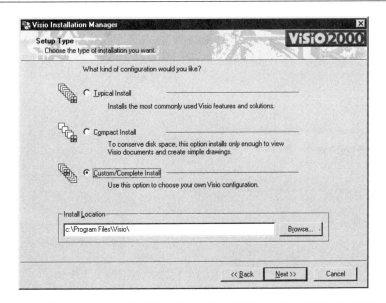

FIGURE 1-5   Setup Type screen

If you want to perform a Complete installation, click the Select All button on the Custom Setup screen (see Figure 1-6).

After you've finished choosing the Visio components to install, click Next. Visio 2000 displays a list of all the Visio 2000 components you've chosen. Look over the list. If anything is incorrect, click the Back button to return to the Custom Setup screen. When you've finished checking the setup list, click Next. The Setup Progress screen appears, as shown in Figure 1-7. The Setup Progress screen shows the progress of your Visio 2000 installation and tells you which options are being loaded onto your hard drive. The Overall Progress bar at the bottom shows how much of the installation has been completed. When the bar reaches the right side, all the Visio 2000 files have been added to your hard drive.

After the Installation Manager finishes the installation, you are asked if you'd like to register your copy of Visio 2000 online. If you choose to register the product, Visio 2000 opens the default Internet connection and registers Visio 2000 using the information you supplied during setup. Then Installation Manager displays an Installation Complete screen, telling you all the program files have been added to the hard drive, as shown in Figure 1-8.

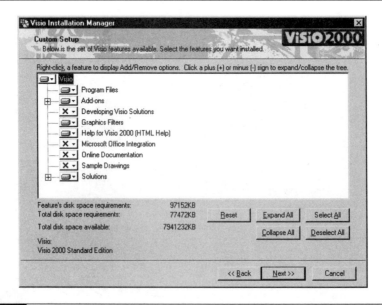

FIGURE 1-6 Custom Setup screen

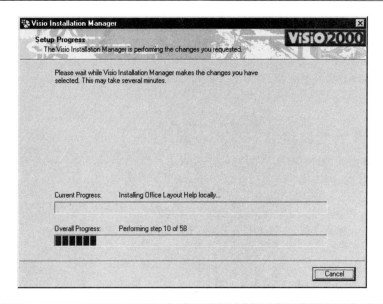

FIGURE 1-7   Setup Progress screen

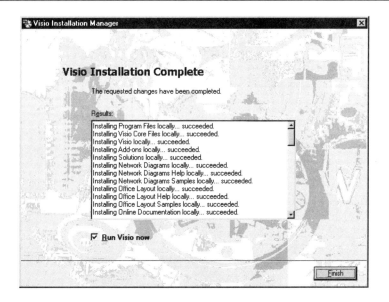

FIGURE 1-8   Installation Complete screen

A "Run Visio now" checkbox appears at the bottom of the screen. By default, the box is checked so that Visio 2000 opens as soon as you finish the installation. If you don't want to run Visio 2000 immediately after the installation, clear the check mark from this box. When you're done reviewing the Installation Complete screen, click Finish. This concludes the installation of Visio 2000.

Getting to Know Visio 2000

After you've installed Visio 2000, you can start the program by going to the Windows Start menu and selecting Visio 2000 Standard from the list.

 You can also start Visio 2000 by selecting the Visio 2000 folder on the Start menu and selecting a type of drawing to open. For now, though, just select Visio 2000 Standard from the list.

When you open Visio 2000 you'll first see the splash screen. Next, you'll see the Welcome to Visio 2000 window, as shown in Figure 1-9. Click the "Create new drawing" option button. After you've opened some drawings in Visio 2000, this dialog box will display drawing types and filenames. For now, select "Choose drawing type," and then click OK. This opens the Choose Drawing Type window, which is shown in Figure 1-10.

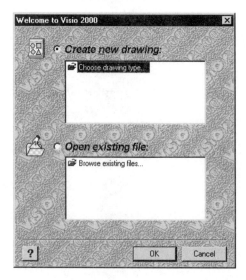

FIGURE 1-9 Welcome to Visio 2000 window

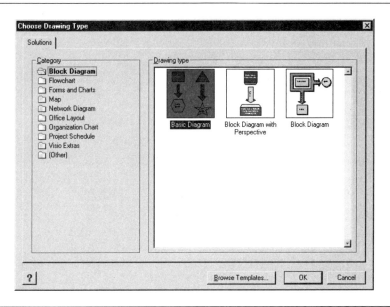

FIGURE 1-10   Choose Drawing Type window

On the left side of the Choose Drawing Type window are categories for each type of Visio 2000 drawing. On the right side are three basic drawing types. Later, we'll discuss what each type of drawing listed in the window does; for now, simply select the Basic Diagram and click OK. The main Visio 2000 window appears, as shown in Figure 1-11.

Take a moment to look at the main Visio 2000 window. Notice the drawing page in the center of the window. This is where you create a Visio 2000 diagram. The three most important parts of the main Visio 2000 window are:

■ The drawing page

■ The menus and toolbars

■ The stencils

Chapter 2, "Creating Your First Diagram," discusses stencils in more detail. For now, we'll focus on the other two parts—the drawing page and the toolbars and menus.

You create a drawing on the drawing page, which is contained in the drawing window. The drawing page is surrounded by a blue background called the *pasteboard*. The drawing page can display a grid, which consists of grid lines like

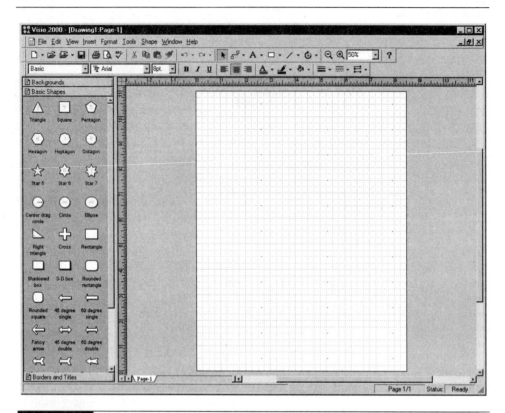

FIGURE 1-11   Main Visio 2000 window

those on traditional quadrille paper. The drawing page is where you'll arrange shapes as you create your diagram.

Drawing pages define the area that will appear on the paper when you print your diagram. You can think of the drawing page as a piece of paper you're working on. The pasteboard—the blue field around the drawing page—is your work surface. Any part of your diagram that is in this blue work surface won't print when you print the rest of your Visio 2000 diagram.

The drawing page title bar is located at the top of the drawing window and lists the page name and number. If you maximize the drawing window, the page name and number are displayed in the title bar of the main Visio 2000 window, as in Figure 1-11.

> **TIP** *The pasteboard (the blue work surface) can be very handy when you have things you'd like to save with a diagram but don't wish to print, such as notes to others or extra pieces of the diagram.*

The menus in the main Visio 2000 window allow you to access all the commands you need to create Visio 2000 diagrams. The toolbars include buttons and tools you can use as shortcuts, instead of choosing menu commands.

Table 1-1 lists the various menus in the main Visio 2000 window and describes the commands they include. We explain how to use these menus and commands in the following chapters.

Visio 2000 has two main toolbars, the *standard* toolbar and the *formatting* toolbar. Each has its own set of buttons. Visio 2000's standard toolbar is much like the toolbars you find in many Microsoft Office products. However, there are several buttons you may not recognize. Table 1-2 describes the buttons on Visio 2000's standard toolbar.

The other main Visio 2000 toolbar, the formatting toolbar, is unique to Visio. Because Visio 2000 is a drawing program, it includes numerous graphics functions with corresponding tools. The formatting toolbar contains many of these functions, such as tools for changing colors of objects, changing font characteristics, and formatting lines. Table 1-3 describes all the tools on the formatting toolbar.

You'll learn more about the tools in Tables 1-2 and 1-3 throughout this book.

Menu	Description
File	Creates, opens, saves, deletes, and prints diagrams and opens stencils.
Edit	Cuts, copies, and pastes information. Also allows reordering and deletion of pages. Finds or replaces text during editing of diagrams.
View	Zooms in and out. Turns on and off toolbars, grids, rulers, and guides. Changes layer properties.
Insert	Inserts pages, graphics, Office documents, hyperlinks, and other objects.
Format	Formats text and shapes, as well as protects documents.
Tools	Checks spelling, changes the layering order of objects. Controls the snap, glue, and grid attributes of a diagram.
Shape	Controls the size, placement, order, and grouping of objects.
Window	Allows movement between open diagrams.
Help	Accesses both basic online and Web help sources.

TABLE 1-1   Menus in the Main Visio 2000 Window

Button	Name	Description
	New Drawing	If you click this once it opens a new blank drawing. Through the drop-down list you can select the drawing type form the list.
	Open	Displays the Open window, allowing you to open any already-saved Visio 2000 diagram.
	Open Stencil	If you click this once it displays the Open Stencil window. Through the drop-down list you can select the stencil from the list.
	Save	Saves the current diagram.
	Print	Prints the current diagram.
	Print Preview	Launches print preview mode.
	Spelling	Starts checking the spelling of the current diagram.
	Pointer tool	Allows you to select and move shapes on the drawing page.
	Connector tool	The first of three tools in this drop-down list, all of which deal with shape functions. The Connector tool creates lines that connect shapes.
	Text tool	One of two tools that handle how text is added and looks on the page. The Text tool adds text to the page.
	Rectangle tool	One of two tools that allow you to create shapes. The Rectangle tool allows you to create freeform four-sided shapes.
	Line Tool	The first of four tools that handle adding lines to the drawing page. The Line tool allows you to create straight lines.
	Rotation tool	One of two tools that handle how shapes appear on the page. The Rotation tool handles the orientation of shapes.
	Zoom Out	Shows the drawing page at one level closer zoom.
	Zoom In	Shows the drawing page at one level farther zoom.
	Help	Launches Visio 2000 help.

TABLE 1-2   Visio 2000 Standard Toolbar Buttons

Button	Name	Description
Basic	All Styles	Lists all the shape styles in the current diagram.
Arial	Font	Lists all the fonts installed on your computer.
8pt.	Font Size	Allows you to change the size of your text.
B	Bold	Bolds the selected text.
I	Italics	Italicizes the selected text.
U	Underline	Underlines the current text.
≣	Align Left	Aligns the selected text block to the left.
≣	Align Center	Aligns the selected text block to the center.
≣	Align Right	Aligns the selected text block to the right.
A	Font Color	Click to change the selected text to the color displayed. Use the drop-down list to change the text to any color you like.
✎	Line Color	Click to change the outline of the selected shape to the color displayed. Use the drop-down list to change the outline to any color you like.
◊	Fill Color	Click to change the interior color of the selected shape to the color displayed. Use the drop-down list to change the interior to any color you like.
≡	Line Weight	Click to change the weight of the selected line to the last-selected weight (the default is 1). Use the drop-down list to change the line to any weight.

TABLE 1-3   Visio 2000 Format Toolbar Buttons

Button	Name	Description
	Line Pattern	Click to change the pattern of the selected line to the last-selected pattern (the default is solid). Use the drop-down list to change the line to any pattern.
	Line Ends	Click to change the ends of the selected line to the last-selected end (the default is none). Use the drop-down list to change the line to any ends.

TABLE 1-3   Visio 2000 Format Toolbar Buttons *(continued)*

Understanding Diagrams

Before you create Visio 2000 diagrams, you need to understand some basic concepts. These concepts are the groundwork you'll use over and over as you create diagrams.

Visio 2000 diagrams are made up of shapes. These shapes can be almost anything—circles, squares, arrows, maps, clip art, and so on. You choose shapes from a *stencil*. Stencils are organized both by topic and by types of shapes. In order to choose a stencil, you should know what types of shapes you'll be using. (Note that some shapes appear on more than one stencil.) There are more than 1000 shapes in Visio 2000 Standard Edition, and each of the other editions has several hundred more shapes.

Templates contain the rules shapes use to relate to each other. They also control such things as the orientation of the drawing page and the stencils that open automatically when you create a new diagram. There are about a dozen templates in Visio 2000 Standard Edition, and several dozen more in the expanded editions. Templates will be covered in detail in Chapter 4. For now, you can think of them as a helping hand that guides you as you create your drawings.

Planning Your Diagram

When you create a new drawing, you must choose a *drawing type*. The drawing type determines the stencils and template that open with the new drawing. Consequently, to select a drawing type, you need a conception of how your drawing will look. This means you must plan your diagram. Carefully planning your diagram parameters will save time and effort later.

The following questions will help you identify some of the necessary considerations before starting a drawing in Visio 2000:

- What's the drawing about?

- What's the drawing for?

- How many different types of shapes are likely to be in the diagram?

- How are the shapes likely to be related?

- How will this diagram be viewed (i.e., printed on paper, viewed on the screen, embedded into another Windows program)?

- What size and resolution will the diagram be viewed at?

- How often will the diagram be updated? Daily? Weekly? Monthly? Never?

- Who will need to read the diagram? Will this diagram ever be passed outside your department or immediate working group?

- What will the diagram be called?

- Will the diagram be part of a larger presentation? How are you going to match the style of the diagram to the other documents?

- Is there a graphical style or look you should be adhering to, for instance a color scheme or design element you already own and want to use?

- Where will the diagram be saved? Who else will have access to see and to change the diagram?

- Will the diagram be used on a Web page?

- Will the diagram include more than one page?

- How many elements are likely to appear in the diagram?

- Will the diagram contain imported images and hyperlink tags?

- What fonts, formats, and colors will the diagram contain?

Perhaps the most important question to ask is, "What is the diagram supposed to convey to the viewer?" You should never start a diagram without the answer to that question firmly in mind. It's the most important question you can ask before you start a diagram. Visio 2000 is a great tool to help you graphically represent ideas to your readers, but to make the most of it you should always do some planning before you begin a new diagram.

> **TIP**   *Keep a list of all the Visio 2000 diagrams you've created and their content. Because the diagrams are reusable—and the shapes are easily rearranged—you can reuse parts of diagrams over and over. A list of your diagrams will help you reuse the work you've already done when creating a new diagram.*

Saving a Visio 2000 Drawing

After you've created a Visio 2000 drawing, you need to save it. To save a drawing, choose Save from the File menu. The Save As dialog box appears, as shown in Figure 1-12. Replace "Drawing1" with the filename for your drawing (for example, "proposal"). Use the Save In drop-down list to navigate to the folder where you want your file to be saved. By default, Visio 2000 saves files in the My Documents folder.

> **TIP**   *If you want to change the default setting for where Visio 2000 saves drawings, select Options from the Tools menu. Click the File Paths tab and update the Drawings field with the name of the folder where drawings should be saved.*

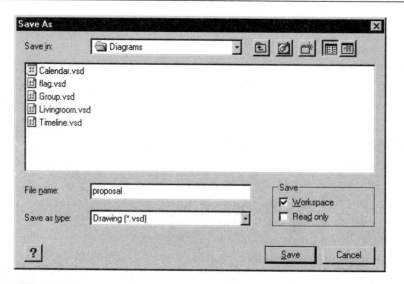

FIGURE 1-12   Save As dialog box

In the lower-right corner of the Save As dialog box, there are two checkboxes. The first enables you to save the entire workspace; this box is checked by default. If you clear the check mark from the Workspace checkbox, Visio 2000 doesn't save the open stencils with the drawing page. When you reopen the file, you'll need to open the stencils yourself. It's a good idea to keep the default setting unless there's some reason you don't want the stencils to open automatically with the file.

The other checkbox enables you to save the file as a read-only file. This checkbox is unchecked by default. If you select the read-only option, you won't be able to alter the file after you've saved it.

After you've provided the filename and adjusted the Save options as necessary, you need to choose the file type. With Visio 2000, you can save your file in any of the formats listed here:

Format	File Extension
Visio 2000 drawing	.vsd
Visio 2000 stencil	.vss
Visio 2000 template	.vst
Visio 5 drawing	.vsd
Visio 5 stencil	.vss
Visio 5 template	.vst
HTML file	.htm, .html
Adobe Illustrator file	.ai
Computer Graphics Metafile	.cgm
Enhanced Metafile	.emf
Encapsulated PostScript file	.eps
Graphics Interchange Format	.gif
IGES Drawing File Format	.igs
JPEG Format	.jpg
Macintosh PICT Format	.pct
Portable Networks Graphics Format	.png
PostScript file	.ps
Tag Image File Format	.tif
Vector Markup	.vml
Windows bitmap	.bmp, .dib
Windows metafile	.wmf
Zsoft PC Paintbrush bitmap	.pcx

After you've selected the file format from the "Save as type" drop-down list, click Save.

 If you need to change the name of a file that has already been saved, choose Save As from the File menu.

Printing a Visio 2000 Drawing

Because Visio 2000 is capable of creating many different types of diagrams, it includes many different printer settings. By default, when you print a diagram, Visio 2000 uses the printer settings for the default printer connected to your computer. These printer settings determine how Visio 2000 sizes the standard drawing page. In other words, your drawing page and your printer settings are linked, so the drawing page matches the size and shape of the paper you'll print on. You can, however, change these settings to alter the size and orientation of the drawing page. To do this, you use the Page Setup dialog box.

Using the Page Setup Dialog Box

You access the Page Setup dialog box by choosing File | Page Setup. The Page Setup dialog box appears with the Print Setup tab displayed by default (see Figure 1-13). The Print Setup tab shows the printer paper size and orientation, along with the drawing page size and orientation. The picture on the right side of the dialog box shows the relative orientations of both, helping you make sure your diagram prints the way you want it to.

If you change the printer paper orientation, by default you also change the drawing page orientation. However, there are options on other tabs of the Page Setup dialog box that may affect page size and orientation. To make sure your drawing prints correctly, verify that your paper orientation and your drawing page orientation are the same.

Troubleshooting Printing Problems

Sometimes Visio 2000 diagrams don't print the way you'd like them to because a page setting has been set incorrectly. Because your drawing page and your printer's paper settings are so dependent on one another, it's important to make sure both have been set correctly before you print a diagram.

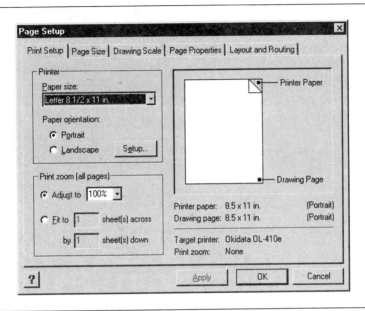

FIGURE 1-13   Print Setup tab of the Page Setup dialog box

TIP   *To resolve a printing problem, view your diagram in Print Preview. This overlays all the page breaks and margins in gray on top of your diagram, allowing you to see how your diagram breaks across pages.*

The most common problem occurs when a large drawing prints across several pages by accident. To avoid this, make sure your drawing page and your printer page have the same orientation. If the diagram still prints across several pages (called *tiling*), try reducing the Print Zoom on the Page Size tab of the Page Setup dialog box. By default, this is set so the drawing page and the printed page have a one-to-one correspondence. If your drawing is large, its size may not allow you to print on one page. By reducing the print zoom, you can fit large drawings on one page.

You can also zoom down in another way—by setting the drawing scale. Architectural drawings and other large-scale drawings have a standard scale they're set to so they print on one page. Many of the architectural or engineering templates have a drawing scale already set up, but you can set one up for yourself in any drawing.

To set up a drawing scale, open the Page Setup window from the File menu. On the Drawing Scale tab you can choose to use a 1:1 scale, any of the standard engineering scales, or define your own scale. All the scale options reduce the size of the shapes on the drawing page so they fit better on the printed page.

If you've kept the drawing page orientation and the printed page orientation the same, you should be able to use these scales to print your drawing on one page and prevent tiling.

> **NOTE**   *If you've used an earlier version of Visio, you might notice that printing has gotten a lot easier in Visio 2000. For the simplest printing settings, make sure the drawing page and printed page have the same orientation by default by not changing the settings on the Page Size tab of the Page Setup dialog box.*

Summary

In this chapter, you've seen how to install and start Visio 2000 and have been introduced to the menus and toolbar buttons. You've also learned the basics of creating Visio 2000 drawings—including how to start, save, and print them.

In the next chapter, you'll learn how to create a basic drawing.

CHAPTER 2

Creating Your First Diagram

The previous chapter showed you how to install and configure Visio 2000 and arrange the contents of the toolbar and menus.

This chapter will introduce you to creating Visio 2000 diagrams. You'll learn how to create a drawing using the standard tools such as stencils, connectors, and templates. You will also be shown how to use the text rotation, drawing, freehand, shapes, view, and pointer tools.

Understanding Shapes and Stencils

In other desktop publishing programs, you create the shapes and lines yourself, using a variety of tools. This can make the diagrams you produce look a little amateurish, and it certainly adds to the time and effort required to make a diagram. Visio 2000 makes creating diagrams easy by providing "smart" shapes that behave predictably when you move or resize them.

SmartShape symbols are shapes you would normally have to draw and refine yourself, like squares and circles. There are tens of thousands of predefined SmartShape symbols that come with Visio 2000, allowing you to quickly add a wide variety of simple or complex shapes to drawings. Figure 2-1 shows examples of three common shapes—a circle, a square, and a five-pointed star. These are examples of SmartShape technology.

Visio 2000 shapes come with dimensions and other features that have been programmed into Visio 2000. They have controls and dimensions that allow you to customize them while still maintaining usable, professional-looking shapes. For

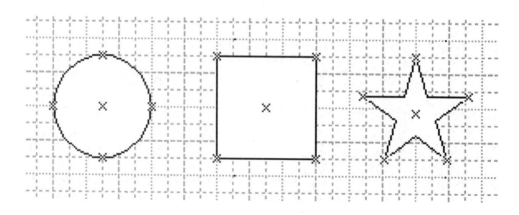

FIGURE 2-1 A SmartShape circle, square, and five-pointed star

example, in other desktop publishing programs, a circle drawn with a standard circle tool can be changed into an ellipse with the wrong click of a mouse. Visio 2000's SmartShape circle, on the other hand, is controlled by a line from its center to its edge. That means the shape will always be a circle, no matter how you manipulate it with the mouse.

Visio 2000 groups shapes into *stencils* so you don't have to browse through all the shapes for every diagram you create. Stencils have been collected in *folders*, so you can easily find the right stencil for the type of diagram you are creating. Visio 2000 ships with dozens of stencils packed with shapes ready for you to use. This means, for example, that you don't have to create a five-pointed star by drawing and assembling each line; instead, you simply choose the five-pointed SmartShape star from the stencil and drag it to your paper. Stencils save a lot of time. You don't have to know every shape in Visio 2000; you just have to pick the right stencil. Stencils also ensure that all examples of one type of shape look exactly the same, because they all come from the same master shape. (Master shapes are explained in more detail in Chapter 4.) This consistency adds a level of professionalism to your drawings.

Opening a Stencil

Most drawing types, called *templates*, have attached stencils that open when you select that drawing type. A basic drawing comes with three basic stencils. For many other drawings, you'll need to open another stencil. In this example, you'll open the Callouts stencil. Here's how:

1. Start Visio 2000 selecting it form the Programs folder on the start menu.

   The Welcome to Visio dialog box appears, as shown in Figure 2-2.

2. Select Choose Drawing Type from the upper window and then click OK.

   The Choose Drawing Type dialog box appears, as shown in Figure 2-3.

3. Open a new drawing by selecting Basic Drawing B from the folder lock Diagram and then click Open.

   The main Visio 2000 window appears with a blank drawing, and three stencils.

4. Select Open Stencil by choosing Stencil from the File menu, or click the Open Stencil button on the toolbar.

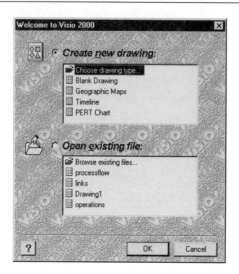

FIGURE 2-2   Welcome to Visio 2000 dialog box

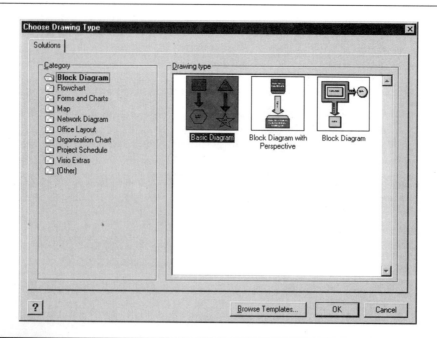

FIGURE 2-3   Choose Drawing Type dialog box

The Open Stencil dialog box appears (shown in Figure 2-4) with a list of all the stencil folders.

5. Now open the Visio Extras folder by double-clicking it or by selecting it and clicking Open.

6. Open the Callouts stencil by double-clicking it or by selecting it and clicking Open.

The Callouts stencil appears on the left side of the window as shown in Figure 2-5.

Now that you have opened a stencil, your Visio 2000 window looks a little different than it did in Chapter 1. Take a moment to look at the screen shown in Figure 2-5. It shows you the names for each area in the Visio 2000 window.

There are five parts to the Visio 2000 window:

- Drawing page

- Toolbar

- Pasteboard

- Status bar

- Stencil

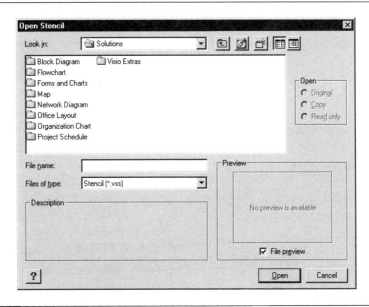

FIGURE 2-4   Open Stencil dialog box

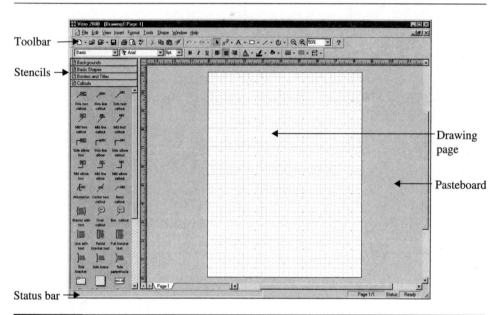

Toolbar

Stencils

Status bar

Drawing page

Pasteboard

FIGURE 2-5   Main Visio 2000 window with Callouts stencil

DRAWING PAGE   The drawing page indicates which part of your Visio 2000 diagram actually prints on paper. It is white with grid lines and has a slight shadow to indicate a 3-D page.

TOOLBAR   The toolbar in Visio 2000 is like the toolbar in most Microsoft Office programs. There are several drop-down buttons that give you access to other buttons. When you use a button, you launch a tool or function that you will use in creating your Visio 2000 diagrams.

PASTEBOARD   The pasteboard is the area on which the drawing page sits. It is indicated by the blue space around the page. You can place objects on the pasteboard; however, because they're not on the drawing page, they won't print.

STENCIL   You drag shapes from the stencil to create your diagram. Figure 2-5 shows the Callouts stencil.

STATUS BAR   The status bar gives information about the object you have selected. This is where Visio 2000 displays the width, height, and degree of rotation of the object. Figure 2-6 gives you a view of a sample status bar showing the width and height of a shape.

Dragging the Shapes

Now that you're familiar with the main Visio 2000 window, you can begin using shapes.

Visio 2000 shapes work on the "drag-and-drop principle." Simply click on a shape and, while holding down your mouse button, drag the shape onto the page and release the button. That's all there is to it! A standard-sized shape appears in the center of the page. It's a separate object you can then pick up and move around with your mouse. Later in this chapter you'll learn how to arrange and resize objects.

NOTE   *No matter how much they might look like buttons, shapes on stencils don't work like standard Windows buttons. You can't double-click to open them or move them to the drawing page; you need to drag them from the stencil to place them on the page.*

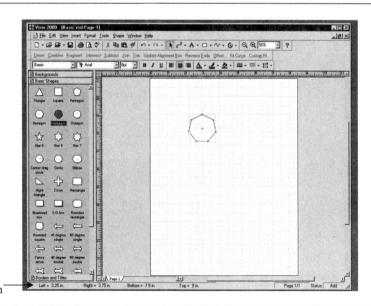

FIGURE 2-6   Main Visio 2000 window with status bar information

Practice dragging a few shapes onto the page until you get a feel for the way shapes and stencils work. It's important to be comfortable with this feature before you begin creating your first diagram—and it's kind of fun to drag the shapes onto the page.

Types of Shapes

On the Basic Shapes stencil you'll notice there are several different types of shapes. For instance, there is a standard square. Further down, in the sixth row, there's a 3-D box. These different types of squares work a little differently. There are three categories of shapes in Visio 2000:

- 1-D shapes
- 2-D shapes
- 3-D shapes

You can use all three categories of shapes in your Visio 2000 diagrams.

1-D Shapes

1-D shapes are connector shapes and are very common in Visio 2000 diagrams. All lines and connectors in Visio 2000 are 1-D shapes, which means they behave as if they just have end points, but no depth or height. Most 1-D shapes come off a stencil, but you can use the line-drawing tool to create them, too. Any single line is a 1-D shape. The Connector tool allows you to create lines very similar to the connector shapes you'll get from the stencils.

To see a 1-D shape, drag the Dynamic Connector shape from the last row of the Basic Shapes stencil. When you drop it onto your page, make sure that it doesn't touch any other shapes, or Visio 2000 tries to connect them. When you select a connector, Visio 2000 displays something like this:

Connectors and all 1-D shapes have only two ends. One end has a green box with a plus, the other a green box with a minus. This allows you to place the 1-D shapes with an arrow at one end in the correct direction. This ensures the connectors know which object is the parent of the two objects you're connecting.

> **TIP** *Make sure the plus end of any 1-D object is on the primary object in your diagram, while the minus end is on the secondary object.*

2-D Shapes

2-D shapes are the most common Visio 2000 shapes. The first three rows of the Basic Shapes stencil are all 2-D shapes, which include things like boxes, stars, and circles. You use 2-D shapes in almost every diagram you create, and they all behave the same way.

Try dragging the triangle from the Basic Shapes stencil onto the page. You'll see something that looks like this:

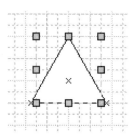

When you select the triangle, the green squares on the surrounding box are the *shape handles*. They allow you to change the size and shape of the object within certain parameters. For instance, you could make the triangle very tall and thin, but it would still have three sides. You can't change the basic parameters of any Visio 2000 SmartShape, and this is most obvious with 2-D shapes. There are some shapes that can change quite a bit and others that cannot. For example, a rectangle can look like a square, but a square can't look like a rectangle.

There are eight resizing boxes on the square surrounding a selected 2-D shape. If you pull on one of the corners, you resize the shape proportionally; in other words, the relative dimensions of the figure stay the same. The boxes on the sides of the surrounding square allow you to change the proportions of the 2-D shape; for example, pulling on the boxes on the left and right sides of a rectangle changes the width without changing the height.

3-D Shapes

3-D objects are the least common of Visio 2000 shapes. There's only one 3-D shape on the Basic Shapes stencil—a box. Drag the 3-D box from the sixth row of the Basic Shapes stencil to your page to see what it looks like. 3-D shapes are meant to represent the most lifelike objects in Visio 2000, and they have an extra handle that allows you to control their depth. Your 3-D box should look like this:

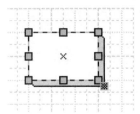

The tiny green square in the lower-right corner of the shape allows you to control the depth of shadow for a 3-D object.

You'll rarely use 3-D objects; however, they can be very useful to indicate the top of a flowchart or some other important part of your diagram. Visio 2000 has two entire stencils dedicated to 3-D images, both in the Block Diagram folder, called Blocks Raised and Blocks with Perspective.

 Make sure all the 3-D objects you use on one page have the same shadow depth. Otherwise, your drawing will look lopsided.

Building Your First Diagram

Once you're comfortable with dragging shapes onto your page and you understand how the basic shapes work, you're ready to put the parts together into a Visio 2000 diagram. This section walks you though each step of the process.

Make sure you have the Basic Shapes stencil open to complete this drawing, and that you have a Visio 2000 window that looks like the one shown earlier in Figure 2-5. Creating your first drawing involves all the normal steps of diagram creation:

- Dragging and arranging

- Sizing

2

- Connecting

- Adding text

Dragging and Arranging

You learned the basic techniques of dragging shapes earlier in this chapter. Now you'll need to drag the shapes for your diagram onto the page. Remember that the shapes on stencils don't work like buttons. Instead, you "pick them up" with the mouse, and "drop" them on the page by clicking and holding the mouse button as you drag the shape from the stencil.

Drag a square, a triangle, two arrows, and a circle to your blank page and place them so they're roughly in the arrangement shown in Figure 2-7.

Once all your shapes are on the page, you're ready to place them in the correct locations. Suppose you want to place all of the shapes in a straight line. You can easily line them up by using the grid to center the objects. Visio 2000 helps you with this by setting shapes to snap to the grid lines by default.

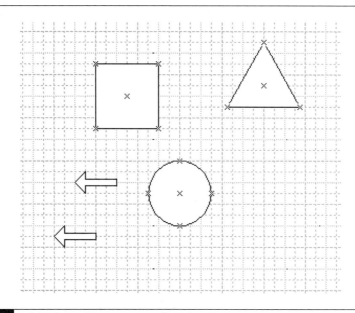

FIGURE 2-7   Add these shapes to your first drawing

Sizing

Now that you have the shapes on your page, you'll notice that the standard circle looks smaller than the standard square. Both shapes have the standard dimensions, but because the circle has rounded corners, it looks a little smaller. This isn't a problem, because Visio 2000 allows you to quickly and easily change the size of a shape.

First, select the circle to resize it. You'll know it's selected, because a box with green squares at the vertices and in the middle of each side appears around it. These are the control handles. Next, click on one of the green control handles and drag it a short distance from the center of the circle. This resizes the circle. Now your drawing should look something like the one in Figure 2-8.

> **NOTE**   *These green control handles appear for any shape you've selected, allowing you to resize the shape. For any shape other than the circle, dragging on the green control handles on the sides of the control box also reshapes the object.*

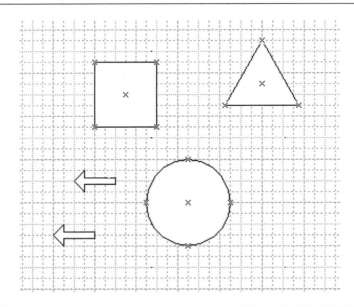

FIGURE 2-8   Resize the circle in your first drawing

Connecting

After your shapes have been arranged and resized, you're ready to make sure they're connected. Connecting shapes is one of the huge advantages of Visio 2000: once a shape has been connected, it takes effort to disconnect it. Connections act like glue, holding your pieces together so you can't accidentally move them.

Connections can only happen at control points. Luckily, there are several control points around shapes, usually at every corner and in the middle of most sides. For shapes like the arrow, there is a control point at the tip and the end. For 1-D objects, there are control points at each end. For circles and round objects, there are eight control points, one on each side of the selection box and one at each corner.

To make sure your shapes are connected, click on the control point of one arrow and move it until it touches the control point of another shape. You know the shapes have touched a control point when a small box appears between the two shapes over their contact point. If you drop the shape there, it loosely connects to the next shape and becomes difficult to move.

Connect the shapes in your diagram as shown in Figure 2-9 so that the arrows are connected to the circle. It is impossible to connect the end of the arrow to the side of the triangle, because there is no control point there. Simply get the end of the arrow as close to the triangle as possible.

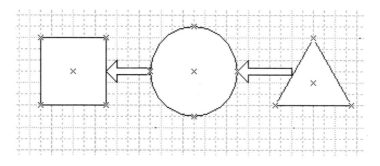

FIGURE 2-9   Connect the shapes in your first drawing

Adding Text

Once you have all the shapes in the correct places, connected with the arrows, you are ready to start adding text.

To add text, you'll need to select the shape and then choose Shape I Edit Text from the menu (or simply double-click on the shape). When you're able to edit the text of a shape, a text box opens over the shape. Select the square, and then choose Shape I Edit Text. The square looks like Figure 2-10.

Simply start typing, and the text appears in the box. For this example, type **Output** in the text box. Figure 2-11 shows the drawing with text added.

By default, text in Visio 2000 is set to center both horizontally and vertically within a shape. You can change that with the tools on the text-editing toolbar, or by selecting Format I Text from the drop-down menu. All the text-editing features of Visio 2000 work like the text-editing features in your favorite word-processing program.

In Visio 2000, the default text size is 8 pt, but you'll rarely want to use that size. Once you've added the text to your square, you can change the point size by selecting another size from the drop-down menu on the toolbar. For this example, the point size is 12 pt.

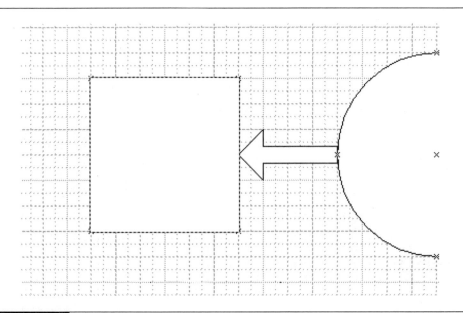

FIGURE 2-10   A text box

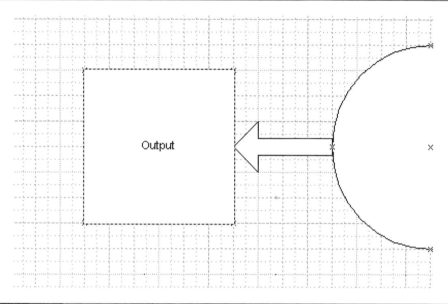

FIGURE 2-11   Add text to your first drawing

 NOTE   *By default, text is set to center horizontally and vertically, and is set to a size of 8 pt.*

Now add text to the circle and the triangle in the same way. As you do, notice how the text is always centered in the middle of the objects.

Saving

Once you have added text to your drawing, you're finished creating your first Visio 2000 diagram. The last step is to save your diagram.

Go to File | Save As, and a standard Save dialog box appears. Select a place to save and a title for your diagram. Click OK. The Visio 2000 Details dialog box appears, prompting you for information about your new diagram. Enter as much information as you'd like, and click OK.

You have now created and saved your first complete Visio 2000 diagram. Congratulations!

Using the Tools

As you created your first diagram, you may have noticed that there are several tools on the toolbar to the right of the stencil and pointer buttons. These are the Visio 2000 tools.

Visio 2000 is packed full of useful and unique tools that help you create stunning, professional-looking diagrams. There are several different tools on the Visio 2000 main toolbar. In Chapter 1, you got a brief outline of the use of each tool, but to make the most of these powerful tools you need more than a quick outline. The tools on the main toolbar are some of the most frequently accessed tools in Visio 2000, and they fall into six main categories, based on their function:

- Text

- Connector

- Drawing

- Rotation

- View

- Shape

 NOTE *You can have only one tool selected at a time, including the Pointer tool. The active tool is highlighted on the toolbar.*

The Text Tool

 There is only one Text tool, and, after the Pointer tool, it's the tool you'll use the most. The Text tool, shown in the left-hand margin, works the same way as the Shape | Edit Text command you used in your first drawing. The Text tool allows you to add text to any shape, or to create a free-standing text block.

To add text to a shape, make sure the Text tool is selected on the toolbar, then select the shape. Visio 2000 zooms in on the shape, and a text-editing box appears with a text cursor blinking in the center. See Figure 2-10 for an example of a text box. Start typing to add text to the shape.

2

 By default all text in Visio 2000 is set to be 8 pt and centered, but 8 pt is usually too small to be seen well on the printed page. To change text size or justification, go to Format | Text.

To create a free-standing text block, make sure the Text tool is selected on the toolbar, then click anywhere on the drawing window that doesn't contain a shape. A text-editing box opens with a text cursor blinking in the center. Simply type to add text. You can resize free-standing text blocks once you have added text, just as you resize any other 2-D shape.

 You can double-click on any shape at any time, and you'll automatically be taken into the text-editing box.

Connection Tools

Connection tools allow you to create connection lines between shapes quickly and easily and help you make sure that shapes connect exactly where you want them to. They also allow you to choose the location of connection points on an object. It's important to note that to make a solid connection with a line on any of the shapes that come with Visio 2000, you'll need to make the two pieces meet at a connection point. Connection points have been set for all SmartShape symbols and are added to any clip art as you import it into Visio 2000.

Connector Tool

 The Connector tool, shown left, creates 1-D connector lines between any two shapes you drag from a stencil. This is very useful when you're creating a flow chart or other diagram with many connections. The connector line is always the same, with the plus end attached to the first object and the minus end attached to the second.

To use the Connector tool this way, simply select it from the toolbar before you drag the shapes from the stencil. As soon as the second shape has been placed on the page, Visio 2000 draws the connection line.

 Visio 2000 attaches the connector line to the closest points on the two shapes, regardless of the shapes between them. You can move the endpoints of the connection line with the Pointer tool.

The Connector tool also allows you to create a connection line between any two legal connection points, even if they're on the same object. This means you can create a 1-D connection line between two points of the same object, if you wish, or between any two objects no matter when you dragged them to the drawing page.

To use the Connector tool this way, simply select it from the toolbar and then click on a connection point and drag the cursor to any other connection point. Visio 2000 draws a 1-D connector between the two connection points.

 You can tell you have the Connector tool selected because the cursor has a small 1-D connector line underneath and slightly to the right.

Connection Point Tool

 The Connection Point tool allows you to add, move, and delete connection points on any shape in Visio 2000. A connection point is a small ×, usually at the corners and center point of a 2-D or 3-D shape, and at the ends of any 1-D object.

The ability to change connection points allows you to make sure your shapes connect exactly where you'd like them to and helps solve the sometimes difficult problem of connection lines behaving in ways you don't like.

 The Connection Point tool always works on the selected shape. It is best if, before using this tool, you use the Pointer tool to select the shape you wish to work with.

To add a new connection point to the selected shape, hold down the CTRL key (the pointer displays a little × above it) and click the shape where you want to add the connection point. The new connection point is magenta while you have the shape selected so you'll be sure to see it.

To delete or move a connection point, you first need to select it. To select a connection point, position the mouse pointer over the connection point (the pointer is a four-headed arrow), and click. The connection point turns magenta when selected, just like it does when you add a connection point. Then, to delete a connection point, make sure it's selected and press the DELETE key.

 You cannot delete a connection point that has something glued to it.

To move a connection point, make sure the connection point is selected, then drag it to a new location. It stays highlighted in magenta until you select another connection point.

2

Drawing Tools

Visio 2000 comes with hundreds of ready-made shapes, but there will be times when you want a shape or line of your own creation. To handle this situation, Visio 2000 comes with six drawing tools to create lines, arcs, and other shapes for your diagrams. Each shape, once created, acts like a standard Visio 2000 shape, with green boxes at its vertices, making it capable of standard resizing operations.

Pencil Tool

The Pencil tool is one of the most powerful tools in Visio 2000. It allows you to draw line and arc segments to whatever length or arc you might need, singly or in groups. It also allows you to edit any shape in Visio 2000 no matter how it was created. The ability to edit shapes, as well as to create lines and arcs, makes this one of the tools you're likely to use often.

To edit existing shapes, make sure the shape you'd like to edit is on the drawing page. Make sure the part of the shape you wish to edit has an endpoint, a control point, or a vertex. Select the Pencil tool from the toolbar, then simply move the Pencil tool over the control point. The cursor turns into a cross with arrows at the tips. Click on the control point and move it where you'd like it to be. If you pull the control point directly away from the center of the shape, Visio 2000 creates straight lines on the sides that are connected to the control point. If you pull in any other direction than straight from the center, Visio 2000 creates an arc on the sides that are connected to the control point.

> **TIP** *When editing shapes with the Pencil tool, it's best to play with it for a while to get used to it. The tool is powerful, but it can be difficult to use well at first.*

To create lines and arcs with the Pencil tool, you need to understand that the tool works on gesture recognition and creates lines or arcs depending on how you move the cursor once you start drawing. There are also several options you can access with the CTRL and SHIFT keys that give you even greater control over how the drawing looks.

To draw a line segment, click on a blank spot on the drawing page and move the cursor straight in any direction. A line starts to appear between the cursor and your starting point.

To draw an arc, click on a blank spot on the drawing page and move the cursor in a circular motion in any direction. If you loop the cursor back toward the starting point, you can create an arc that is almost a full circle. However, if you try to complete the circle, the arc collapses.

> **NOTE** *Visio 2000 looks for the slightest motion away from a straight line to draw an arc, so it's easy to end up with an arc when you intended a line.*

To draw a line at 45-degree intervals, hold down the SHIFT key as you click and move away in a straight line. Visio 2000 forces you to one of the 45-degree intervals on its grid.

To draw a perfect half arc, hold down CTRL as you click and move away in a circular motion. Visio 2000 lets you go only halfway around and creates a perfect arc. You can control the size and depth of the arc by going closer or farther from the starting point.

To draw a group of lines or arcs, start drawing a line or arc, and then hold down both SHIFT and CTRL. Make sure you start a shape first, or you'll end up zooming in on the page instead. As long as you hold down both keys as you draw, every line and arc you create becomes part of a group. You may need to make a wider gesture to create arcs and the lines can only be at 45-degree angles. This grouping can also be done using the Freeform, Line, and Arc tools, as long as all the shapes in the group are made at one time.

You can also create a closed shape by linking several lines or arcs head to tail by starting the next shape at the exact endpoint of the old one. Once you've completed enough parts, and the end of the last one reaches the head of the first, Visio 2000 creates a completed shape out of the drawing, which then acts like any other 2-D shape.

Freeform Tool

The Freeform tool allows you to create a 1-D line of any shape. Visio 2000 simply evens out some of the curves while you move the cursor across the page. These smooth curves are sometimes called *splines*, which allow you to create a very specialized shape for your diagram.

To create a spline, make sure the Freeform tool has been selected from the toolbar. Then click on the page and start drawing. While you hold down the mouse button, Visio 2000 creates one continuous line. The line has control points at every Visio 2000 ruler mark and can be edited further with the Pencil tool.

You can also create a 2-D shape with the Freeform tool, an ability that allows you to create a shape to fit any need. Simply start and end your freeform drawing in the same place. Visio 2000 makes the figure into a 2-D shape.

Line Tool

The Line tool allows you to create straight lines of any length. These straight lines will be 1-D objects unless you add another shape to the end as described here.

To draw straight line segments, make sure the Line tool is selected. Then click and drag the cursor in any direction, and a line appears between the starting point and the cursor.

To draw a line at a 45-degree interval, hold down the SHIFT key as you click and move away in a straight line. Visio 2000 forces you to one of the 45-degree intervals on its grid.

Adding other line or arc segments creates a 2-D shape. After you've finished making the first part of your shape using the Line tool, use any other 1-D drawing tool and start the next part of the shape where the line ended. Continue adding 1-D shapes until you connect the end of the last shape to the head of the first. Visio 2000 creates a 2-D shape.

To change a line to an arc or to edit a line segment in a 2-D shape, use the Pencil tool. You can switch between the Arc tool, Line tool, Pencil tool, and Freeform tool to draw shapes consisting of several segments.

Arc Tool

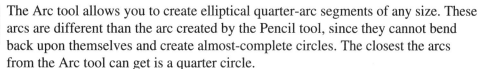

The Arc tool allows you to create elliptical quarter-arc segments of any size. These arcs are different than the arc created by the Pencil tool, since they cannot bend back upon themselves and create almost-complete circles. The closest the arcs from the Arc tool can get is a quarter circle.

To draw an arc with the Arc tool, first make sure it has been selected from the toolbar. Then click and drag the cursor away from the starting point. The way you drag the mouse determines whether the arc has a horizontal axis (the endpoint is right or left of the beginning point) or vertical axis (the endpoint is above or below the beginning point). If the end point is exactly horizontal or vertical to the beginning point, the arc becomes a straight line.

To add other arc or line segments and create a 2-D shape, first draw an arc. After you've finished making the first part of your shape using the Arc tool, use any other 1-D drawing tool to start the next part of the shape where the line ended. Continue adding 1-D shapes until you connect the end of the last shape to the head of the first. Visio 2000 creates a 2-D shape.

Rectangle Tool

The Rectangle tool allows you to draw 2-D squares and rectangles. Although Visio 2000 comes with shapes for both squares and rectangles, this tool can be useful when you need to create a standard 2-D shape on your own. The shapes created by the Rectangle tool and the shapes you can drag off the Basic Shapes stencil behave identically after you complete the drawing process. For both rectangles and squares, Visio 2000 displays the size of the 2-D object you're creating in the status bar.

To draw a rectangle, first make sure you have the Rectangle tool selected on the toolbar. Then click and drag diagonally in any direction. A rectangle starts to appear between the cursor and the starting point, with the cursor at the corner diagonally away from the starting point.

To draw a square, hold down the SHIFT key as you drag. Instead of a rectangle appearing below the cursor as you drag, which happens when you're creating a square, a square appears below and slightly to the right. Also, when you create a square your cursor will be on one of the sides adjacent to the corner of the starting point, and you'll define the square by one side alone.

To edit a square or rectangle you created using the Rectangle tool, first create the shape. Then, depending on what you wish, you may either use the standard Pointer tool or the Pencil tool to change the shape. If the shape simply needs to be resized, use the Pointer tool and the green shape handles to resize as you would any other shape. If the shape needs to be altered more fundamentally, use the Pencil tool on one of the control points to change the orientation of one of the sides. Remember that the Pencil tool creates lines if you pull directly away from the center, but it makes arcs if you pull in any other direction.

Ellipse Tool

The Ellipse tool allows you to draw 2-D circles and ellipses. Although Visio 2000 comes with shapes for both circles and ellipses, this tool can be useful when you need to create a standard 2-D shape on your own. The shapes created by the Ellipse tool and the shapes you can drag off the Basic Shapes stencil behave identically after you've completed the drawing process. As you draw circles and ellipses, the status bar displays the size of the rectangle that would encompass your 2-D object.

To draw an ellipse, make sure the Ellipse tool is selected on the toolbar. Then click and drag in any direction. An ellipse appears between the cursor and the starting point. As you draw, the cursor has a small ellipse below it and slightly to the right.

To draw a circle, hold down the SHIFT key as you move the cursor. The cursor has a small circle below and slightly to the right.

Both ellipses and circles are closed shapes made up of two arc segments. There are control points at four places on either shape, so you can change the way they look with the Pencil tool.

Like any 2-D shape, you can change the size by using the green handles and the Pointer tool.

> When you use the Pencil tool to reshape an object created by the Ellipse tool, the results can be surprising. Make sure you practice with this tool and these shapes before you attempt your final shape.

Any circle or ellipse you create with this tool allows you to change its shape, unlike the SmartShape circles.

Rotation Tools

Visio 2000 diagrams often need their shapes to be a different orientation. The rotation tools are one way you can change the orientation of shapes and text to make sure they work well in your design. Both rotation tools allow you to rotate the shapes to any degree.

Rotate Shape

This rotation tool allows you to rotate any shape to any degree. Both 1-D and 2-D objects rotate exactly the same way, and everything listed here applies to both types of shapes. 3-D shapes rotate similarly, but they take their shadow with them as they move, so it can look very odd to rotate them very far. You want to make sure all 3-D shapes in a diagram have been rotated similarly, or you'll lose the effect of their three-dimensional shape.

To rotate a shape, make sure the Rotation tool is selected from the toolbar, then select the shape you wish to rotate. The green handles at each corner of the square selection box changes from boxes to circles. Grab one of the circles and rotate the shape. As you do, the degree of rotation appears on the status bar as well as the snap to degree. This is the amount of control you have over the rotation—a smaller number indicates a finer control over the rotation angle. To get finer control over the rotation angle, move the cursor farther from the point of rotation.

> **NOTE** *In the full-page view, Visio 2000 sets the default minimum and maximum degree control at 15 degrees at the point of rotation and .1 degrees at the largest point away from the center of rotation. The more you zoom into the page, the finer is the degree of control.*

You can resize while using the Rotation tool, but only in one of the stretching directions using the square handles on the side of the selection box.

The shape rotates around the default rotation point, usually set as the center for Visio 2000 shapes and all the shapes you create yourself. The rotation point looks like the green rotation handles with a dot in the center. You can change the shape's center of rotation by making sure you have the Rotation tool selected, and then clicking on and moving the rotation point. When you pick up the rotation point, the cursor turns into a small circle with a dot in the middle. The shape rotates around wherever you set as the new rotation point.

Text Block Rotation Tool

The Text Block Rotation tool allows you to control the orientation of your text block. All text that you attach to shapes is orientated to display at the default set for that shape. The default assumes the shape will be used with a certain orientation, and the text block is set to be read at that orientation. If you rotate a shape, the text rotates to stay in the same relationship to the shape and may become unreadable. For example, if you rotate a shape ninety degrees to the right, the text rotates with the shape and would now need to be read from the bottom on the page to the top. To solve this problem, Visio 2000 created the Text Block Rotation tool, which works in much the same way as the Rotation tool, except it rotates just the text on a shape.

To rotate a text block, first make sure the Text Block Rotation tool is selected from the toolbar. Select the text block, if it is a stand-alone block, or the shape that contains the text block. The same circular handles appear at the corners of the shape, but when you select one and begin to rotate, instead of the entire shape moving, only the text block rotates. For some rectangular and irregular shapes this is indicated by a lightly grayed version of the selection box, showing how much rotation you've given to the text block.

Just as with the standard Rotation tool, the degree of control you have with the Text Block Rotation tool is controlled by the distance from the rotation point for the text block, with the same set of defaults. The Text Block Rotation tool also controls the rotation point for the text block exactly as the Rotation tool controls it for shapes.

View Tools

Visio 2000 diagrams can be very complicated, and no screen is large enough to display all of a complicated drawing at full size. To deal with this issue, Visio 2000 has included easy-to-find View tools that allow you to zoom in and out on your diagram as you work.

 Holding CTRL and SHIFT while you click always allows you to zoom in, centered on the place where you click.

Zoom In

 The Zoom In tool allows you to zoom in one level as defined by the default levels.
    This tool doesn't work like the drawing and other tools you've already seen. Simply click on it to zoom in one level, centered on the currently selected object. If no object is selected, Visio 2000 zooms in on the center of the page.

 Always have something selected when you zoom in; otherwise, you'll have to use the scroll bars to find the object you want to see.

Zoom Out

 The Zoom Out tool allows you to zoom out one level as defined by the default levels.
    Simply click on it to zoom out one level, centered on the currently selected object. As with the Zoom In tool, if no object is selected, Visio 2000 zooms out from the center of the page.

Shape Tools

The shape tools were created to make it easier to create more of or modify shapes that already exist. These tools are a huge help when you have to create lots of copies of a shape, or when you need to change the look of a shape you've imported as clip art.

Stamp Tool

 The Stamp tool allows you, with one click, to make a copy of any object on your page or any object in any open stencil. These copies are called *instances* in Visio 2000. You can create an infinite number of any shape you would like.

To create instances of a shape, first make sure you select the shape you want to copy. If the shape is on your drawing page, simply select it. If you'd like to copy a shape on a stencil, click on it, but don't drag it to your desktop. A dark-blue box appears around the shape on the stencil to show it has been selected. The selected shape becomes the master from which all your copies are made. Once the shape has been selected, then select the Stencil tool from the toolbar. The cursor changes to a shape similar to the one on the tool button. If you click anywhere in the drawing area, a replica, or instance, of the shape appears.

 This is a particularly great tool for when you need lots of copies of an object you've imported from another program. Instead of importing and reimporting, you can simply copy it.

Crop Tool

 The Crop tool allows you to change the visible amount of any object you have imported or of any of the clip art that comes with Visio 2000. With the Crop tool, you can resize the border that surrounds each shape. When you do this with clip art, it reduces the amount you can see on the page, thereby cropping the piece. You can also move the shape within its border, changing how much of it is visible on the page but leaving the border the same size.

 You can't use this tool with any of Visio 2000's shapes. It's only for use with clip art and objects imported from other sources.

To crop a shape, first make sure the Crop tool is selected from the toolbar. Then select the shape, and the green control handles appear. Simply move the control handles until they have cropped the part of the shape you wish to have obscured.

To move an imported image within its border, select the Crop tool from the toolbar, and then select the image to be moved. When you move the cursor inside the border, it changes to a hand shape. Click and drag the image inside the border until the part you wish to have obscured is no longer visible. Visio 2000 dynamically redraws your image while you do this, so you are able to see what's happening.

Summary

This chapter introduced you to the basics of creating Visio 2000 diagrams. You saw how to create a drawing using SmartShapes, stencils, and connectors. You also saw how to use tools to rotate text, draw freehand shapes, and view, edit, and copy objects on the page.

In the next chapter you will see how to take your basic knowledge of Visio 2000 even further by learning to use layout tools, adding pages and backgrounds, and including graphics in your Visio 2000 diagrams.

2

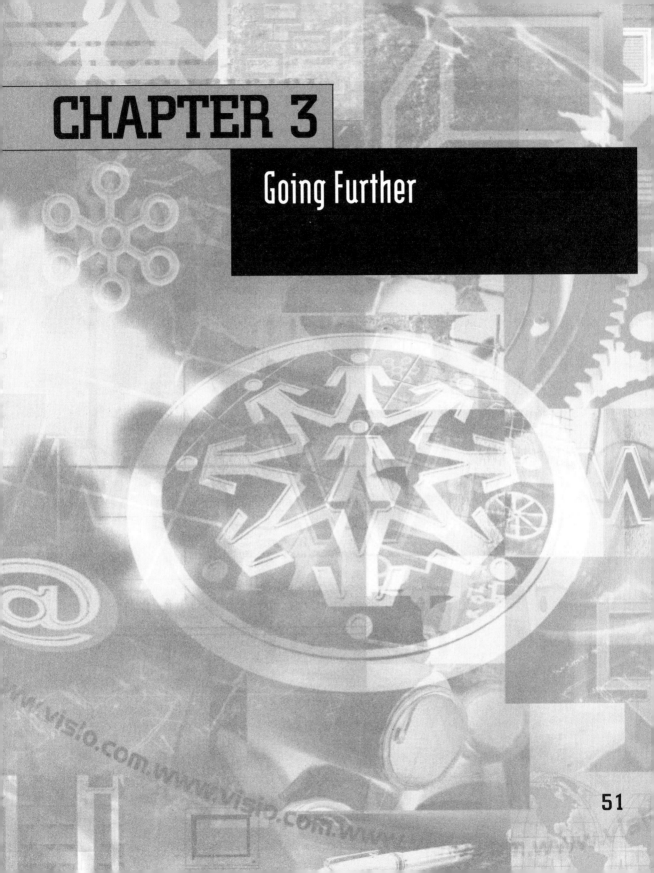

CHAPTER 3

Going Further

In the last chapter, you created your first Visio 2000 diagram, toured the main Visio 2000 window, and learned about the basic Visio 2000 tools.

In this chapter, you will see how to take your basic knowledge of Visio 2000 even further by learning to use layout tools, adding pages and backgrounds, and including graphics in your Visio 2000 diagrams.

Understanding Layout Tools

You've learned about all the basic tools that Visio 2000 offers; however, as you create more drawings, layout tools help you take your diagrams to a new level. Layout tools allow you to precisely place your shapes using rules, grid lines, and guides, as well as giving you control over how the shapes in your diagrams stack and group together.

Exploring Rulers

The rulers are the most commonly used tools in Visio 2000. You may not have realized it, but the rulers were probably a huge help when you created your first drawing, allowing you to align the shapes and helping you see their relative sizes.

By default, the rulers are turned on in Visio 2000, and, in the U.S. version, are set to measure the pasteboard and drawing page in inches. For the international version of Visio 2000, the default units are metric. Figure 3-1 shows the default rulers for the U.S. version.

Grid lines and guides are tied to the rulers, so the scale and zero points on the rulers affect how Visio 2000 behaves when you move shapes.

 As you zoom in on a page, the ruler changes scale. If you need a finer ruler, just zoom in. Visio also zooms in the grid lines.

Shape Shadows

Rulers also help you place your shapes, because they show you exactly where the selected shape is at any given time. Visio 2000 does this by placing a *shape shadow* on the ruler for the selected shape. The shape shadow is a series of faint lines on each ruler showing the outer edges of the shape you have selected. For 1-D shapes, these lines correspond to the endpoints. For 2-D shapes, these lines correspond to the outer edges of the shapes, with another line corresponding to the center point.

Shape shadows help you know exactly where a shape is, enabling you to line it up with other shapes on the page, even if those shapes are very far apart. Figure 3-1 shows shape shadows for a heptagon.

Zero Point

The zero point for your ruler defines where the ruler counts from and is set by Visio 2000 for both rulers. The horizontal ruler's zero point is the left edge of your drawing page; the vertical ruler's zero point is the lower edge of your drawing page. This makes the 0,0 point for the drawing page in the lower left-hand corner, known as the *origin*.

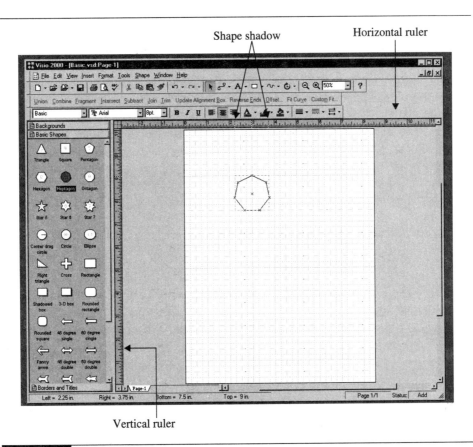

FIGURE 3-1   Visio 2000 rulers

For some people this origin can be a little counterintuitive, since they think the page should have an origin in the upper left-hand corner. To move the origin to the upper left-hand corner, you leave the horizontal ruler the same as the default setting and flip the vertical ruler so it starts with zero at the top of the page. Here's how to change your ruler's zero point settings so they start at zero in the upper-left corner:

1. Start Visio 2000.

2. Open a new drawing.

3. Select Tools | Ruler & Grid. The Ruler & Grid dialog box appears, as shown in Figure 3-2.

4. Select the "Ruler zero" box for the vertical ruler.

5. Set the ruler zero to 11 inches and click OK.

NOTE   *Changing your zero point to this setting causes the vertical ruler to show negative numbers, but at least you'll have a better orientation, because the zero will be in the upper left-hand corner of the drawing page.*

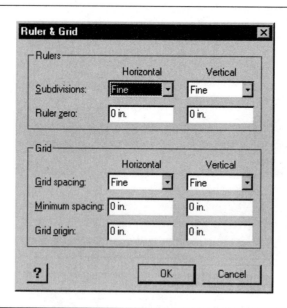

FIGURE 3-2   Ruler & Grid dialog box

3

You might also want to change the ruler's zero point to help you find the end of the printed page as you lay out diagrams. Just as you changed your zero point to the upper-left corner of the page, you can set the zero points on either ruler to reflect the actual printing edges of your page. Most printers don't print within half an inch of the edge of a piece of paper, so you may find it useful to set your rulers so their zero points are half an inch from the edge of the drawing page.

Ruler Units

Ruler units give you a lot of control over how you place shapes with Visio 2000. Ruler units can have a large impact on how your diagrams look because you use the ruler with all the shape placement and creation tools. Subdivisions are the most common settings to change on your rulers. By default, Visio 2000 sets your ruler to open with inch units in 1/4-inch subdivisions. To get finer control over shape placement, you may want to increase the subdivisions.

NOTE *The number of subdivisions within an inch increases as you zoom in on the drawing page.*

Here's how to change your ruler units:

1. Open a new drawing.

2. Select Tools | Ruler & Grid. The Ruler & Grid dialog box appears as shown in Figure 3-2.

3. Select the drop-down list for subdivisions on the horizontal ruler.

4. Select Fine from the list.

5. Select the drop-down list for subdivisions on the vertical ruler.

6. Select Fine from the list, and click OK.

TIP *Make sure your grid and ruler subdivisions work well together. For example, set them both to fine, instead of one to fine and one to coarse. It can be confusing to work with them set too far apart.*

Understanding Grid Lines

Grid lines, the small gray lines that cover the Visio 2000 drawing page, are a powerful tool for arranging shapes in your diagram. They form a grid that follows the ruler subdivisions, much like the grid lines on a page of graph paper. Here's what grid lines look like on the drawing page:

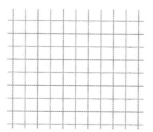

Grid lines are turned on by default in Visio 2000, so every new drawing includes them. However, by default, grid lines do not print with the rest of your diagram.

In Chapter 2, you used grid lines when you created your first diagram. They helped you arrange the shapes in a straight line. Grid lines are vital to making your diagrams look well-organized and carefully laid out. They also help you create great-looking diagrams quickly and easily.

 Grid options are easy to change and can help you create diagrams much easier. It's worth your time to change these options, since the right settings save you time later.

Changing the Grid Options

You can change lots of grid options. From the Tools menu, choose Ruler & Grid. The Ruler & Grid dialog box opens, as shown in Figure 3-2. Here's what each of the options controls:

GRID SPACING   This option sets the distance between the grid lines on the drawing page. You can choose Fine, Normal, Coarse, or Fixed. Fine, Normal, and Coarse allow the grid to resize as you zoom in and out. Fixed forces the grid to maintain the same grid spacing as you zoom.

Fixed grids can get in the way when you need to zoom in. It's best to choose one of the variable grids if you'll be working at several sizes. However, fixed grids can be invaluable for placing objects in line if there are just a few. The distance between the grid lines for fixed spacing is set in the minimum spacing box. For most purposes, it's best to choose one of the variable grid spacing options.

3

| NOTE | *The intervals of the grid correspond to the units of measure set in the Options dialog box.* |

MINIMUM SPACING   This option sets how close the grid lines can get no matter how far zoomed in you are. Grid spacing of Fine, Normal, or Coarse gives the minimum possible distance between grid lines. A grid spacing of Fixed gives the exact distance between the grid lines.

GRID ORIGIN   This option sets the grid's zero point. The default is set to start in the lower-left corner. Grid Origin works very much like ruler origin from the previous section. You only need to set this if you've set your ruler increments and grid increments differently.

Understanding Snapping

Snapping is the action that forces any shape you drag to the Visio 2000 drawing page to attach to the nearest grid line, connection point, guide, or ruler subdivision. This feature helps you create diagrams with shapes in straight lines with a minimum of effort.

Snapping also affects how you use the drawing tools, which are also set to snap to the nearest grid line. This makes it easier for you to draw shapes of the same size as well as helps you create straight lines.

By default, all shapes you drag or create on the Visio 2000 page snap to the closest grid lines in both horizontal and vertical directions. Since the snapping function is closely tied to the ruler and its settings, as well as the grid lines, make sure you've chosen the ruler options first.

Using the Snap & Glue Options

As you work with your diagram, you may want to turn on and off some of the snap and glue options. You can set how different screen objects snap and glue to the grid lines, connection points, guides, and ruler subdivisions, and you can change these settings at any time without affecting shapes already positioned or glued.

To change your snap and glue settings, choose Snap & Glue from the Tools menu. The Snap & Glue dialog box appears, as shown in Figure 3-3.

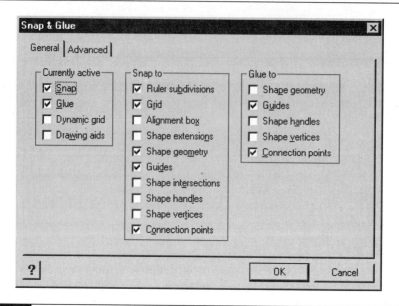

FIGURE 3-3   General tab of the Snap & Glue dialog box

TIP   *For placing shapes, you'll find the most useful Snap & Glue options are Ruler subdivisions, Grid, and Guides. The other options can be useful when gluing shapes.*

"SNAP TO" AND "GLUE TO"   The "Snap to" and "Glue to" areas of the General tab list the various screen elements you can select.

NOTE   *If you want to both snap to and glue to a particular screen element, you need to have that element checked in both lists. You can snap to something but not glue to it, and vice versa.*

When an element is checked in the "Snap to" and "Glue to" lists, Visio 2000 automatically snaps and glues to that element when you create a new shape or drag an existing shape onto the page. Table 3-1 lists the elements to which you can snap and glue shapes, and it describes how the settings affect objects on the page. The table also shows the default settings for the screen elements.

Element	Effect	Default
Ruler subdivisions	Shapes stick to the nearest ruler subdivisions.	On
Grid	Shapes stick to the nearest grid line.	On
Alignment box	Shapes stick to another shape's alignment box.	Off
Shape geometry	Shapes stick to any part of the nearest shape, no matter which part of the shape that is.	Off
Guides	Shapes stick and/or glue to guides.	On
Shape handles	Shapes stick and/or glue to any handle of the nearest shape's selection box.	Off
Shape vertices	Shapes stick and/or glue to any vertices of the nearest shape.	Off
Connection points	Shapes stick and/or glue to any connection point of the nearest shape.	On

TABLE 3-1   Snap & Glue Settings

CURRENTLY ACTIVE   These checkboxes allow you to turn on and off the snapping and gluing actions without changing the selections in the "Snap to" and "Glue to" lists. When you select the Snap or Glue checkbox, all the selected elements in the respective list become active. When you clear the Snap or Glue checkbox, all the selected elements in the respective list become inactive.

> **TIP**   *You can also press F9 to toggle Glue on and off, or press SHIFT+F9 to toggle Snap on and off.*

The Currently Active checkboxes allow you to turn off all snapping or gluing with one click, without having to reselect all the elements when you want to turn them back on again. For example, if you're working on placing a shape you'd like to move slightly, snapping can sometimes get in the way. You can clear the Snap checkbox, place the shape, and then reselect the Snap checkbox without changing the individual selections in the "Snap to" list. You can turn both Snap and Glue off to get complete control of shape placement or turn both on to use the grid lines and other screen elements to help with placing shapes.

> **NOTE**   *Unlike earlier versions of Visio, Visio 2000 has a nudge function you can use by selecting the shape and using the arrow keys to move it slightly.*

The Snap & Glue dialog box has another tab, Advanced, which is shown in Figure 3-4.

SNAP STRENGTH   The sliding bars in this section set the distance (in pixels) that screen elements pull when snapping is active. The strength of the grid, guides, rulers, or points (connection points, vertices, or handles) is set here. The higher the number, the farther away shapes can be when pulled to the element.

 For most Visio 2000 diagrams, guides should be set to about 5; rulers, grids, and points should be set to about 2.

SHAPE EXTENSION OPTIONS   These options control how the *drawing aids* function in Visio 2000. They help you place shapes, but only if set correctly. By default, none of these options are checked. If you want very fine control of how your shapes snap and glue, you may want to review these thirteen options and select some to help you create more precise drawings.

ISOMETRIC ANGLES   By holding down the SHIFT key as you rotate a shape, Visio 2000 constrains your angles to 30, 45, and 60 degrees. You can change the rotation

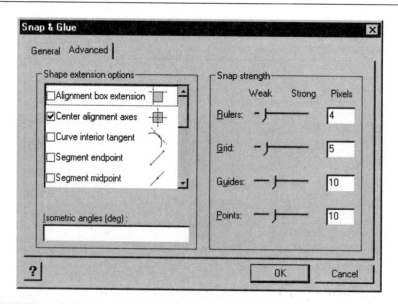

FIGURE 3-4   Advanced tab of the Snap & Glue dialog box

angles by adding new values to the Isometric Angle field. Separate the angles with commas. Visio 2000 will cycle through the list.

Using Guides

When you create diagrams, you often need to line up several shapes. *Guides* can help you do this with precision to give your diagrams a professional look. Although grid lines can be very useful for aligning objects, the grid lines are all over the page. That can make it confusing when you're trying to get perfect alignment. Guides, however, act like straight edges you can place *anywhere* on your page and use to align objects consistently. In addition, guides are easier to see on the drawing page than grid lines. With guides, you can be assured you're placing objects precisely.

There are two types of guides in Visio 2000: guide points and guide lines. *Guide points* give a single point to which you can affix the connection point of any shape. *Guide lines* provide a solid line you can use to connect two or more connection points. Both are useful in placing your objects on the page precisely.

 Gluing and snapping for guides can be set in the Snap & Glue dialog box (refer to Figure 3-3), as explained earlier in this chapter.

Making Guide Lines and Guide Points

Guide lines and guide points are created using the standard rulers in Visio 2000. All Visio 2000 drawing pages come with rulers turned on by default, so you should be able to create guides without changing any default settings.

 If you've turned off the rulers in Visio 2000, you can turn them back on by selecting View | Rulers.

To create a guide line, place your cursor over one of the rulers, and then click and drag the cursor onto the drawing page. A blue line appears under the cursor. Move it to the drawing page and then release the mouse button. This blue line is a guide. When you release the guide, it turns green.

To create a guide point, place your cursor where the two rulers meet. The intersection has two crossed blue lines. Click on the intersection and drag the cursor onto the drawing page. A blue crosshair appears, centered on your cursor. This is your guide point. As you drag the guide point to the drawing page the cursor turns into a four-headed arrow.

Figure 3-5 shows examples of guide lines and guide points.

 Both guide lines and guide points lightly snap and glue to grid lines. You can use this to make sure you have properly placed the guide.

Gluing and Snapping

Once you have your guides on the page, you need to know how to use them. Snapping and gluing to guides is similar to snapping and gluing to grid lines. By default, the strength is set stronger for snap and glue to guides than for grid lines. These features can be turned on and off for guides in the same way they are with grid lines, by using the Snap & Glue dialog box, shown earlier in Figure 3-3.

 Snapping and gluing are the best features of guides. They help with shape placement and don't get in the way of creating your drawing. Leaving them on is usually for the best.

When an object snaps to a guide, Visio 2000 brings at least two of the shape's connection points in contact with the guide. For guide *lines,* Visio tries to get two connection points in contact with the guide; for guide *points*, Visio snaps two adjacent sides of a shape's selection box to the guide points.

Gluing allows you to move attached shapes with the guide. If you glue a shape to a guide, the connection points of the shape turn red when you move them over the guide. Figure 3-6 shows a square with one side glued to a guide. By gluing

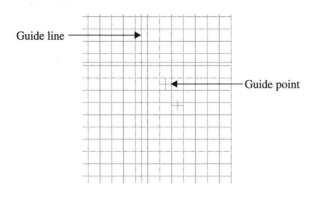

FIGURE 3-5   Guide lines and guide points

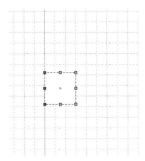

| FIGURE 3-6 | Square glued to a guide

several shapes to one guide you can make sure that all the shapes always line up, no matter where you move the guide.

To get a shape to snap or glue to a new guide, move the guide near the shape, and then drag the shape onto the guide. Snapping and gluing should happen automatically. If a shape doesn't snap or glue where you want it, try moving the shape a little and then put it back in place.

TIP   *For precise placement of shape, right-click on the shape and select Size and Position.*

Moving Guides

Guide lines and guide points are great for shape placement, especially when they are snapped and glued to shapes. When you move the guide, you also move all the shapes that are glued to it. This gluing action allows you to quickly rearrange your diagram to incorporate new ideas or a new layout without picking up each piece individually and replacing it. To take advantage of this feature you need to move the guides.

To move a guide, place the cursor over the guide away from any shape. The cursor turns into a double-headed arrow for a guide line and from a black arrow to a white one for a guide point. Click the guide and it turns green. Once a guide is green, you have selected it and can move it. Click and hold on a guide and move it to the new location. All the shapes glued to the guide move with it.

Guides have the same shadow on the ruler that lines and points do. Use the shadow to help you place guides as you move them. Guides also attempt to snap to the grid by default. This can make it difficult to get the precise placement you need

as you move your guides. You can turn off snapping to the grid in the Snap &
Glue dialog box, explained earlier in this chapter.

TIP	*To remove a guide, select it and press DELETE.*

Grouping

Grouping shapes allows you to place shapes in relation to each other and then
make sure that relationship always stays the same. Grouping in Visio 2000 helps
you manage shapes by helping you collect them into sets that work together.

Creating and Dissolving Groups

There are two ways to group shapes. One way is to hold down SHIFT, select all the
shapes for the group, and then click the Group button on the standard toolbar.
Alternatively, you can go to the Shape menu, select Grouping, and then select an
option from the submenu, as shown in Figure 3-7.

The toolbar buttons are useful when you simply want to group a set of shapes
(or dissolve an entire group of shapes). The Shape | Grouping menu commands
give you several submenu commands for grouping shapes.

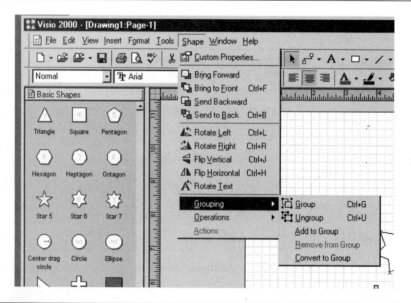

FIGURE 3-7   Shape | Grouping submenu

Formatting, Adding, and Removing Shapes in Groups

Once you've created a group, you may wish to format, add, or subtract member shapes within the group structure. Groups of shapes behave like a single shape, so dealing with a shape in a group often requires more steps than simply dealing with a single shape on your drawing page. Formatting a shape that has been grouped requires selecting the individual shape without selecting the entire group.

To format a shape in a group:

1. Deselect everything by clicking on an unoccupied part of the drawing page.

2. Select the group containing the shape you wish to format.

3. Select the shape within the group. You might notice the shape handles are slightly different than normal ones. They have small ×'s inside them to indicate that the shape is part of a group, as shown in Figure 3-8.

4. Format the shape.

Formatting a shape can change the group size, making the group smaller or larger than the group window. To adjust this, right-click on the group and select Format | Behavior.

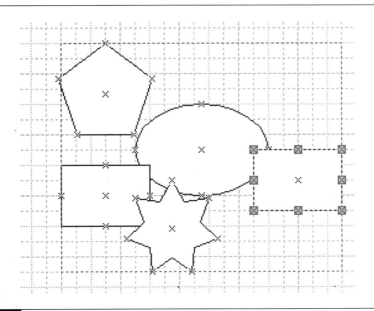

FIGURE 3-8   A selected shape within a group

Adding or removing shapes is best accomplished by using the Shape | Grouping menu commands.

To add a shape to a group:

1. Deselect everything by clicking on an unoccupied part of the drawing page.

2. Select the group to which you wish to add the shape.

3. Hold down SHIFT and select the shape to be added. The shape has a selection box with blue control points.

4. Select Shape | Group | Add to Group. A box appears containing the original group and the new shape.

Add to Group adds the new shape to the group without affecting the original group or the new shape in any way other than expanding the group. The added shape remains in its place, and Visio 2000 repositions the group's selection rectangle to encompass it. You can also add a group to another group.

To remove a shape from a group:

1. Deselect everything by pressing ESC or by clicking on an unoccupied part of the drawing page.

2. Select the shape you wish to remove from the group. The shape has a selection box with green control handles with crosses inside them.

3. Select Shape | Group | Remove from Group, or press the DELETE key.

Remove from Group takes the selected shape out of the group without changing the group or the shape in any other way. Both the selected shape and the remaining shapes in the group stay where they were. Once you've removed a shape from a group, you're free to place it as you would any other shape.

| NOTE | *After repositioning, adding, or removing shapes within a group, the alignment box for the group may be the wrong size. To adjust it, right-click on the group and select Format | Behavior.* |

Convert to Group

When you import Windows metafiles or linked objects from other programs into Visio 2000, they don't automatically come in as a Visio 2000 shape. Instead, when you import these into Visio 2000, they're placed as one single shape and act very differently from Visio 2000 shapes.

Convert to Group allows you to change these imported shapes into groups that act much more like you expect shapes to act. Usually, the conversion allows you to ungroup and manipulate parts of the imported shape.

To convert an imported object into a group, first you need to import the object. Select the correct type of object (usually Picture) from the Insert menu and proceed with the insertion. Once the object has been inserted, select the new shape and nothing else. Select Shape | Grouping | Convert to Group. The shape should now be a group and you can format, add, or remove shapes from the group using the other Shape | Grouping options. Not all objects can become Visio 2000 groups, so test this before relying on your object being able to do it.

CAUTION *If you use this feature on a linked object that has been embedded or linked in another program, you'll become unable to edit it in any program other than Visio 2000.*

Stacking Order

Stacking order determines how shapes overlap other shapes on the page and the order in which shapes are selected. You can change the stacking order by using the Bring to Front, Bring Forward, Send to Back, and Send Backward commands on the Shape menu. You can also use the Send to Back and Bring to Front buttons on the toolbar.

NOTE *Shapes on a background always appear behind shapes on a foreground. Layers, however, have no effect on stacking order.*

The selection order is important when you select multiple shapes by dragging a selection net around them. The shape at the front of the stacking order becomes the primary shape, displaying green handles. When you select multiple shapes by holding SHIFT and clicking, the stacking order doesn't affect the selection order. The first shape you click becomes the primary shape.

Adding Pages, Layers, and Backgrounds

Visio 2000 diagrams can have hundreds of shapes and cover topics that require dozens of pages of diagrams. Sometimes a diagram has shapes in a complicated arrangement, or there can be different diagrams on separate pages that need to look like part of a set. Visio 2000 has created three ways for you to manage these issues: pages, layers, and backgrounds.

Pages, layers, and backgrounds allow you to create diagrams that are more than just what you see on the drawing page. Pages allow you to create diagrams that have more than one page. Layers allow you to work with shapes in a complicated diagram without worrying about moving shapes you've already placed. Backgrounds make it easy to create several different diagrams that have a similar look.

Working with Pages

Visio 2000 diagrams are divided into two parts: foreground pages and background pages. So far you've just dealt with foreground pages, and only one page at a time.

Visio 2000 diagrams can contain several foreground and background pages, allowing you to create multipage diagrams that have the same look throughout. When you decide to create a multipage diagram, you need to first make sure you know what the page will look like. Good planning is essential when working with multipage diagrams, since you won't be able to see all the diagram at once, making it easy to become confused about where shapes are located. Planning helps reduce confusion and increases the effectiveness of pages.

 Visio 2000 windows can only display one page at a time.

The distinction between the drawing page and a page in Visio 2000 can get confusing, especially because as you add pages they look just like the drawing page you have dealt with so far. It may help to keep the following distinctions in mind: The page you see on the screen is called the *drawing page.* When you print the diagram you do so on the *printed page.* When you add a page to your Visio 2000 diagram, you're adding a whole new Visio 2000 document that is linked to the one you have open, with its own desktop and possibly its own stencils.

Using pages allows you to keep related diagrams together and gives you the option of using backgrounds.

 Have all the versions of a single diagram saved as different pages. That way, you can keep the progression of the diagram together for later reference.

3

Pages also let you present a series of diagrams like a slide show. Using full screen view, you can navigate through a series of pages to see how they would look when presented in that manner. You can also place links between pages that are saved together and then navigate through them like a Web site.

You can also rotate pages individually. If you have part of a diagram that needs to be set differently on the printed page, you can add another Visio 2000 page and rotate it to make it easier to edit the material.

> **NOTE** *Most Visio 2000 templates are set up with the drawing page, printed page, and printed drawing sizes all the same, so you don't have to change any settings or sizes to get the printed drawing you expect.*

Adding Pages

If your plan calls for layers, backgrounds, or multiple pages, the first step is to add a new page.

> **NOTE** *To move between pages, use the page tabs at the bottom of the Visio 2000 window.*

To create a new page, make sure you're on the page that directly precedes the new page. New pages inherit their properties from the page being displayed when they are added. Choose Insert | Page. The Page Setup dialog box opens, as shown in Figure 3-9. This dialog box allows you to change the size, scale, and other settings for a drawing page by using five tabs: Print Setup, Page Size, Drawing Scale, Page Properties, and Layout and Routing.

Page Properties   Specifies the type of page and to name the page. This portion of the tab also lists the assigned background page and the unit of measure set for the rulers. The type of page, background page settings, and ruler settings are inherited from the page that was displayed when you added the new page.

> **TIP** *Make sure to give your pages meaningful names describing their content or placement. This becomes invaluable when you have several pages to work with simultaneously.*

Shape Shadow Offset   Specifies the location of shadows in relation to shapes. All shadows on a page have the same offset. By default, shadows

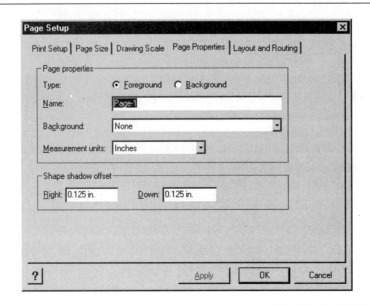

FIGURE 3-9   Page Setup dialog box

appear 0.125 inches down and to the right of the shape. For shadows above or
to the left of a shape, type negative numbers.

Layout and Routing   Add line jumps to a page. A *line jump* is a small,
uneditable arc that Visio 2000 draws on one of two crossed lines, showing the
lines are crossed, not connected. Add line jumps to specify which line of the
two has the small arc. Jumps can be set for horizontal or vertical lines only or
set to happen on the last line that was created or adjusted. If you choose Last
Routed Line, jumps occur on both horizontal and vertical lines.

Page Size   Displays the page size settings for Visio 2000. By default, the
page size is set to match the paper size set for the printer.

Print Setup   Displays the current printer settings for Visio 2000.

Drawing Scale   Displays the current scale set for the drawing, which is 1:1
by default. You can edit the scale here, but remember that the page size and
printer settings directly affect how this looks on the printed page.

Once you're satisfied with the information in the Page Setup dialog box, click OK, and Visio 2000 adds the new page. Visio 2000 takes you to the new page, which is blank, ready for you to start another part of your diagram.

Deleting Pages

You can delete pages when you no longer need them. Visio 2000 cannot undo a page removal, and all information on a page will be lost when you remove it. Be very sure that you don't need any information on the page when you delete it.

CAUTION *Always save your diagram before you remove pages. That way, if you need to go back, you can use your saved file.*

To delete a page, right-click on the tab for the drawing page and select Delete Page. After the page is deleted, Visio 2000 renumbers your pages if you haven't named them. If you delete the last page in a file, Visio 2000 replaces that page with a blank page.

Sizing and Reordering Pages

After you've added pages, you often need to reorder or resize them. This ability to customize pages can be useful; however, make sure you verify that the printed page settings are correct so the diagram prints the way you expect. (Printing settings can be accessed by selecting File I Print.)

If you print a diagram that's larger than the printed page, the drawing prints across several pages. This is called *tiling*. You can verify whether and where your drawing breaks across pages by choosing View I Page Breaks. Gray lines appear to show the page breaks.

You may resize pages by placing the mouse over an edge of the drawing page, holding down CTRL, then clicking and dragging. The page dynamically resizes as you do this. You can also alter the page size by choosing File I Page Setup and selecting the Page Size tab.

Since new pages inherit the attributes of the page that was displayed when they were added, it usually works best to add the page next to a very similar page and then reorder it so it appears in the right place in your page flow.

To reorder pages, right-click on any page tab and select Reorder Pages. The Reorder Pages dialog box appears, as shown in Figure 3-10. Move the pages around by selecting them and using the Move Up and Move Down buttons. Once they're in the order you need, click OK.

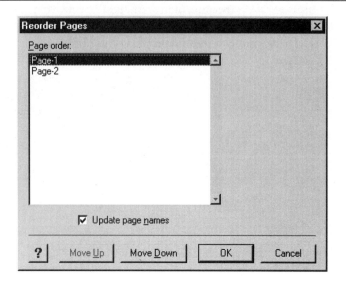

FIGURE 3-10   Reorder Pages dialog box

 NOTE   *Visio 2000 automatically renumbers or renames pages if you select the "Update page names" checkbox and don't rename the pages yourself.*

Using Layers

Layers give you control over how you edit a diagram. With layers, you can work with or display some parts of your diagram without the other parts being visible or movable. Layers also allow you to print part or all of a diagram at a time.

Layers are there to help facilitate the diagram-creation process. They allow you to look at a set of shapes at once, possibly even making them all one color so you can see where they are. They help you lock down shapes you've already placed so they aren't accidentally moved as you edit other shapes. Layers also help you control the snapping and gluing action of shapes in your diagram, since snapping and gluing can be set differently for each layer. You can even print reports listing the shapes in each layer, a feature that is particularly useful when doing office diagrams or floor plans.

Layers are so useful in floor plans that templates for office diagrams and floor plans come with shapes already assigned to the layers. For example, you can lay out the walls and computer networks and assign them to one layer. Then, when you start to place furniture and cubicles, the walls and network wiring won't be accidentally moved. If the furniture is on its own layer, you could then run a report of all the furniture shapes, greatly helping you plan your purchases and organize your office needs.

Adding Layers

In Visio 2000, a *layer* is a named category of shapes. Any single shape can be assigned to multiple layers or no layer, and every page in a drawing can have a different set of layers. To add a layer to a diagram, select View | Layer Properties. The Layer Properties window appears, as shown in Figure 3-11.

> **TIP** *You can also get to the Layer Properties window from the View menu on the Preview screen.*

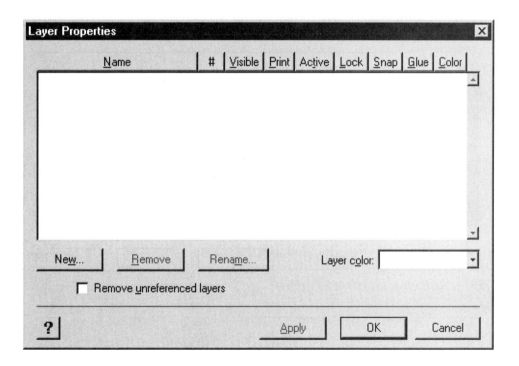

Layer Properties	✕

Name | # | Visible | Print | Active | Lock | Snap | Glue | Color

New... | Remove | Rename... | Layer color:

☐ Remove unreferenced layers

? | | Apply | OK | Cancel

FIGURE 3-11 Layer Properties window

New   Allows you to create a new layer. A dialog box asking for the name of the new layer appears when you click this button.

Remove   Deletes the selected layer.

Rename   Changes the name of the selected layer. A dialog box asking for the new name appears when you click Rename.

Name   Lists the names of the layers. Clicking the Name button opens the Rename Layer window for the currently selected layer. You can also use the Rename button to rename the selected layer in place.

Lists the number of shapes in each layer.

> **TIP**   *The numbers in the # column only tell you how many shapes are on each layer; they don't provide an accurate count of how many shapes are in the entire drawing. A single shape may be assigned to two or more layers.*

Visible   Allows you to set whether the shapes on a given layer are visible or hidden. Place a check mark in the column to show the layer; clear the check mark to hide the layer.

Print   Allows you to set whether the shapes on a given layer print. Place a check mark in this column to have the layer print; clear the check mark to have the layer not print.

Active   Specifies the default layer to which shapes are assigned. More than one layer can be active at a time, so any shape added belongs to all active layers if you don't assign it a specific layer. You may find it useful to change your active layer or layers as you progress through your diagram, making sure that the shapes you add attach to the correct layer.

> **NOTE**   *Active layers cannot be locked.*

Lock   Prevents shapes on a given layer from being selected or changed. An active layer cannot be locked, and a locked layer cannot have any of its Visible, Print, Snap, Glue, or Color properties changed.

3

Snap   Specifies whether any other shapes can snap to shapes assigned to this layer. A shape on a layer that has Snap unchecked can still snap to other shapes, no matter what their layer, but other shapes cannot snap to it.

Glue   Specifies whether any other shape can glue to shapes assigned to the layer. A shape on a layer that has Glue unchecked can still glue to other shapes, no matter what their layer, but other shapes cannot glue to it.

Color   Specifies the color for all shapes on that layer. Use this option to identify all the shapes assigned to a color, or to help move shapes on different layers within a complicated diagram. This option doesn't permanently change the color of the shapes; it simply overrides the shape's color in favor of the layer color. To return a shape to its original color, uncheck this option.

> **NOTE**   *Layers do not determine how shapes appear on the page, so layer order has very little effect on the page. The way shapes overlap on the drawing page is determined by their stacking order and background settings.*

Once you have added all the layers you need and selected their options, click OK.

Removing or Renaming Layers

When you have created a drawing with many layers, you may find that you have more layers than you need, or that layers you added and named earlier now need to be renamed. You can accomplish both of these tasks in the Layer Properties window, shown in Figure 3-11.

> **CAUTION**   *If you select the checkbox for Remove Unreferenced Layers, Visio 2000 automatically deletes any layers that don't contain shapes.*

To remove a layer, first make sure that you don't need any shape on the layer; shapes on removed layers are deleted. Once you are sure, select the layer and click Remove. A window appears asking you to confirm the removal, warning you that the shapes on that layer will be deleted. Click OK.

To rename a layer, select it from the list, and click Rename. The Rename dialog box appears. Once you enter the new name, click OK.

Understanding Backgrounds

Pages and layers help you create complicated diagrams; however, they aren't the best tool to allow you to create a seamless look for all the pages in a diagram. A special type of page, called a *background*, can be added to every drawing page to help your diagrams look the same for a whole set of pages.

Backgrounds are added like pages and behave somewhat like layers. Like layers, they allow you to have shapes in your diagram that cannot be edited as you place other shapes on the drawing page. Unlike layers, backgrounds hold shapes completely static and won't allow you to snap or glue any shape on the drawing page to the background.

Add a background when you want the same shape in the same place to show on more than one page. Backgrounds allow you to place a common graphic element and use it to create a seamless look from page to page. For example, you can place your company logo in the lower-left corner of the background and then assign that background to all your pages. The element appears exactly the same size, shape, and placement on each page you assign that background to, significantly adding to the professional look of your diagrams.

Backgrounds act like the company logo on an office letterhead: they're visible on the page, but not editable. Backgrounds are also inherited as you add new pages. You can edit the background itself separately, as a page on its own, and the changes update on all the pages that reference that background.

Visio 2000 diagrams can have several backgrounds, just as they can have several pages; however, each page can have only one assigned background. Fortunately, backgrounds can have backgrounds, allowing you to make a multilayered page with several backgrounds working together. For example, you could place your company logo on one background and a border on another, allowing you to move them separately.

NOTE	*When adding backgrounds to backgrounds, make sure you have carefully planned the diagram and know which elements will be on which backgrounds; otherwise you might get lost as you try to edit the shapes on a page.*

Adding Backgrounds

You can create a new page as a background or convert a foreground page to a background. When you create a background, Visio 2000 automatically adds it to the list of available backgrounds for other pages in the Insert Page and Properties windows.

> **NOTE**   *The Page Layout Wizard creates a background for your diagram and puts in placeholders for elements such as title blocks, borders, and logos. To edit these placeholders you must display the background page.*

To create a background, add a page by choosing Insert | Page. The Page Setup dialog box appears, as shown earlier in Figure 3-9. Add the page as you would any other, but make sure to select Background for the Type. The background inherits the page size and drawing scale from the page on the screen when you added it, but you can change that just as you would for any other page. Click OK when you're done.

To convert an existing foreground page into a background page, display the foreground page you wish to convert in the Visio 2000 window. You can move between pages by using the page tabs at the bottom of the Visio Page.

Select File | Page Setup. The Page Setup dialog box appears. Click the Page Properties tab. The dialog box should look like the one shown earlier in Figure 3-9. Change the Type option from Foreground to Background and then click OK.

Assigning a Background Page

Once you've created a background page that didn't exist before (either by creating a new page or by converting a foreground page) you need to set a foreground page to use it. This is called *attaching a background*.

To attach a background, select the page tab to go to the foreground page you'd like to attach a background page to, then go to File | Page Setup. The Page Setup dialog box opens, as shown earlier in Figure 3-9. On the Page Properties tab, set the Background for the new background page. Its name should be in the drop-down list of backgrounds.

The background appears behind the foreground. Remember to save your diagram after you do this to make sure you have all the changes saved.

Editing Backgrounds

Since a background's main purpose is to remain unchanged as you edit the foreground, you need to go through some extra steps to edit a background. To edit a background, you must first open the background by selecting Edit | Go To and going to the page. If the background is attached to the page currently displayed, you can simply open the background by choosing Background. If the background isn't attached to the current page, you need to select it by name from the list. It may be easier to open the background in a new window. That way, you can have both the page and its background open simultaneously, allowing you to edit both at once. To display a background in a new window, choose Edit | Go To | Page, select Open Page In New Window, and then click OK. To see both pages at once, choose Window | Tile.

Once a background is open, you can edit as you would any other page. The edits you make are reflected on all the pages with that background established. Those pages are updated as soon as you finish editing the background and move to another page.

> **TIP** *If you'd just like to view, edit, print, or lock shapes down individually on one page, use layers. Backgrounds are for forming a cohesive look across pages.*

Once you've finished editing the background, you need to return to the foreground page to continue constructing your diagram by selecting the Page tab from the bottom of the Visio window.

Deleting Backgrounds

Backgrounds are special types of pages, so deleting them works very similarly to deleting pages—with one difference. As in other pages, everything on a background page will be deleted when you remove the page. However, any background page that is still attached to a foreground page cannot be removed. You need to remove all the attachments to a background before you delete it.

> **NOTE** *If you try to delete a background page while it is still assigned, Visio warns you to remove it from the foreground page and takes you to that page in order to use the Page Setup window.*

To cancel a page's background assignment, display the foreground page it's attached to. Choose File | Page Setup. The Page Setup dialog box appears, as shown earlier in Figure 3-9. On the Page Properties tab, select None from the Background drop-down list and then click OK.

Once the background page is detached from all foreground pages, you can delete it by right-clicking on the Page tab and selecting Delete from the list.

Adding Graphics

Graphics in your Visio 2000 diagrams add personalization and panache to the finished product. There are two ways to add images to your Visio 2000 diagrams—you can import images or embed them. Imported images such as bitmaps and JPGs are supported by Visio 2000 and work best when you plan to integrate them into your diagram as shapes, annotate an image, or when file size is a concern. This section discusses imported images.

> **NOTE** *Embedded images usually come from Object Linking and Embedding (OLE) programs, such as the Microsoft Office Suite. For information on OLE functions with Visio 2000, see Chapter 6.*

When you import an image created in another program into Visio 2000, it only exists as a picture in Visio 2000 and has none of the properties of Visio 2000 shapes. You can only reposition, resize, or crop imported images in Visio 2000, so you should make sure all the image editing that needs to be done is finished in the image's original creation program.

You cannot edit imported pictures in Visio 2000 because the images go though a filter that translates the image, stripping away the information added by the original creation program so it can be displayed by Visio 2000. You also need to make sure that you save the image in a format Visio 2000 can read. A list of all importable formats is in the next section.

Images you import into Visio 2000 go though two translations—one when they are saved from the creation program and one when they are imported into Visio 2000—so they may not look the same in Visio 2000 as they did in the original program. Make sure you have verified, by both viewing it on the screen and by printing the imported image, that the translated image works for your purposes.

> **TIP** *Bitmaps and JPGs undergo the least conversion when imported into Visio 2000.*

Importing Formats

Visio 2000 has translators for many file formats, which are listed in Table 3-2.

Most files you import into Visio 2000 as graphic images are translated into metafiles. However, bitmap files (such as .dib, .bmp, and .pcx files) remain bitmaps in the Visio 2000 drawing.

Vector-based graphic programs or formats, such as Adobe Illustrator (.ai), CorelDraw (.cdr), Encapsulated PostScript (.eps), and Micrografx Designer (.drw) files, do not import as smoothly as metafile formats like bitmaps. Their lines sometimes appear jagged when the images are imported into a Visio 2000

File Extension	Creation Program or Interchange Formats
.af3, .af2	ABC FlowCharter 2.0, 3.0, 4.0
.ai	Adobe Illustrator
.dwg	AutoCAD Drawing
.dxf	AutoCAD Drawing Interchange
.dwf	AutoCAD Drawing Web
.gif	CompuServe Interchange
.cgm	Computer Graphics Metafile
.cmx	Corel Clipart
.cdr	CorelDRAW Drawing, versions 3.0, 4.0, 5.0, 6.0, and 7.0
.cfl	CorelFLOW 2.0
.eps	Encapsulated PostScript
.igs	Initial Graphics Exchange Specification
.jpg	Joint Photographic Experts Group
.pct	Macintosh Picture
.drw	Micrografx Designer Version 3.1
.dsf	Micrografx Designer Version 6.0
.png	Portable Network Graphics
.tif	Tag Image
.txt and .csv	Text and Comma Separated Variable
.bmp and .dib	Windows Bitmap
.wmf	Windows Metafile
.pcx	ZSoft PC PaintBrush Bitmap

TABLE 3-2   Importable File Formats

drawing. You'll usually get better results if you save these types of files in a
metafile format before importing them into Visio 2000.

TIP   *Metafiles are the best type of images to import into Visio 2000, since the
Convert to Group command allows you to deconstruct them into groups
and then edit the pieces individually.*

Importing Images

Visio 2000 adds imported images to your diagram as simple shapes with a rectangular selection box and control handles. It's best to add images early in the diagram process to make sure the translation worked well and that the image works for your planned diagram.

Importing images into Visio 2000 is a simple process. First, make sure you're on the page where the image is to be placed, then choose Import | Picture. The Picture window appears, as shown in Figure 3-12.

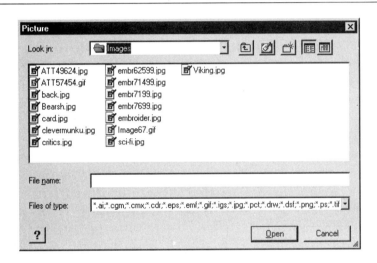

| FIGURE 3-12 | Picture window |

Locate the image file. Once you have selected it, click Open. Depending on the image's file type, Visio 2000 may display an Import dialog box like the one shown here:

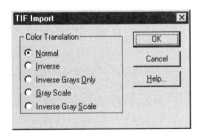

The Import dialog box allows you to set the color and gradient for some image formats. Select the import settings, and click OK. An importing progress bar appears, like the one shown here:

Once the image has been imported, it appears centered on the drawing page you selected. You can now place and resize the image as you would a Visio 2000 SmartShape image. However, the imported image will not resize in a way that retains its dimensions or image clarity.

Cropping

Imported images are a special type of shape in Visio 2000. They don't work like SmartShape images, so Visio 2000 created a special tool to help you edit imported images: the Crop tool. The Crop tool doesn't work on Visio 2000 images, only on imported ones, and is the only tool you have to edit images that don't use the Convert to Group or Fit to Curve functions.

The Crop tool allows you to edit imported images in two ways—you can remove a portion of the image by *cropping* or you can move the image within its selection box by *panning*. To learn how the Crop tool works, see Chapter 2.

You should try to keep cropping to a minimum. Although the cropping tool hides a piece of a graphic, the entire graphic is still stored in the drawing and sent to the printer, causing a lot of unnecessary data pushing. It's best to do major cropping in another application so that the copy stored in the Visio drawing is as small as possible.

Summary

In this chapter, you learned how to use the many Visio 2000 layout tools, how to add graphics to your Visio 2000 diagrams, and how to take advantage of pages, layers, and backgrounds. In the next chapter, you'll learn how to choose, use, and create stencils and templates.

CHAPTER 4

Using Stencils and Templates

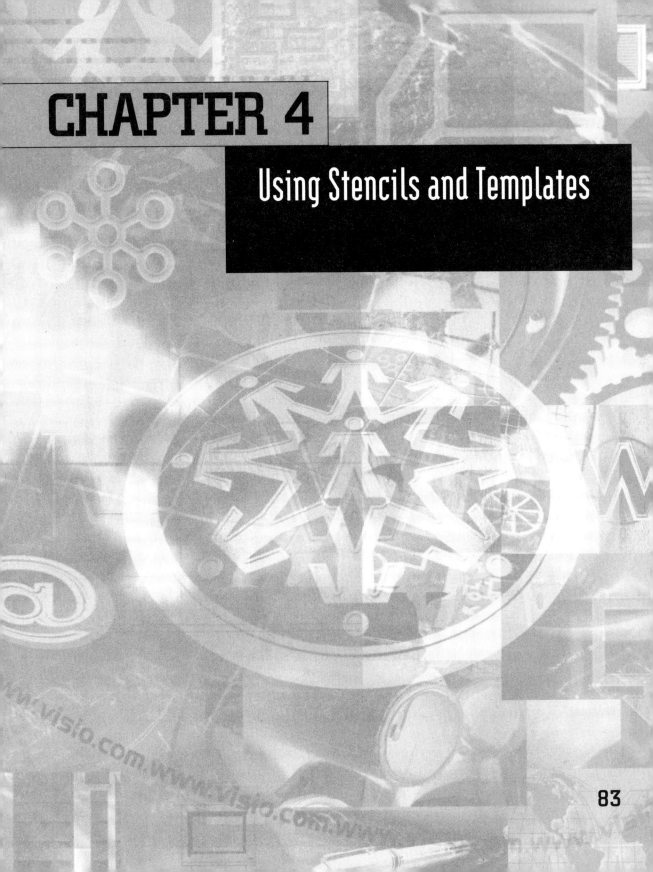

In the last chapter, you learned how to use Visio 2000's layout tools and how to add graphics to your diagrams.

In this chapter you'll learn how to:

■ Find, use, modify, and create stencils

■ Create master shapes and include them in your stencils

■ Find, use, modify, and create templates

Getting to Know Stencils

Stencils are the workhorses of Visio 2000. They allow you to add shapes to your diagrams with minimal effort, and they ensure that the shapes in your diagrams have a consistent appearance. Ease of creation and uniformity are what set Visio 2000 apart from other graphics programs.

Stencils are collections of shapes that are related in some way. The Callouts stencil, for example, has all the shapes you need to create callouts in diagrams—including lines, callout bubbles, and brackets. These shapes are included on one stencil to help you complete your diagrams quickly and easily. To use the shapes in a diagram, you simply open the Callouts stencil and drag the shapes from the stencil to your drawing page. Figure 4-1 shows the Callouts stencil.

> **NOTE**   *A shape can appear on many different stencils. For example, some of the shapes on the Callouts stencil appear on other stencils, as well.*

Stencil files, which have a .vss extension, contain information about the various stencils, including information about the shapes they contain. The shapes on a stencil are *master shapes,* which become individual shapes when you drag them off the stencil onto the drawing page. The information that determines a shape's attributes and behavior is contained in the master shape.

Choosing the Right Stencil

When you create a new diagram, you should first have a plan for it. Knowing the types of shapes you're likely to include is invaluable when you start using stencils. If you know what shapes you'll be using, you can determine which stencils to open.

FIGURE 4-1   Callouts stencil

| TIP | *You can open as many stencils as you like while working on a diagram.* |

Choosing the right stencils for the job may seem a bit confusing at first, because Visio 2000 includes a tremendous number of stencils. But the people at Visio have worked very hard to make the process as painless as possible. Stencils have been grouped into folders by topic to help you locate the ones you need. In addition, Visio 2000 includes a search engine—the Shape Explorer—to help you find stencils containing particular shapes. Visio 2000 also includes many templates that open certain stencils automatically. For now, though, we'll only discuss opening stencils using the folders and the Shape Explorer. We explain templates later in this chapter.

Navigating Stencil Folders

Stencils can be added to any diagram. But first you need to know how to choose the right stencils from the large selection included in Visio 2000.

Visio 2000 Standard has nine folders containing stencils. Table 4-1 lists these folders and describes the types of stencils they contain.

Folder	Description of Stencils
Block Diagrams	Basic diagrams and simple connections, usually used in conjunction with more complicated stencils
Flowcharts	Complete flowcharting tools with hundreds of different shapes
Forms and Charts	Simple charts and graphs, basic forms, and marketing-support diagrams
Maps	Tools for creating maps of any location and for integrating maps into diagrams
Network Diagrams	Computer and network shapes for basic network outlines and other related diagrams
Office Layout	Shapes for diagrams of office layouts
Organizational Charts	Shapes for creating organizational charts
Project Scheduler	Calendar, process-mapping, and timeline shapes
Visio Extras	Miscellaneous stencils, including clip art and callout stencils

TABLE 4-1 Stencil Folders in Visio 2000

 Appendix A of this book lists all of Visio 2000's stencils, the folders where they're located, and the shapes they contain.

Using Shape Explorer

Sometimes, you'll want to use a particular shape or set of shapes, but you won't know which stencil you need. Visio 2000 has included the Shape Explorer to help you find the right stencil. You can use the Shape Explorer to search for shapes by entering keywords. The Shape Explorer tells you the stencils on which a particular shape appears and the folders where the stencils are located.

 The Shape Explorer also helps you find templates and wizards. For now, though, we'll focus on how it can help you find shapes and stencils.

To use the Shape Explorer to find a shape, open the Shape Explorer window by selecting Tools | Macros | Shape Explorer. The Shape Explorer window opens, as shown in Figure 4-2.

To see the Shape Explorer in action, type **diamond** in the "Search for" box and click Find Now. The Shape Explorer searches Visio 2000 for the keyword and returns a list of shapes, as shown in Figure 4-3.

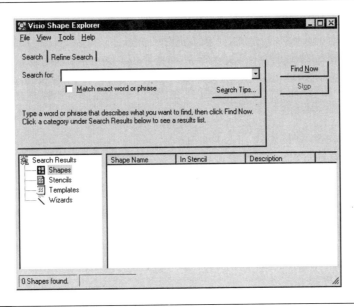

FIGURE 4-2   The Shape Explorer window

The lower half of the Shape Explorer window is divided into two panes. The left-hand pane lists the different types of search results that are possible. The four types are Shapes, Stencils, Templates, and Wizards. When you perform a search, the Shape Explorer tells you how many matches there are for each type. For example, if you search for the keyword "diamond," the Shape Explorer comes up with six matches for shapes, but no matches for stencils, templates, or wizards. (Refer to Figure 4-3.) Click on a result type in the left-hand pane to view the results for that type in the right-hand pane.

The right-hand pane lists the actual search results. For example, when you search for the keyword "diamond," and select Shapes in the left-hand pane, the right-hand pane displays all the diamond shapes found. Double-click on one of these shapes to bring up a Properties window, as shown in Figure 4-4, giving you detailed information about the shape.

Right-click on the diamond shape that is located in the Clip Art stencil (the filename for the stencil is clip art.vss). Select Open Containing Stencil from the shortcut menu. This automatically adds the stencil to your diagram. Now you can use this diamond shape in your drawing. You can use this process for any shape or stencil you find with the Shape Explorer.

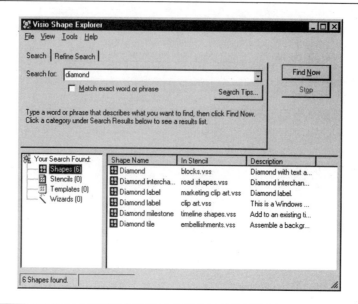

FIGURE 4-3   The Shape Explorer window with search results

The Shape Explorer has a database of all the shapes, stencils, templates, and wizards that come with your version of Visio 2000. With the Shape Explorer, you can perform two kinds of searches: standard and refined. When you perform a

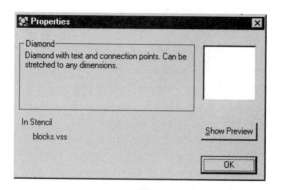

FIGURE 4-4   The Properties window for a diamond shape

standard search, the Shape Explorer searches everything in its database for the keywords you enter. When you perform a *refined* search, the Shape Explorer searches for only the type of results you need. For example, you could search for just shapes or just stencils. By default, the Shape Explorer performs a standard search and looks for everything in its database that matches the keywords. However, standard searches can give you more information than you need.

> **TIP** *To view everything in the Shape Explore database that matches your keywords, use the Search tab in the Shape Explorer window to perform a standard search.*

To get only a specific type of result, you need to use the Refine Search tab of the Shape Explorer window. The Refine Search tab allows you to narrow the scope of your search by modifying the search parameters. For example, you could search for all stencils with rectangles, while excluding shapes and templates from your search results. To include a category in your search, leave it checked on the Refine Search tab. If you'd like to remove a category from the search, clear the check mark beside the category. Using the Refine Search tab helps you avoid getting too many matches in your search results.

> **TIP** *It's usually helpful to exclude the Wizards category from searches. It takes time for the Search Explorer to search through all the wizards, and typically you'll be interested in finding only shapes and stencils.*

Working with Stencils

Stencils are essential for creating professional-looking Visio 2000 diagrams. To get the most out of Visio's stencils you need to know how to open them and how to reposition them onscreen. As you'll see, it can be very handy to have multiple stencils open at the same time.

Opening Stencils

In addition to using the Shape Explorer to open stencils, you can open a new stencil using Visio 2000's menus. To open a stencil, in the main Visio 2000 window, select File | Stencils | Open Stencil. The Open Stencil dialog box appears, as shown in Figure 4-5.

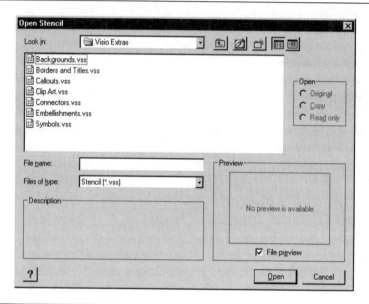

FIGURE 4-5   Open Stencil dialog box

 You can also display the Open Stencil dialog box by clicking the Open Stencil button on the toolbar.

The Open Stencil dialog box allows you to choose from several dozen stencils. Double-click a folder in the window to see a list of the stencils it contains. Each stencil contains a different set of shapes. (Remember, however, that a particular shape may appear on more than one stencil.) Visio 2000 helps you choose between stencils by providing a description of each stencil in the lower left-hand corner of the Open Stencil dialog box. Select a stencil (without opening it) to view its description.

Once you've found the stencil you need, select it and click Open. The Open Stencil dialog box closes and the stencil appears in the main Visio 2000 window.

 You can have more than one stencil open at a time. To view an open stencil that's hidden behind another stencil, click the stencil's title bar to bring it to the front.

Moving Stencils

When you open new stencils, they automatically appear on the left-hand side of the main Visio 2000 window. Having all your stencils on the left side of the window can be inconvenient, though—especially if you've rotated the drawing page and zoomed in. Then the stencils can get in your way. Visio 2000 gives you a couple ways around this problem, though. You can move stencils to other sides of the window, and you can "undock" them.

When a stencil appears on the left side of the window, as you've seen so far, it is considered *docked,* or locked to the pasteboard. A docked stencil is locked in place and can't be dragged from its location. Although by default stencils are docked on the left side of the main Visio 2000 window, you can dock them on any side of the window. To dock a stencil on a different side, right-click on the stencil's title bar, select Position, and then choose the new place to dock the stencil.

In addition to docking stencils on different sides of the window, you can undock stencils so they can be moved around freely within the main Visio 2000 window. You can move undocked stencils, which are called *floating stencils,* by dragging them. This makes them much easier to move out of the way than docked stencils. Floating stencils are also handy because they can be *rolled up.* When you roll up a floating stencil, only its title bar is visible. This enables you to keep many stencils open without using up a lot of valuable screen real estate. Figure 4-6 shows three floating stencils, two of which are rolled up.

To make a docked stencil become a floating stencil, right-click on its title bar. A shortcut menu appears, as shown here:

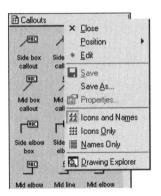

On the shortcut menu, select Position and then Float. The stencil detaches from its docked position and becomes a floating stencil. The stencil can be redocked by clicking on the title bar and dragging it back to the upper-left or upper-right corner of the pasteboard.

TIP *You can also make a stencil float by clicking anywhere on its green background and dragging the stencil onto the pasteboard.*

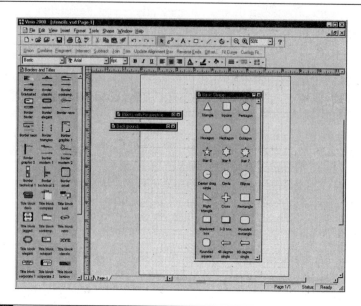

FIGURE 4-6 Docked and undocked stencils

To roll up a floating stencil, click the minimize button on the stencil's title bar. This minimizes the stencil so you see only its the title bar. By rolling up floating stencils, you can make more room for your diagram without loosing access to the stencils should you need them. To unroll a stencil, click the maximize button on its title bar.

Closing Stencils

To close a stencil, right-click on the stencil's title bar and choose Close from the stencil's shortcut menu. Alternatively, you can click the Close button, the small × in the upper-right corner of the stencil. This removes the stencil from your diagram.

Moving Further with Stencils

Having mastered choosing, opening, moving, and closing stencils, you're ready to tackle the slightly more complicated processes of modifying stencils and creating new stencils. However, before you can do this, you need to understand the concept of *master shapes,* which comprise stencils.

Master Shapes and ShapeSheets

Master shapes are the shapes on the stencils. To modify or create new stencils, you'll be dealing with master shapes. Master shapes contain all the information that goes into making SmartShapes smart. This includes not only the number of sides and the color of the shape, but also how it's resized, how it behaves under rotation, and how added text behaves, as well as all the custom properties that come with some shapes.

All information for master shapes is stored in *ShapeSheets,* which are databases that contain the programming information for the master shapes. ShapeSheets are discussed in more detail in Chapter 11, "Using Advanced Visio 2000 Features."

To modify an existing stencil or create a new one, you change master shapes. There are hundreds of master shapes that come with Visio 2000, and there's also a way to make master shapes of your own.

Modifying a Stencil

Modifying a stencil means changing the order, arrangement, content, or number of master shapes on it. The most common type of stencil modification is the addition of a master shape to a stencil.

No matter what kind of change you're making to a stencil, the first step should always be to open the stencil so you can change it. This means you need to open the stencil in *read/write mode.* Normally, when you open a stencil, you open it as *read-only,* meaning you can't make any changes to the original stencil. All changes you might attempt to make are blocked.

NOTE *If you try to make changes to a read-only stencil, Visio 2000 asks if you'd like to open the stencil in read/write mode.*

To open a stencil so you can change it, select File I Stencil I Open Stencil. Select the stencil you'd like to modify. Then, on the right-hand side of the Open Stencil dialog box (shown earlier in Figure 4-5), select the Copy radio button. Click Open to open a copy of the stencil in read/write mode.

CAUTION *Never open the original file for a stencil unless you intend to delete it. Open a copy instead.*

You can also convert an open stencil from read-only mode to read/write mode by selecting Edit from the Stencil menu.

Copying Existing Master Shapes

To copy an existing master shape from one stencil to another, make sure both stencils are open, and then drag the master shape from the original stencil to the stencil you're modifying. The new master shape appears on the modified stencil along with the other shapes, which automatically move aside to make room for the new shape.

 When you close a modified stencil by clicking the Close button, Visio 2000 asks if you'd like to save the stencil.

When you're satisfied with the arrangement of the master shapes on the stencil, select Save from the File menu. The Save As dialog box appears, as shown in Figure 4-7. Make sure to save the stencil in a place where you can find it again. The best place to save a modified stencil is where Visio 2000 keeps its stencils— in the Visio 2000 directory, under Solutions.

 If you create several stencils, you may want to group them in a folder of their own (under Solutions).

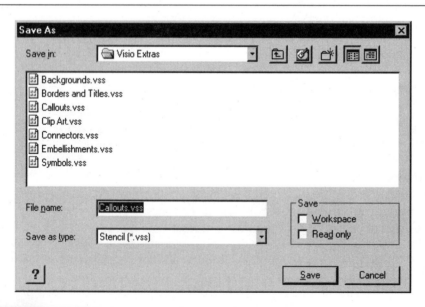

FIGURE 4-7 The Save As dialog box for a stencil

Removing Master Shapes

To remove a master shape from a stencil, open the stencil in read/write mode and right-click on the master. Choose Delete from the menu. This removes the shape from the stencil. The other shapes automatically rearrange themselves to fill in the gap. Make sure to save the modified stencil by selecting the stencil and choosing Save from the File menu.

Changing How Master Shapes Appear

To change how master shapes appear on a stencil, first open the stencil in read/write mode. Then right-click the master shape and choose Master Properties. This allows you to change the name and other display properties for the master shape. If you'd like to change the icon for a master shape, right-click on the shape and choose Edit Icon. This opens a dialog box for editing the icon. Make sure to save the stencil after any modifications.

To reorder the master shapes on a stencil, first open the stencil in read/write mode. You can then reposition the master shapes by dragging them. When they are arranged in the proper order, save the stencil.

Creating New Master Shapes

If the shape you'd like to add to a stencil doesn't already exist in Visio 2000, you need to create the master shape yourself.

To create a master shape, first you must create the shape you wish to convert into a master. You can use the drawing tools to create the shape, you can modify an existing shape, or you can import a shape from another program.

NOTE *Imported objects are often turned into clip art master shapes, not Visio 2000 SmartShape objects.*

Once you've created the shape, open a copy of the stencil you would like to add it to and then drag the shape to the stencil. By default, the new master shape is named Master.*x*, where *x* is the number of existing shapes in the stencil plus one. To change the name of the master shape, right-click on the shape and select Master Properties. The Master Properties dialog box opens, as shown in Figure 4-8. Enter a new name for the master shape, and set other options as described in the following subsections.

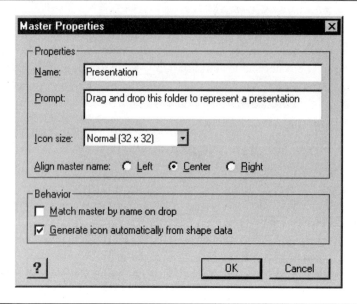

FIGURE 4-8   Master Properties dialog box

Name   Sets the name that appears beneath the master shape's icon in the stencil window. Master shape names can be up to 31 characters.

Prompt   Specifies the text that appears when you hover the mouse pointer over the master shape's icon in the stencil window.

TIP   *Keep your icon names and prompts short.*

Icon Size   Sets the size of the master shape icon. The default setting for an icon's size is Normal. The Tall setting is the same width as Normal, but twice the height. The Wide setting is the same height, but twice the width. The Double setting is twice as wide and twice as tall as Normal.

Match master by name on drop   When checked, allows you to make sure that no matter which stencil a shape comes from, it will always be formatted the way you have it formatted. When this box is checked and a shape is dragged from the stencil, Visio 2000 automatically checks to make sure that no other versions of that shape are on open stencils. If there is another version shape on an open customized stencil, Visio 2000 makes sure the new formatting is carried over to the shape you just added, even if it was dragged from a standard stencil.

Generate icon automatically from shape data When checked, Visio 2000 automatically creates the master shape's icon from the shape.

> **NOTE** *You can edit an icon so it displays better at a different size by right-clicking on the master shape on the stencil and choosing Edit. This opens a dialog box for editing the icon.*

4

One you've chosen all the options needed for the new master shape, click OK, and the Properties window closes. Complete your changes to the stencil and save it.

Remember that all the master shapes supplied by Visio 2000 are copyrighted. You may not sell or distribute original or modified Visio 2000 masters. Feel free to copy, reorganize, and modify them for your own use, though. You may also distribute drawings that contain them.

Creating a New Stencil

Creating a new stencil allows you the flexibility of collecting the shapes you use most often together on one stencil without the hassle of deleting shapes from an already existing stencil. New stencils, like all Visio 2000 stencils, can contain any master shapes that come with Visio 2000 or new master shapes you've created.

To create a new stencil, select File | Stencil | Blank Stencil. A new blank stencil opens, as shown in Figure 4-9.

Once the blank stencil is open, add shapes to it as you would any stencil you're modifying. Remember to save the stencil in a place where you can find it again. It's best to save stencils where Visio 2000 stores its stencils, in the Solutions folder in the Visio 2000 directory. You may even want to create another folder in the Solutions directory to hold your new custom stencils.

Getting to Know Templates

With stencils, you can create shapes quickly and uniformly. However, a Visio 2000 diagram consists of more than just shapes; page dimensions, shape colors, and backgrounds are all important features of professional looking diagrams. To help you with these other features, Visio 2000 includes a variety of drawing types, called *templates,* with preformatted information. Templates handle much of the formatting for you when you create standard types of diagrams.

A template is a Visio 2000 file that opens one or more stencils and can contain styles and settings for a particular kind of drawing. You can create a new drawing with a specific template's styles and settings by opening that template. When you

FIGURE 4-9   A blank stencil

open Visio 2000 and choose a drawing type (other than Basic Drawing), you automatically open a template.

When you start a drawing with a template, a Visio 2000 file opens containing:

- One or more stencils containing related shapes

- A blank drawing page using a grid and measurement system that's appropriate for the type of drawing you're creating

- A drawing page set up with the correct scale and page size, if appropriate

- Styles for text, lines, and shape colors appropriate to the type of drawing you're creating, saving you the time it takes to define your own styles

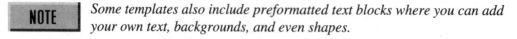

NOTE   *Some templates also include preformatted text blocks where you can add your own text, backgrounds, and even shapes.*

Using templates ensures consistency in your diagrams. The templates in the Solutions folders were created to help you with many common tasks. These templates save you time and energy by automatically setting formatting and other options. They let you get right to the task at hand.

Choosing the Right Template

When you open a new diagram, Visio 2000 asks you to choose a drawing type. At that point, it helps to know which template is likely to be the most useful. Like stencils, Visio 2000 makes the job of choosing the right template easy by grouping templates into folders. Templates and stencils have been organized into the same structure, so the template folders are the same as the ones listed earlier for stencils (refer to Table 4-1).

> **NOTE** *Appendix A includes a complete list of all the templates that come with Visio 2000 Standard and describes what each template contains.*

Working with Templates

To get the most out of templates, you need to know how to open a template, and you should understand how a template differs from a basic drawing. This section walks you though the use of a basic template.

Opening a Template

A template can be opened with a new diagram, or it can be added to a diagram that already exists.

To open a template for a new diagram, select File | New and then choose a template from the list. A new diagram opens on a new page, in a separate window. The new diagram has all the formatting and stencils included in the template. Figure 4-10 shows a new diagram with the Basic Flowchart template attached. As you can see, diagrams with templates attached look just like normal Visio 2000 diagrams, but they have stencils and styles already included.

> **NOTE** *You can open more than one diagram at a time in Visio 2000, allowing you to have several templates open at once.*

To attach a template to an existing diagram, first make sure the diagram is open in the main Visio 2000 window, and then select File | Open. Navigate to your Visio 2000 directory (usually in the Program Files folder) and then to the

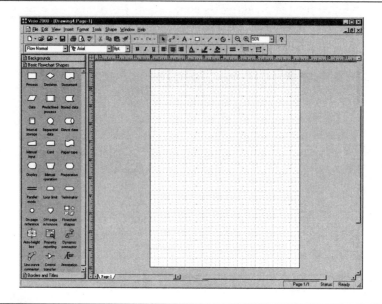

FIGURE 4-10   Basic Flowchart template

Solutions folder. Find the template you want, and click Open. The template attaches to the open diagram, overwriting all conflicting formatting.

 Because templates contain formatting to help you create diagrams, they can overwrite your own formatting when you add them to existing diagrams.

Identifying Included Formats

To make the most of a template, you need to know all the formatting it includes. The template's formatting acts like defaults, often working behind the scenes. This section discusses the diagram features that are usually affected when you attach a template. You'll also learn where to look to identify the new settings.

STENCILS   The most noticeable addition to a blank document is a stencil. When you open a template, at least one stencil will usually open with it. All stencils that open with templates are docked on the left-hand side of the screen.

If you should need stencils other than the ones that automatically open with a template, you are free to open more. To learn how to open additional stencils, see the section entitled "Opening Stencils" earlier in this chapter.

TEMPLATE HELP   Each template includes online help that explains the most efficient way to draw, the best way to use and combine shapes, how to perform specific actions using shape and page right-mouse menus, how and when to access wizards that automate tasks, and more. To access the help for a particular template, open Visio 2000 Help by choosing Template Help from the Help menu. Choose the name of your template from the list. The help document contains many useful tips for getting the most out of a template.

STYLES   A template often includes many styles. Styles for lines, text, and fills give you formatting options and are an important part of a template. To see the added styles, use the drop-down lists on the toolbars.

TIP   *Styles only work for you if you use them. Be sure to take advantage of the styles in your templates.*

PAGE FORMATTING   Units, page size, layer settings, and many other formatting options can be set in a template. To make creating diagrams easier, Visio 2000 has included templates with page formatting. Some page formatting changes are obvious, such as page orientation. Other page formatting is less obvious, such as layer settings.

To find the page formatting settings, you may need to look in a couple of places. The File | Page Setup menu is one place. So is the Ruler & Grid dialog box, which you access from the Tools menu. Page formatting changes vary widely from one template to another, so it's best to check for these changes whenever you open a template for the first time.

Moving Further with Templates

Now that you understand the basics of template use, you're ready to move on to modifying templates and creating templates of your own. Templates, like stencils, always need to be opened in read/write mode before any alteration can take place.

To open a template in read/write mode, you need to specify this mode when you attach the template. In the Open dialog box, shown in Figure 4-11, make sure

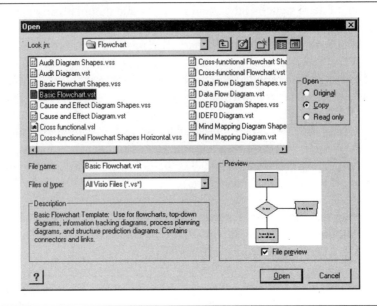

FIGURE 4-11   The Open dialog box

the Copy radio button is selected. Once you're sure you're opening a read/write copy of the template, click Open.

 Don't open the original file for a template unless you intend to delete it. Open a copy of the template instead.

Modifying a Template

If you're creating several diagrams that need to look the same, you may wish to modify one of Visio's templates to include your own style and page formatting settings and the stencils you're likely to use. Modifying a template saves you the repetitive steps required to open the appropriate stencils, create styles, and establish page settings for each drawing.

To modify a template, first open a copy of the template in read/write mode. Then make all the setting changes you need to create the new template. The most common setting changes are:

- Adding or subtracting stencils
- Creating new stencils with special master shapes

■ Changing page formatting options

■ Changing backgrounds or layers

■ Adding styles

If you need to define a new style, choose Define Styles from the Format menu. The Define Styles dialog box appears, as shown in Figure 4-12.

Defining styles assumes you're creating a new style and not simply modifying an old one.

Style   Shows all the current styles in the document. If a shape is selected, the style for that shape is highlighted in the list. If you're naming a new style, type the name here.

Based on   Selects the parent style for your newly created style. If you don't want to base your new style on an existing style, choose No Style in this box.

Includes Text, Line, Fill   Specifies whether the style includes attributes for lines, fills, or text.

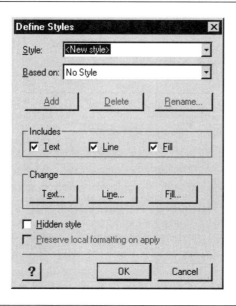

| **FIGURE 4-12** | The Define Styles dialog box |

Change Text, Line, Fill   Allows you to change the styles for text, line, and fill. The buttons open the Font, Line, and Fill dialog boxes so you can change attributes for the style. By default, these dialog boxes show the attributes for the style listed in the Style box. If the style is listed as New Style, they show the Visio 2000 default styles. Choosing OK in the Line, Fill, or Text dialog box returns you to the Define Styles dialog box.

Hidden style   Makes the style unprintable (and possibly unseen onscreen). All shapes with this formatting are hidden.

Preserve local formatting on apply   If checked, prevents the style's attributes from replacing formatting you have applied directly to the shape. Uncheck the "Preserve local formatting on apply" checkbox if you want the style to replace all previous formatting.

> **NOTE**   *If you try to close a modified template by clicking on the Close button, Visio 2000 asks if you'd like to save the template.*

Once satisfied that you've made all the setting changes you need, you're ready to save the template. Select Save As from the File menu. It's vital that you save the file with a .vst extension, since the only difference between a template and a diagram is the extension. Also, make sure you save the new template somewhere you can find it again. It's best to save the template where Visio 2000 has its templates, under the Visio 2000 directory in the Solutions folder. This location guarantees the template will be available to you in both the File | New and Open menus.

Creating a New Template

There are times when you find you're changing the same settings over and over again as you work on new diagrams; or maybe you always open the same stencils when you create a certain diagram, stencils that aren't included in an already existing template. If you find yourself repeating tasks and including the same information over and over, making a brand new template will save time and energy.

You might want to create a new template when you create drawings that:

- Require customized settings such as page size or scale, window size and position, or shape or text styles.

4

■ Often use a particular background or set of layers. For example, if you place your company logo in every drawing, you can create a template with that background or set of layers in place.

A new template allows you to start from scratch. You don't need to find out what settings have been modified in an existing template, helping assure that your diagrams look uniform and are exactly the way you want them.

Creating a template completely from scratch is almost exactly like modifying a template with one small difference—instead of opening a template's read/write mode to start the process, all you need to do is open a new document. However, it's just as vital to make sure your template gets saved with a .vst extension, since it becomes a document if you do not.

| CAUTION | *Make sure the Workspace checkbox is selected when you save a new template.* |

Summary

In this chapter you've learned how to find, use, and create stencils, how to create master shapes and include them in your stencils, and how to find, use, and modify templates.

In the next chapter, you'll learn the how to create and use flowcharts. You'll also learn how to use databases to create flowcharts as well as how to use flowcharts to create databases.

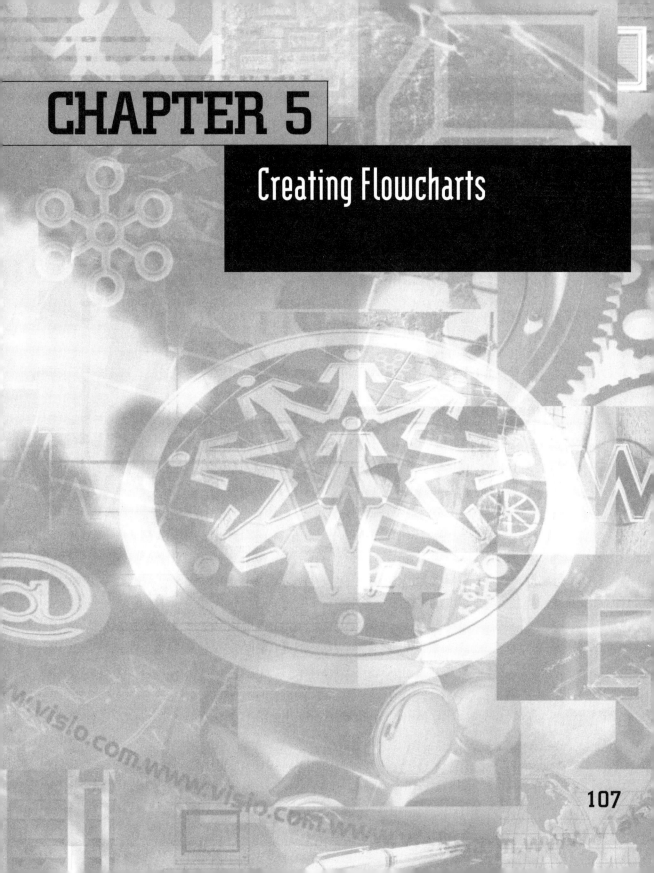

CHAPTER 5

Creating Flowcharts

In the last chapter, you learned how to use stencils and templates, how to create your own shapes, and how to add master shapes to stencils.

In this chapter, you'll learn about flowcharting in Visio 2000 and how to create several types of flowcharts. You'll also learn how to use databases to create flowcharts, and how to use flowcharts to create databases.

Understanding Visio 2000 Flowchart Diagrams

With Visio 2000, flowcharting is easy. Flowcharts are diagrams you can use to represent a business's organization and processes. Flowcharts make it easy for people to visualize a business or process in action. With a variety of simple ways to create many different kinds of flowcharts, Visio 2000 may well be the best product on the market for flowcharting.

TIP	*To get the most out of Visio 2000's flowcharts, make sure you always plan out a diagram before you start creating it on the drawing page.*

The word *flowchart* generally refers to a diagram outlining a process of data-flow; however, it can also refer to any type of diagram with shapes and connections. One of the simplest types of flowcharts is an organization chart. Organization charts illustrate how people in a business (or other organization) work together. Organization charts show who reports to whom, how pay structures and management structures operate, and how departments are linked. They're a powerful tool for creating better-organized and more dynamic business structures. In this chapter, we explain organization charts in detail to introduce you to the general format of flowcharts.

Getting to Know Visio 2000 Flowcharting

Flowcharts are composed of shapes and lines. The shapes usually represent people or steps in a process. Lines indicate the exchanges between these people or steps, and they also indicate relationships and hierarchies. In Visio 2000, there are hundreds of shapes specifically for flowcharts, but you can use any shape you wish. One important tool, the Connection tool, has been designed specifically to create flowchart lines. Figure 5-1 shows a basic Visio 2000 flowchart. It is an organization chart that depicts the business structure of a small company.

A good flowchart is like a house. The foundation is the flowchart's shapes, the walls are the connections, and the roof is the text. Without all these parts, a flowchart cannot stand. The following subsections provide some guidelines for effectively using the various parts of a flowchart.

Using Shapes

Shapes in flowcharts are information containers. They represent the people in a business or the steps in a process. In the organization chart shown in Figure 5-1, there are three different types of boxes. These boxes are standard Visio 2000 flowchart shapes, and their differences convey information about the different positions held by the people represented in the diagram.

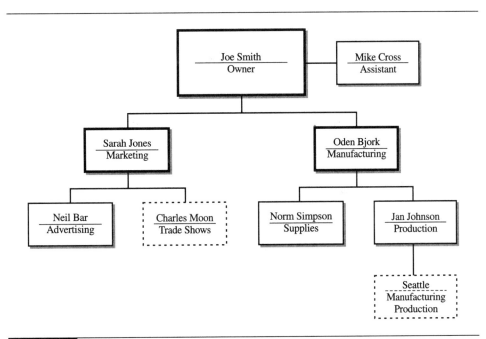

FIGURE 5-1   A basic Visio 2000 flowchart

While the placement and connection of shapes are important features of a flowchart, the most important feature is its shapes. People can tell a lot about a flowchart simply by looking at its shapes. The shapes in a flowchart provide basic information, beyond what can be learned by reading the text and looking at the connections.

> **TIP**   *The shapes you select affect the way Visio 2000 builds reports based on your flowcharts. Choose your shapes carefully to make the reports informative.*

Here are some things to consider as you choose shapes for a flowchart:

- The most complicated shape should always represent the top level or highest position on a flowchart page. People who read your flowchart will equate the more complicated shapes with higher positions, and they may be confused if the chart isn't organized accordingly.

- The bottom or lowest position in the flowchart should be a simple shape that can be repeated many times. Flowcharts can get very cluttered if you repeat a complicated shape many times, so it's best to choose a simple shape for low-level positions.

- Use shapes with light or dotted borders for temporary positions—or for work that has been out-sourced. The different border immediately conveys that the position is somehow different from other positions with the same shape on the same level.

- Use no more than five different shapes on one page, and use no more than ten different shapes for an entire flowchart. Although you can convey more information by using more shapes, your flowcharts may be confusing if they include more than ten different shapes.

Using Connections

When used correctly, flowchart connections can give people a clear picture of how a business operates.

There are two main types of connections: with arrows and without arrows. For most flowcharts, use simple 1-D connection lines without arrows. Simple connection lines are usually sufficient to indicate relationships, and they help you avoid cluttering diagrams that have a lot of shapes and text. Simple connection lines are especially useful in complicated flowchart diagrams.

If necessary, you can use connection lines with arrows to show information flowing in a particular direction. Don't overuse connections with arrows; they can make your diagrams more complicated than they need to be.

Using Text

Text in flowcharts gives the reader information about the shapes. The text may be the first thing readers grasp consciously, so make sure you've made careful choices about what you include in the text.

Text in flowcharts should be simple and easy to read. The font should be fairly uniform throughout. Sometimes it can be helpful to use boldface text for the position at the top of each page. Using a larger font size for certain high-level positions can also be useful. It's important to remember, though, that no matter how you format the text at the top of the tree, the text at the bottom also needs to be legible. Also, no matter which fonts you choose, never exceed three fonts on one page. This maximum of three fonts includes both the title font and the font you use to label the shapes.

Using the Organization Chart Template

There are two ways to create an organization chart in Visio 2000: using the Organization Chart template and using the Organization Chart Wizard. This section deals with the template; for most simple organization charts, the template is the best way to start. For charts based on databases, you'll want to use the Organization Chart Wizard, as described later in this chapter.

The Organization Chart template can be used to diagram the personnel structure of a business. Positions, job descriptions, and even managerial styles all affect the way a business works, and organization charts help you to understand them better. The diagram in Figure 5-1 is an organization chart that depicts a small computer company; it illustrates how reports and managerial duties flow through the company.

To create your own organization chart, first you need a list of positions and employees. When you've collected all the information you need, you're ready to open the Organization Chart template. Open the template as you would any other Visio 2000 template. When the Organization Chart template opens, it changes the orientation of the drawing page to landscape, opens the Organization Chart Shapes stencil, and opens a floating Organization Chart toolbar. A newly opened Organization Chart template is shown in Figure 5-2.

The Organization Chart toolbar has five buttons, which are explained in Table 5-1. The first three buttons are drop-down buttons.

To help you to create organization charts, the template has additional features beyond its own toolbar and stencil that help you create and organize the shapes.

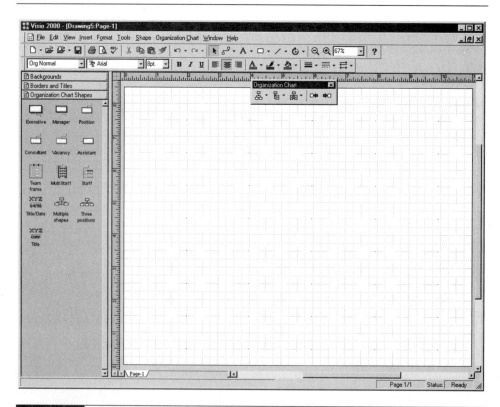

FIGURE 5-2   The Organization Chart template

Button	Function
	Allows arrangement of subordinates horizontally
	Allows arrangement of subordinates vertically
	Allows arrangement of subordinates in groups
	Moves the selected shape to the left
	Moves the selected shape to the right

TABLE 5-1   Organization Chart Toolbar Buttons

Dragging Positions to the Page with Automatic Connection

Organization charts use lines to indicate business relationships between them. These lines are usually 1-D connection lines that are glued to both the position and its superior. Creating all the lines in an organization chart manually would take a great deal of time and effort, so Visio 2000 has an automatic connection feature for shapes in the Organization Chart Shape stencil.

For the automatic connection feature to work, shapes need to be added from the top of the structure down. To use this feature, you need to have a plan for your diagram before you start.

To connect shapes from the Organization Chart Shape stencil, first drag a superior shape to the drawing page. Once you've placed the superior shape, drag one if its subordinates to the drawing page and drop it on top of the superior shape. Visio 2000 places the subordinate and connects it to the superior with a 1-D connection line.

To add another subordinate to a superior, drag it from the stencil and drop it on the superior. Any subordinates that already exist for the superior rearrange themselves to make room for new subordinates. This reorganization occurs because of the "dynamic glue" that Visio 2000 uses when it connects shapes in this way.

Moving with Dynamic Connectors

Dynamic glue, which is discussed in more detail later in this chapter, allows shapes to stay glued together even though one of them moves. Dynamically glued connectors act slightly differently. Not only do they stay connected even if the shape moves, but dynamically glued connectors change shape and orientation automatically as you move the shapes they connect.

 You can break a connection by moving the connector instead of one of the connected shapes.

Dynamic connectors route themselves around shapes that lie between the shapes they connect. Because dynamic connectors have this capability, you can maintain connections even though you move shapes around the page. Your diagram stays neat and tidy as you rearrange shapes. Dynamic glue is the default setting for all shapes in the Organization Chart template, so you can add as many positions as you like, and the shapes always stay neatly connected to their superiors.

 Connector shapes are added automatically when you drop a subordinate shape on top of a superior shape.

Arranging Subordinates and Superiors

By default, dropped subordinates arrange themselves horizontally underneath their superior. However, if your diagram has three levels or more, this arrangement can be cumbersome—using the width of the page without making use of the height. You can alter the arrangement of subordinates by using the arrangement buttons on the Organization Chart toolbar. If you have too many positions arranged horizontally beneath a superior, select the superior, click the second button on the Organization Chart toolbar, and then choose a vertical orientation for the subordinates.

 The different orientations are a bit difficult to see on the Organization Chart toolbar. Look closely to choose the correct orientation and connection scheme.

The superior is now set with a new organizational scheme, and all new subordinates dropped on it arrange themselves according to the new scheme.

Placing Multiple Positions at Once

There are times when it's useful to add multiple positions to an organization chart simultaneously. The Organization Chart Shapes stencil includes two special master shapes for those cases: the Three Positions master shape and the Multiple Shapes master shape. Both of these master shapes allow you to drag and drop several subordinates at once.

> **TIP** *To quickly convert a shape into a different type, right-click the shape, then choose Convert Shape and select the type you want.*

The Three Positions master shape creates a set of three position shapes, exactly like the position shape in the second row of the stencil. When you drag it onto a superior, it adds three position shapes arranged by the method set as the default for the superior.

The Multiple Shapes master shape adds a designated number of organization chart shapes to your diagram. When you drag the Multiple Shapes to the drawing page and drop it on a superior, an Add Multiple Shapes window opens, like the one shown here, where you can choose the type of shape and the number of shapes to drop:

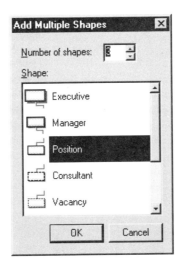

To show or hide subordinate positions in organization charts, select the shape representing the top-level position, and then choose Organization Chart | Hide Subordinates.

Select the shape type and number, and click OK. Visio 2000 automatically arranges and connects the shapes.

Adding Text

The default text style for the Organization Chart template is 8-point Arial. In addition, by default a divider line appears between the names of people represented on the chart and their titles. The default divider line helps keep the diagrams neat by separating text that might otherwise be confusing.

As you add text to your organization chart, remember to be brief. Textual information tends to be secondary to the shapes and their connections.

When you're satisfied with the placement of the shapes and the text, you're done with your organization chart. Remember to print the chart at least once during the final stages to make sure you like the way it looks on the printed page and then save the diagram.

Using the Organization Chart Wizard

The Organization Chart Wizard helps you create organization chart diagrams based on databases. Since most companies keep their human resource information in some sort of database, Visio 2000 includes an easy way to turn that database information into organization charts.

The Organization Chart Wizard asks you for the location and name of a data source. Although the wizard allows you to create a new database on the fly, usually the database will already exist in a format the wizard can import.

Visio 2000 can import data from the following formats:

- Text files (.txt)

- Microsoft Excel spreadsheets (.xls)

- Microsoft Exchange Server directories

- ODBC-compliant database applications

Most often, organization charts are built from text files or Excel files, but the other two formats can be useful in some cases.

Formatting Text and Excel Data Files

In text files and Excel files, the source data needs to be formatted in a way that Visio 2000 can use.

For text files, the data in each line should be separated by commas, and hard returns should be inserted at the end of each line. Also, when you use a text file as the data source, it needs to have the following first line, which specifies the headings for the data:

```
Name,Reports_To,Position,Department,Telephone,Master_Shape
```

 CAUTION   *The heading line needs to appear in the exact format shown here. There should be no spaces before or after the commas.*

Every line in the text file becomes its own shape, and must include *at least* the Name and the Reports_To fields. All other fields should be represented by commas, even if there's no corresponding text between the commas. Each line must include a unique name; otherwise, Visio 2000 won't accept the file. The Master_Shape data is not required and is used only if you want to control which Organization Chart Shapes are applied to specific positions. If you choose not to define a master shape for each line, leave the Master_Shape field out of the heading line.

For Excel files, the data should be organized into columns and rows. The Excel file should have the following headings in the first row of cells:

```
Name Reports_To Position Department Telephone Master_Shape
```

for a total of six columns. Each row of the spreadsheet then becomes a shape in the organization chart.

NOTE   *You may have more than six columns if there are "custom properties" for the shapes. Custom properties are explained later in this chapter in the section "Creating Reports from Flowcharts."*

The fields in text and Excel files are as follows:

Name   Defines the name that appears on the corresponding shape in the organization chart. Capitalization and spacing are carried over into the diagram.

Reports_To   Defines the shape's superior. The data must exactly match the Name field of another line in the text file or another row in the Excel file. This field should only be blank for the shape at the top of the chart.

Position   Defines the title that appears on the corresponding shape in the organization chart. Remember, the title appears below the divider line that separates the name and title.

Department   Specifies the department for the position. This information appears as part of the custom properties for the shape.

Telephone   Specifies the telephone number for the position. This information appears as part of the custom properties for the shape.

Master_Shape   Defines the shape assigned to a position. Visio 2000 assigns shapes based on the total number of lines in the file and the number of Reports_To relationships. This optional field allows you to select a shape for each line or row. Entries in this field should match shape names that appear in the Organization Chart Shapes stencil.

Using Other Data Files

Open Database Connectivity (ODBC) is a Microsoft standard that allows applications to access, view, and modify data from a variety of databases. Examples of ODBC-compliant database applications include Microsoft Access, Microsoft SQL Server, and Oracle SQL Server. For example, Visio 2000's interpretation of a Microsoft Exchange Server directory creates an organization chart based on information set up in the address book. It is a fast and easy way to translate your e-mail information into graphical form.

Importing the Data

When you have a database with the source data in the proper format, you're ready to use the Organization Chart Wizard to import the data. Open the Organization Chart Wizard as you would a template. The opening screen of the wizard appears, as shown here:

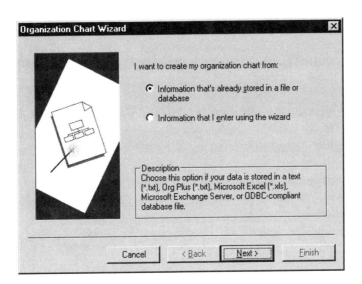

Choose to create your chart from information already stored in a file and click Next.

The second wizard screen appears, as shown here:

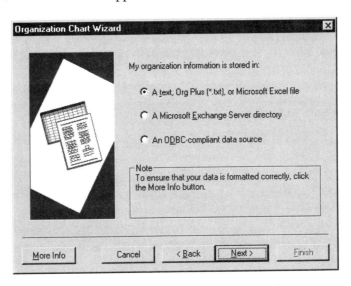

This screen lists all the types of files Visio 2000 can use to create organization charts. Choose the correct file type for your data file and click Next. The next screen appears asking for the file location. Click Browse and an Open File dialog box appears. Locate the file, then click Open. The Open File dialog box closes.

The next wizard screen appears, as shown here:

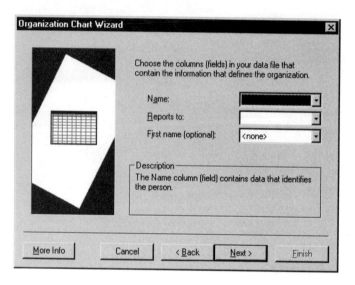

This screen allows you to identify which of the fields define the relationships between the shapes in your organization chart. For most charts, leave the fields as they are listed. Then click Next. Another screen appears, allowing you to define the text that displays in the shapes for your organization chart. As with the previous screen, it's best to leave the drop-down menus with their default and click Next.

The following wizard screen appears:

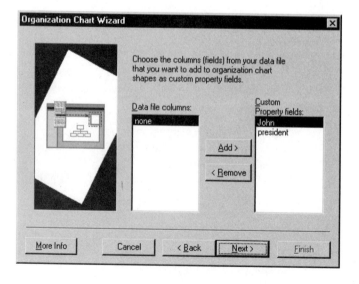

This screen asks if you want to add information to the Custom Properties field for your chart. Select all the data fields in the left-hand box, then click Add. They appear in the right-hand box. Click Next.

The next wizard screen appears, as shown here:

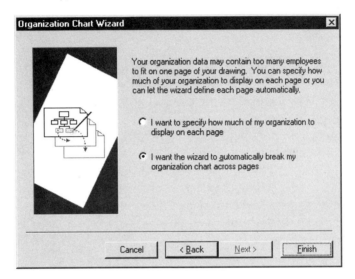

This screen allows you to decide how your organization chart breaks across pages. You can choose how the chart breaks, or you can let Visio 2000 decide automatically. For most cases, Visio 2000 does a nice job of deciding how your charts should be laid out, so that has been set as the default. Visio 2000 calculates the number of shapes that would appear on a page and breaks across levels when including all of a level would mean more than 50 shapes on a page.

Choosing to manually decide how your chart breaks across pages opens another wizard screen where Visio 2000 prompts you to make additional decisions.

When you've determined how the chart will break across pages, the wizard has all the information it needs. Click Finish, and Visio 2000 begins creating your organization chart. Process bars appear on the page as Visio 2000 reads and uses your data file to create the chart. As the wizard creates the chart, it may need to add pages to the diagram.

When Visio 2000 has finished your organization chart, the wizard closes, and the chart appears on the drawing page. The Organization Chart template should be open, allowing you to make any changes as necessary.

 Remember to save your new organization chart before closing the drawing.

Understanding Visio 2000 Flowcharts

Visio 2000 flowcharts are like the big brothers of Visio 2000 organization charts. They're more complicated and often require more steps to complete; however, the basic concept of connections and shapes conveying information still holds.

Just as in organization charts, Visio 2000 has two ways to create flowcharts: creating a flowchart from scratch with a template, and creating a flowchart from a data file. Unlike organization charts, there are several different kinds of flowcharts—in fact, there are so many that they have their own folder titled Flowcharts. For this section we discuss only one type of template: the Basic Flowchart template.

 To understand how to use the other templates in the Flowchart folder, see Appendix A. Every template is listed there with information about when to use it.

Using the Basic Flowchart Template

When you select the Basic Flowchart template from the Open dialog box, Visio 2000 opens a new blank page and the Basic Flowchart stencil.

The shapes on the stencil work the same as the shapes on the Basic Shapes stencil; simply drag and drop them onto the page to create shapes based on the master shape. However, connections don't work the same way as for the shapes on the Organization Chart Shapes stencil. You'll need to create the connections between shapes yourself by using the Connection tool.

Using the Connection Tool

The Connection tool helps you create flowcharts in two ways: by giving you a quick way to connect shapes that are already on the drawing page, and by connecting two shapes as you drop them. Connecting shapes that are already on the drawing page is the easier method. However, using automatic connections as you drag shapes from stencils may be more efficient and has, as a default, the added advantage of a special Connection tool feature: dynamic glue.

Dynamic glue is a type of connection that allows the endpoints of a connector line or shape to move around the object it's glued to as the shape and those around it move. Like Visio 2000's normal gluing action, dynamic glue can only be removed by clicking on the attachment point and moving the connector away. However, unlike normal gluing, connectors that have dynamic glue never overlap other shapes on the page. The jumping action as dynamically glued connectors move around the page is triggered by moving the shape or the connector.

To connect shapes that are already on the drawing page with the Connection tool, select the Connection tool from the toolbar, click on a connection point of the first shape, and drag to a connection point on the second shape. Visio 2000 creates the connector and the gluing of the shapes.

You can get the benefit of dynamic glue with shapes already on the drawing page if you hold down CTRL as you join the shape. While holding CTRL, click on a connection point for the first shape, and then drag to the next shape, creating a connector that is dynamically glued to each shape.

TIP *You can also connect a shape to itself with the Connection tool by selecting it from the toolbar, then clicking on one of the shape's connection points, and then dragging to another of the shape's connection points.*

When you've successfully connected two shapes, the endpoints of the connector turn red when the connection is selected. The shade of red varies according to the type of glue: dark red is static, bright red is dynamic.

To connect shapes as you drag them from a stencil:

1. Choose the Connection tool from the toolbar. The cursor now has a connector with an arrow below it.

2. Choose any 2-D shape from the Flowchart or Flowchart (Additional) stencil and drag and drop it on the page. 2-D shapes are indicated by a gray background on the stencil.

3. With the first 2-D shape selected, drag and drop a second 2-D shape. Visio 2000 connects the shapes using dynamic glue.

4. Drag and drop enough shapes to complete your flowchart. As long as you have the tool selected, each new shape you drop connects to the shape selected on the drawing page.

5. When you're done with the Connection tool, choose the Pointer tool from the toolbar.

The shapes are connected with an instance of the Connector master shape selected in the stencil. If no master shape is selected, Visio 2000 creates an instance of the dynamic connector to connect the shapes.

 Don't forget that you can add additional information to your shapes by including custom properties. Right-click on the shape and select Properties to open a dialog box where you can add custom properties.

Creating Flowcharts from Databases

Often when you wish to create a flowchart of a process, you already have some or all of the data for the flowchart in a file or program somewhere on your computer system. Visio 2000 has a process by which you can turn that data quickly and easily into a flowchart—the Import Flowchart Data Macro.

 Always create the data file before you start the macro. You can do it the other way around, but it wastes time.

The first step to creating a flowchart from a data file it to make sure your data file is complete and in the correct format. Visio 2000 can import data from these formats:

■ Text files (.txt)

■ Microsoft Excel spreadsheets (.xls)

■ Microsoft Project Exchange files (.mpx)

■ Microsoft Exchange Server directories

■ ODBC-compliant database applications

 ODBC stands for Open Database Connectivity, a Microsoft standard that allows applications to access, view, and modify data from a variety of databases.

For most flowcharts, you'll work with a text file (.txt) or Microsoft Excel spreadsheet (.xls). The macro requires the data file to include specific column headings, so it's best if you use one of the data file templates that come with Visio 2000, located in the Flowchart folder in the Solutions folder under the Visio 2000 program directory.

If you plan to use an ODBC database application, the database must be set up as an ODBC data source. You can set up a database as a data source using the ODBC Database Administrator, which you can run from the Windows Control Panel.

Whichever type of database you choose, you need to make sure to attribute a shape to each entry in the database. The shape should correspond to the proper name of one of the hundreds of shapes in Visio 2000. The Shape ID field in the database should list the name of the shape to be used for the information in that row. It's very important to make sure the name is an exact match for the shape, or Visio 2000 may reject your data file.

When you have the data source set up correctly, you're ready to run the macro.

Using the Import Flowchart Data Macro

The Import Flowchart Data Macro is the quickest and easiest way to create a flowchart using data. This macro launches a wizard that helps you create a standard data flowchart using a data file you have already created.

To create a flowchart using the wizard, select Tools | Macros | Import Flowchart Data. The first screen of the Import Data Flowchart Wizard opens, as shown here:

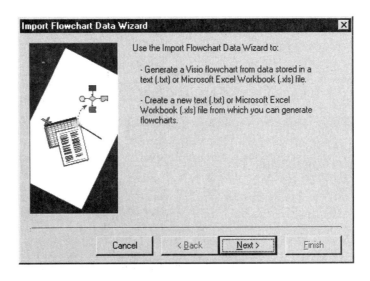

Behind the first wizard screen, a new blank drawing opens—the Basic Flowchart template. Click Next.

The next window opens, asking for the data source, as shown here:

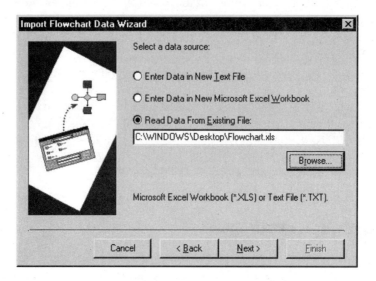

You can create flowcharts with this wizard that have several different data sources or no data source at all. The options on the second wizard screen are as follows:

Enter Data in New Text File   If you select this option, you'll need to create a text file with the data in tab-delimited format. This option is most useful when data has been exported from some other program, because most database and accounting programs can export data as text.

Enter Data in New Microsoft Excel Workbook   If you select this option, you'll need to enter data in a new Excel workbook or spreadsheet, with the data organized in simple columns. This option is only useful if you've already stored a record of all the data in Microsoft Excel.

Read Data from Existing File   If you select this option, the wizard uses an existing file, such as an Excel workbook or plain text. Visio 2000 can import data from only certain kinds of files, Microsoft formats chief among them. See the discussion earlier in this section for more information about the types of files from which Visio 2000 can import data.

NOTE   *It's best to create a data file before running the wizard. (The previous section details the requirements for Visio 2000 data source files.) If you choose to create the data file from within the wizard, Visio 2000 walks you through the creation process and then drops you out of the wizard, forcing you to start over again. To save time, create the data file first, and then start the wizard.*

Select Read Data from Existing File, and click Next. The third wizard screen appears, telling you the wizard is ready to create your flowchart. Click Finish. A progress bar appears, letting you know Visio 2000 is attempting to read your data file. Once it has verified your file works, a screen appears, indicating that Visio is converting your file.

The File Converter asks which character has been used in the data file to indicate columns, as well as the characters used as "text delimiters" and "comment separators." The *text delimiter* is the character you put around anything you want Visio 2000 to display as is, be it standard ANSI text or extended characters (such as the end-of-line character). The text delimiters should surround the text, one at the beginning and one at the end. The *comment separator* is the character you use to add comments to your data file that you don't want Visio 2000 to use in the flowchart. They go at the very front of the field with the comment. Once you've set all the conversion parameters, click OK.

Visio 2000 creates the flowchart on the drawing page, and the Import Flowchart Data Wizard closes. You can now alter your flowchart using the techniques outlined in the section "Using the Basic Flowchart Template" earlier in this chapter.

    You can include number shapes in your flowchart by selecting Tools | Macros | Visio Extras | Number Shapes.

Creating Reports from Flowcharts

Creating reports for flowcharts you've made in Visio 2000 can be an important part of your business process. For example, if you've done a lot of fact-finding about your company's supply process and kept the data as a Visio 2000 flowchart, you can retrieve that data by creating a report, which can then be imported into a database program. You can also use the reporting feature of Visio 2000 to create a printed report that you can hand out during presentations in which you use the flowchart as a visual aid.

The ability to create reports from flowcharts is based on the "custom properties" of shapes. The custom property fields of shapes populate the fields, or columns, in the database table.

A *custom property* is a Visio 2000 database field that holds specific information about a shape. Many Visio 2000 master shapes come with property fields already assigned. You can always add custom property fields of your own to a shape by right-clicking and selecting Properties. If the shape doesn't have any custom properties assigned, you're asked if you'd like to add them.

By default, every 2-D flowchart shape has three property fields: Cost, Duration, and Resources. You can enter data into the fields by right-clicking the shape, and then choosing Properties from the shortcut menu.

Using the Property Reporting Wizard

If you've entered data for the properties associated with the shapes in your flowchart (including custom properties), you can run the Property Reporting Wizard to generate inventory or numerical reports based on your flowchart. The Property Reporting Wizard produces a report like the one shown in Figure 5-3.

Property Report

ITEM	TOTAL
Cost	1009
Data 1	0
Data 2	0
Data 3	0
Duration	37
Height	13.63
Master	0
Name	0
NameID	0
Qty	19
Resources	52
Text	0
Type	0
Width	7.88
X	70.81
Y	118.31

FIGURE 5-3 A report created with the Property Reporting Wizard

Visio 2000 creates the report as a shape and includes it on your drawing page. You can choose the type of information it includes; however, the Property Reporting function is fairly limited and is only meant for simple numerical summaries and inventories of shapes.

To use the Property Reporting Wizard, first you must create your flowchart, and the shapes must have some information in their custom properties fields. When you have all the necessary data, you can run the wizard by selecting Tools | Property Report. The opening Property Reporting Wizard screen appears; it tells you that the wizard creates two types of reports based on flowchart data. Click Next.

The second wizard screen appears, as shown here:

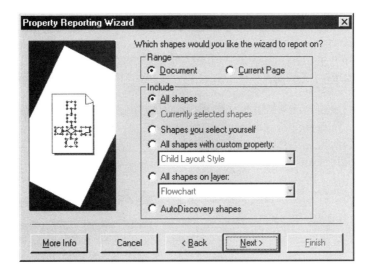

This screen asks you to identify which of the shapes you'd like to have included in the report. The default is for all shapes to be included, but you can choose a report on just one type of shape, to only include shapes from one layer, or you can select shapes manually. When you've decided which shapes to include, click Next.

The third screen of the wizard appears, as shown next:

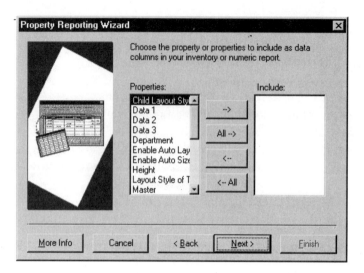

The left column in this screen contains a list of all the properties—both standard and custom—that you can use to create the report. Many of the properties are totals or combinations of information from the shapes. Scroll down the list and highlight the properties you'd like in the report, clicking the arrow button to move the property to the right-hand column. When you've chosen all the properties you'd like to include in the report, click Next.

The fourth screen of the wizard appears, as shown here:

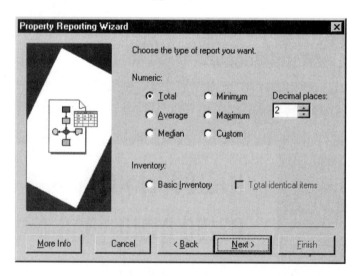

This screen asks you what type of numeric computation you'd like to perform on the property numbers you selected in the previous window. For flowcharts, only the numeric values mean anything. The inventory values are for office layout functions. To learn more about office layout, see Chapter 8, "Organizing Your Business with Visio 2000."

As a general rule, you want to report either totals or averages for the properties. You also choose how many decimal places are reported here, usually two is sufficient. When you're done choosing the computation options, click Next.

The fifth screen of the wizard appears, asking for the report title and the page you'd like the shape to be dropped on:

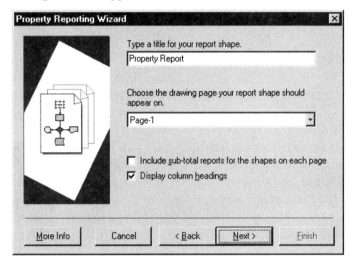

When you've completed the information, click Next.

The sixth screen of the wizard appears:

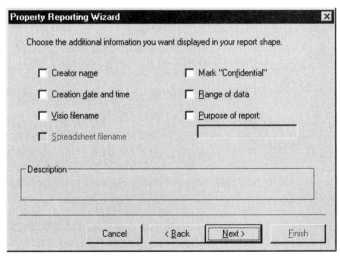

This screen asks what type of time information and what kind of heading you'd like to include in the report. This includes not only the time the report was created, but the creator and other custom text. If you need to label the report in some way, use the "Purpose of report" checkbox.

When you've made your selection, click Next. The last screen of the wizard appears, telling you it's ready to create the report. Click Finish, and a progress bar appears to show Visio 2000 is creating the report.

When Visio 2000 has completed the report, Visio 2000 places it somewhere near the bottom of the drawing page.

Using the Database Export Wizard

If you need a report in some format other than a Visio 2000 report, or if you need to create a database from flowchart data, you can export the data from a flowchart into standard ODBC-compliant format using the Database Export Macro. The Database Export Macro launches the Database Export Wizard. The Database Export Wizard is available for a few templates from which you may incorporate frequently-used data into your databases, such as flowcharts, office layouts, and organization charts.

You can create an entirely new database or insert new tables into an existing database. To run the Flowchart Database Wizard, you must have the database program you wish to use to read the data installed on your computer.

 It's best to run through this wizard at least once before attempting to create or modify a functional data source file.

To run the wizard, choose Tools | Macros | Visio 2000 Extras | Database Export. This launches the wizard.

The Database Export Wizard has almost a dozen screens, and many of them look like the option screens for the Property Reporting Wizard, which is explained in the previous section.

As you follow along with the Database Export Wizard, you are asked to make the following choices and specifications in the order listed here:

1. A filename to export to.

2. The shapes you would like to export (every shape or selected layers of shapes).

3. The information from those shapes that you would like to export.

4. The Data Source File to export to.

5. If the data source file doesn't already exist, you're asked to create one. At the very least you are asked to browse and locate the file.

6. Database export details, including the Table Name.

7. The way each piece of information will be represented in the table.

8. A right-mouse option for exporting the data from the drawing page.

9. Verification of the data to be exported.

5

When you run the Database Export Wizard to export shape data, the wizard stores export-related information with the drawing page. If you make changes to the shapes and want to re-export the data, you can right-click the drawing page and choose Database Table Export.

NOTE *The exact information asked for in each Data Export Wizard Screen depends a great deal on the type of data source you're exporting to.*

When you've completed all the information for the export, the Data Export Wizard informs you it's ready to finish and create the report. When you click Finish, Visio 2000 creates or updates the data source as a background process and then tells you when it's completed.

Summary

In this chapter, you learned how to create organization charts and flowcharts by hand and with an imported data file. You also learned how to export data from flowcharts into reports or into their own data sources.

In the next chapter, you'll learn how to make the most of using Visio 2000 with Microsoft Office.

CHAPTER 6

Using Visio 2000 with Microsoft Office

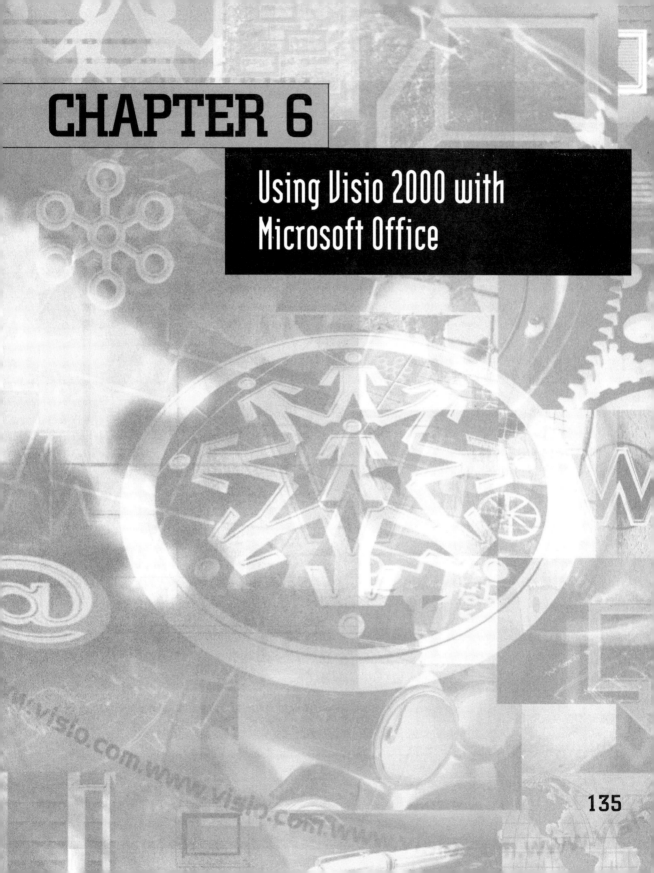

In the last chapter, you learned how to create flowcharts using Visio 2000, as well as how to import and export data into and out of your Visio 2000 diagrams.

In this chapter, you'll learn how to use Microsoft Office software and Visio 2000 together. You'll see how to include Office documents in your Visio 2000 diagrams, how to include Visio 2000 diagrams in your Office documents, and how to link two documents to create automatic updates. You'll also learn the most common ways Microsoft Office programs are used with Visio 2000.

Using Visio 2000 with Other Software

During the business day, you need to accomplish tasks that require many different kinds of software, of which Visio 2000 is only one. One task alone—creating a report, for example—may require several programs working together to generate text, diagrams, and tables. And collecting all the information into a presentation requires yet another program. For many businesses, the standard business productivity programs are Microsoft products. Businesses use Microsoft Office to create the text and tables and to collect the data from different programs into unified documents. Many businesses also use Microsoft Outlook or Exchange for e-mail. All these products work with Visio 2000 to create a seamless environment for accomplishing tasks.

Visio 2000 was designed to work with these other programs, allowing you to use data and diagrams created in Visio 2000 in other programs and allowing information from other sources to be added to Visio 2000 documents. There are many ways you can use Visio 2000 with Microsoft products.

| NOTE | *Many of the figures in this chapter use Microsoft Word 2000 as an example. Most other Microsoft products work similarly.* |

Understanding Object Linking and Embedding

When a Visio 2000 diagram is included in whole or in part in another program, it is done in one of three ways:

■ As an image saved in Visio 2000 and inserted into the new document.

■ As an embedded object included in the new document but editable as if it were in Visio 2000.

■ As a linked object included in the new document in such a way that the changes are reflected, no matter where you edit the diagram.

These last two options require the use of Object Linking and Embedding. *Object Linking and Embedding*, or OLE, is the main way Visio 2000 is designed to work with Microsoft Office products. OLE allows programs to "speak the same language" when they exchange data. Microsoft first incorporated a common language for programs to exchange data when it developed Windows 3.1. Since then, OLE has become an industry standard, greatly increasing the productivity of business software by allowing different programs to work together seamlessly.

> **NOTE** *Visio 2000 uses an updated version of OLE, specifically OLE2. Only OLE2-compliant programs can use some of the features discussed in this chapter. Some of the OLE functions discussed here may not work with older versions of Microsoft products (for example, Word for Windows 95).*

Visio 2000 has a complete set of OLE functions that allow you to trade Visio 2000 information between it and other OLE-compliant programs. Programs in the Microsoft Office Suite are the most widely used products with which Visio 2000 can interact.

Creating Visio 2000 Drawings in Other Programs

The best way to see OLE in operation is to create a Visio 2000 diagram right inside another program. OLE embeds a Visio 2000 diagram when you do this.

When you install Visio 2000, Visio tells other programs installed on your system about itself. It notifies them what type of program Visio 2000 is, what Visio 2000 is capable of, and how to interact with Visio 2000 if they require its services.

To create a Visio 2000 diagram in the document of another product (for example, Microsoft Word 2000), first place the cursor where you'd like the Visio 2000 diagram to appear. Then choose Insert | Object. The Object dialog box opens, as shown in Figure 6-1.

Choose Visio 2000 Drawing from the list of object types, and click OK. The Choose a Drawing Template dialog box appears, as it does when you open a new drawing within Visio 2000 (see Figure 6-2).

The program inserts a Visio 2000 drawing page, opens the selected Visio 2000 template, and replaces the program's standard toolbars with Visio 2000's standard

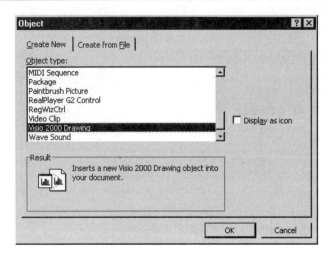

FIGURE 6-1   The Create New tab of the Object dialog box

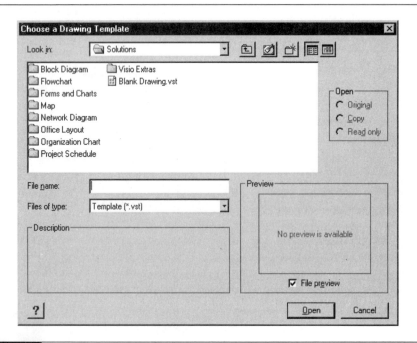

FIGURE 6-2   The Choose a Drawing Template dialog box

toolbars. You can create the diagram as you would any new diagram in a Visio 2000 window, including drawing and dropping shapes, adding text, and even adding connections.

When you're done editing the Visio 2000 drawing, click somewhere on the document outside the embedded Visio 2000 window. This closes Visio 2000 and restores the program's standard toolbars. After Visio 2000 has closed, you're able to move the diagram around as you would any inserted image.

> **TIP** *If you accidentally close Visio 2000 while editing a linked or embedded drawing, double-click on the drawing to open Visio 2000 again. You'll learn more about this process in the following section, "Embedding."*

6

Embedding

As explained earlier, an embedded object is data created by one program (the *native* program) that is included in the document of another program in such a way as it can still be edited in its native program but saved in a document created in the new program.

When you're adding an embedded object into a program, there are several ways it can be done and several special issues that affect how you edit the object. This section discusses these issues both for embedding data from other programs into a Visio 2000 diagram and for embedding Visio 2000 diagrams in other programs.

> **CAUTION** *Remember, when you embed data into another program, it becomes part of that program's file, and you can only edit it as an embedded object from then on.*

You should only embed data into another document when you don't want to keep a separate file for the data. Embedded data doesn't refer back to the original file in which it was created, and it has no link back to its original program. Embedded data is useful when you want to transfer a diagram or other data to another computer; you can send all the data in one file, and the receiver need not have Visio 2000 to view the diagram. The downside of embedded images is that they can increase the file size dramatically, so make sure you check the file size before sending the document over a network.

Embedding Another Program's Data in a Visio 2000 Diagram

Embed data from other programs when you want to include that data as part of a Visio 2000 diagram but don't want to maintain a separate file for the data. For example, you may want to include a Microsoft Excel spreadsheet listing the operating costs of a factory under the shape for that factory on a production chart.

Remember, when you embed data from another program into a Visio 2000 diagram, Visio 2000 becomes the holder of that data. The embedded data is saved as part of the Visio 2000 file and can only be edited there. When you double-click on the data in the Visio 2000 diagram, the native program for that data opens up and you can edit it, but any change you make exists only in the Visio 2000 diagram. This may make it easier for you since you need not keep track of a separate file. The data doesn't exist as a separate file; it's incorporated into the Visio 2000 document.

To embed another program's data into a Visio 2000 diagram, first open the file that has the data you want to include in the Visio 2000 diagram. Copy the data out of the file, usually by selecting it and then choosing Edit | Copy. This copies the data to the clipboard.

With the data on the clipboard, open the Visio 2000 diagram into which you want to embed it. To make sure nothing in the diagram is selected, click on a blank portion of the drawing page, and then choose Edit | Paste (or click the Paste button on the Visio 2000 toolbar).

The data appears in the center of your Visio 2000 window as an embedded object. Move the object as you would any Visio 2000 shape, placing it wherever you want on the drawing page.

 Always save the file before and after embedding an object. The process can be memory-intensive and if there are any computer problems, you want to make sure you don't lose data.

Embedding Visio 2000 Shapes in Another Program's Document

There are two ways you can include Visio 2000 shapes in the documents of other programs: you can drag the shapes or you can copy and paste the shapes. Both methods work in a similar manner.

To drag a Visio 2000 shape into another program's document, first make sure both the Visio 2000 diagram and the document into which the shape will be embedded are open and visible on the Windows desktop.

> **TIP** *To arrange the programs so both are visible, launch both programs and then right-click on the taskbar. Select one of the options for tiling the windows, either horizontally or vertically.*

With both programs open and visible, select the shape in the Visio 2000 diagram and drag it to the new document. This *moves* the shape, deleting it from the Visio 2000 diagram and placing it in the new document. If you want to *copy* the shape, select it in the Visio 2000 diagram and hold down CTRL as you drag the shape to the new document. This leaves a copy of the shape in the Visio 2000 diagram and embeds a copy in the new document.

To copy and paste Visio 2000 shapes into another document, first make sure both Visio 2000 and the other program are open. Then select shapes in the Visio 2000 diagram and choose Edit | Copy. This copies the shapes to the clipboard. While the shapes are still on the clipboard, display the document in which you want to place them. Move the cursor where you want the shapes to appear in the new document and then paste the shapes, usually by choosing Edit | Paste.

To move a shape from a Visio 2000 page to another document, use the same process as for copying and pasting, but instead of choosing Edit | Copy, choose Edit | Cut. This places the shape on the clipboard and removes it from the Visio 2000 diagram. Then paste the shape in the document.

No matter how you embed the shapes, the Visio 2000 window opens inside the other program. When you're done placing the shapes, click outside the box containing the embedded Visio 2000 shapes, and the Visio 2000 toolbars and rulers disappear. Make sure to save the new document after embedding the Visio 2000 shapes.

Embedding a Whole Visio 2000 Page in Another Program's Document

What if you want to embed more than just one or two shapes from a Visio 2000 diagram? You can embed an entire Visio 2000 drawing page in another document by using the Copy Drawing feature.

First, open the Visio 2000 diagram that contains the page you'd like to copy. Then open the document you'd like to copy the page into. Make sure your diagram and the document have been saved. In the Visio 2000 window, display the page you want to copy and click on a blank portion of the page to be sure nothing on the page is selected. Then, in your Visio 2000 diagram, choose Edit I Copy Drawing. This places the entire drawing page onto the clipboard, including all the shapes, backgrounds, and connections.

With the drawing page on the clipboard, click on the document into which you'd like to insert the page. Place the cursor where you'd like to embed the Visio 2000 drawing page and paste the Visio 2000 data, usually by selecting Edit I Paste.

> **NOTE** *This procedure only pastes the page displayed when you selected Copy Drawing. To copy more than one page of a multiple-page drawing, you need to repeat this process for each page you want to embed.*

Editing Embedded Visio 2000 Data in Another Program

Once you've placed your Visio 2000 data into a document in another program, the beauty of OLE becomes apparent when you need to edit that data. No matter what type of data you've embedded—one shape, a drawing page, or an entire diagram—the editing process is the same.

First, open the document containing the embedded Visio 2000 data. Then double-click on the data, which usually appears inside its own box. When you double-click on your embedded Visio 2000 data, OLE automatically opens Visio 2000 and temporarily replaces the toolbars of the new program with the Visio 2000 standard toolbars. If the data is a drawing page or a whole Visio 2000 diagram, Visio 2000 also opens any stencils attached to the original drawing. Figure 6-3 shows a Visio 2000 diagram embedded in a Microsoft Word document.

When you edit the Visio 2000 data in the new document, the Visio 2000 rulers appear on two sides of the Visio 2000 diagram, indicating that you're editing the diagram in Visio 2000 running inside the other program. Also, the menus and toolbars temporarily become Visio 2000 menus and toolbars.

> **NOTE** *If you need a stencil in the new program, use the Open Stencil button on the Visio 2000 toolbar, which temporarily replaces the program's toolbar.*

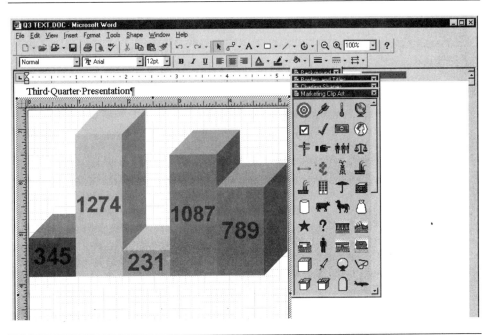

FIGURE 6-3   A Visio 2000 diagram embedded in a Microsoft Word document

Edit the Visio 2000 diagram as you would if it were running in the main Visio 2000 window. If you need more space or a larger drawing page, resize the drawing by moving the cursor to the bottom-right corner of the diagram until it turns into a double arrow, then click and drag the corner until the drawing page is the correct size.

When you're satisfied with your changes to the diagram, click on the new document's page somewhere other than on the embedded diagram. This returns the native program's toolbars and removes the Visio 2000 rulers and stencils.

TIP   *If you accidentally click outside the embedded diagram, you can return to the editing function by double-clicking on the embedded diagram.*

After you've restored the native program's toolbars, remember to save the document. Because your diagram only exists as part of the new document, if you don't save the new document, you'll lose all changes.

Managing the Space Around Embedded or Linked Visio 2000 Diagrams

Because the program into which you embed a Visio 2000 diagram sees the diagram as a type of image, by default, a blank border exists around the diagram. This space is kept free of text and other data to avoid crowding the diagram, but you may want to set the amount of white space yourself for a couple of reasons.

- For small diagrams or single shapes embedded as Visio 2000 diagrams, the white space is too little and the shape becomes crowded when other text or data is added to the document. You may need to add a white border shape around your shape to compensate for this.

- When you copy and embed an entire drawing page into another program, extra white space can appear around the Visio 2000 diagram. This white space represents the parts of your drawing page that didn't have shapes, but were included when you used the Edit | Copy Drawing command. You may need to remove some of the white space around your diagram so it doesn't cover part of the new document.

To adjust the amount of white space around your embedded or linked Visio 2000 diagram, first select the diagram in the new document. Do not double-click to open the Visio 2000 editing capability, but instead edit the Visio 2000 diagram in a Visio 2000 window. To edit the diagram in the Visio 2000 window, you need to choose Edit | Visio 2000 Object | Open after you've selected the embedded diagram on the drawing page. This opens the diagram in an independent Visio 2000 window like the one shown in Figure 6-3.

NOTE   *The diagram may appear as though it is zoomed in.*

Once you have the diagram open in a Visio 2000 window, you can change the amount of white space around the diagram by changing the size of the page.

To change the size of the Visio 2000 page, choose File | Page Setup and select the Page Size tab, shown in Figure 6-4.

Choose the page size and orientation that most fits your needs. Here are the options available on the Page Size tab:

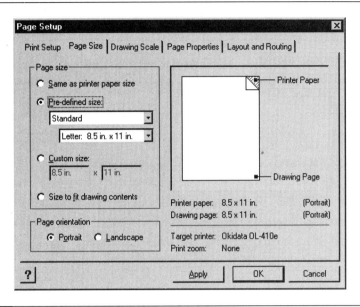

FIGURE 6-4   Page Size tab of the Page Setup dialog box

Same as printer paper size   Sets the drawing page size to be the same as the paper size set in the printer.

Pre-defined size   Sets the drawing size to one of four standard page-size sets: Standard U.S. sizes, Standard E.U. sizes, Architectural sizes, or Engineering sizes. Once you choose the page-size set, then the second drop-down menu allows you to choose the exact page size.

Custom size   Sets the exact size of the page. This is one of the two most useful settings for managing white space.

Size to fit drawing contents   Shrinks the drawing page to include only the shapes with no white space outside them. This setting is also very useful for handling white space.

Page orientation   Changes the orientation of the drawing page to have the long side vertical (portrait) or the long side horizontal (landscape).

There is more discussion of page size and printer settings in Chapter 1, "Visio 2000 Basics."

Once you've selected the drawing page size, click OK and the Page Setup dialog box closes. Visio 2000 has now changed the drawing page containing your embedded diagram according to your choice.

You can alter the diagram in any way you like in the Visio 2000 main window, because it is actually open in Visio 2000. You can open and close stencils and add shapes and text. Also, while you have the diagram open in the Visio 2000 window, you can save a copy of the diagram in Visio 2000 file format or as an image by choosing File I Save Copy As.

When you're finished altering the page size of your diagram, and you're ready to return to your document, choose File I Exit and Return to (document). This closes the Visio 2000 window and returns you to the document in the main window of its resident program. Remember to save the document as soon as you close the main Visio 2000 window.

 For advice on troubleshooting problems with embedded data, see "Troubleshooting Linking and Embedding Problems" at the end of the next section.

Linking

A linked object is data created in one program (the native program) that is included in a file of another program in such a way that the data can be edited both in the original file *and* in the file of the other program. Both files (the original and the one containing the linked data) reflect changes to the data regardless of where those changes are made.

 Linking data can happen between more than two programs. You can link to the same data from as many programs as you like. However, only linking between two programs will be covered in this chapter. For more information about linking, see the online help for your OLE-compatible program.

Link data when you want to be able to update the information from both programs. Data included via linking can be altered in its original document in its original program, and the link updates the data and incorporates the change when the new document is opened again.

For example, if you have text describing the confidentiality of company data that you'd like to include at the bottom of your Visio 2000 diagram, you can create that data in another OLE-compatible program, then link to the data. If you later need to change the wording of the text, simply alter it in its original program, and Visio 2000 automatically updates the data on the diagram page.

One of the biggest benefits of linking to data instead of embedding it is that when you link to data from another program, Visio 2000 only keeps a reference to the data instead of containing it. This lack of inclusion in a new document means that linking to data doesn't increase file size, so your documents remain small.

 Because linking adds a reference to the data via the filename and location, if you change the filename or move the files related to each other, you'll break the link. If you need to move linked files you must move them all together.

The advantage of linking is that files are updated no matter where the data is changed. This ability can be a huge time-saver, but adding links to data and managing linked data has its own special procedures. This section explains how to add links, change them, edit the data, and make sure they're updated correctly.

Preparing Documents to Be Linked

You need to make some preparations before you can add linked data to a document. Make sure you have completed all of these steps before you begin the linking process.

- Make sure the document containing the data you're linking to has been saved.

- Make sure that both programs—the native program and the one for the document in which you're creating the link—are loaded on your system.

- Make sure the two files are saved in the same locations, or at least in the same relative locations, where they will reside when you have finished editing them.

Inserting Linked Data into a Visio 2000 Diagram

There are two ways to add linked data to the drawing page. One is to insert the data as an object, and the other is to create a link while copying the data. This subsection explains how to insert the data as an object. The next subsection explains how to link data while copying it.

To insert linked data into a Visio 2000 diagram using the first method, make sure your Visio 2000 diagram has been saved. Because linking involves adding a reference to another document, both documents must be saved to create the reference.

After you've saved both documents, you're ready to create the link. On the Insert menu in the main Visio 2000 window, select Object | Create from File. The Insert Object dialog box opens, as shown in Figure 6-5. Select the checkbox for Link to File, setting the object to be inserted to automatically update as the file changes. Click Browse to display the Browse dialog box, shown in Figure 6-6. Browse to the file, select the filename, and then click Insert. The file path you select appears in the File Name text box of the Insert Object dialog box.

NOTE   *In the Insert Object dialog box, you can also select to display the object as an icon. This choice puts a placeholder in your diagram instead of displaying all the data in the document you link to.*

When you're satisfied with the path and options set in the Insert Object dialog box, click OK. The Insert Object dialog box closes, and Visio 2000 places a copy

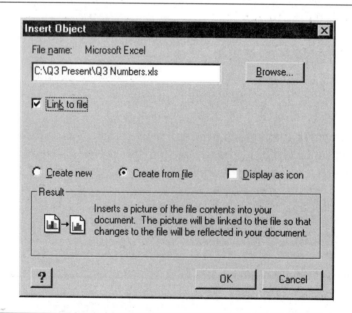

FIGURE 6-5   The Insert Object dialog box

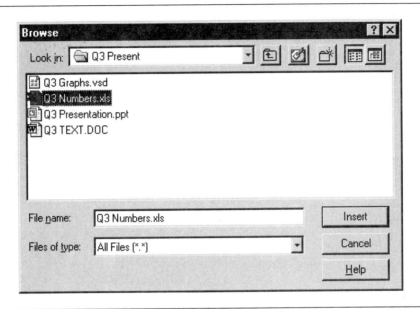

FIGURE 6-6   The Browse dialog box

of the first page of the linked data in the center of your drawing page. Remember to save your diagram after setting a link.

Copying Linked Data into a Visio 2000 Diagram

To copy linked data into the drawing page, first make sure both the Visio 2000 document and the document containing the data have been saved.

In the document containing the data, copy the data to the clipboard, usually by selecting it and then choosing Edit | Copy.

After you have the data on the clipboard, open the Visio 2000 diagram you wish to add the data to and choose Edit | Paste Special. The Paste Special dialog box appears, as shown in Figure 6-7.

Choose to paste the data in any format you wish, but make sure to select the Paste Link option button. This option pastes the data on the clipboard as a link instead of as an embedded object.

When you've set all the options in the your data, click OK. The Paste Special dialog box closes, and the pasted data appears in the center of the drawing page. You can move it around the drawing page like any other shape. Remember to save your diagram after you have pasted the linked data into the drawing page.

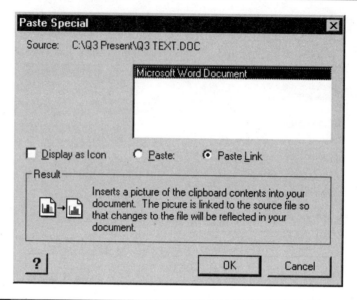

The Paste Special dialog box

Deciding How Linked Data Updates

After you've linked data on your drawing page, you need to decide how Visio 2000 updates those links. There are two types of link updating: manual and automatic. By default, all links are set to be updated automatically. Visio 2000 updates the data in a linked object every time you open up the Visio 2000 diagram containing it. Manual updating changes the data in a linked object only when you request that it be updated.

Usually, automatically updated links work well. When you use automatic updating, you can still manually update links without closing and reopening the file. If a link is set to be updated automatically and Visio 2000 cannot find the linked file when you open the diagram, Visio prompts you for the file's location. If you plan to do a lot of editing on a diagram and won't have consistent access to the linked document, it's best to use manually updated links.

To change the update method for a linked object, select it on the drawing page. Then choose Edit | Links. The Links window appears, as shown in Figure 6-8. The Links window shows the file paths for all the linked objects on the drawing page.

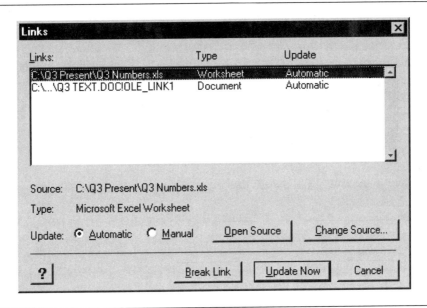

FIGURE 6-8   The Links window

The path for the selected link is highlighted. Below the list of links, the Source field shows the path for the highlighted link, and the Type field shows what kind of file it is.

To set the update method, select either the Automatic or the Manual option button at the bottom of the Links window. (In the next section, you'll learn how to use the other options available on the Links window.) After you've selected the update method, click OK. The Links window closes, and Visio 2000 uses the new update method for the linked data.

Managing Linked Data in Visio 2000

In addition to the setting that determines how linked data is updated, there are several other settings you can adjust using the Links window. If you have set linked data to be manually updated, it's important to know how to use these settings. These settings are also important if the data is set to be automatically updated and you later move or rename the original files.

If you open a drawing containing linked data and Visio 2000 cannot find the original file, Visio 2000 asks you to update links manually.

All settings for your linked data are set on the Links window. To open the Links window, choose Edit I Links. The Links window appears, as shown in Figure 6-8. Here's a list of the available settings on the Links window:

Links List Lists all linked data on the current page. This area of the dialog box lists the path, type, and update method for each link.

Source Shows the file path for the highlighted link in the Links list.

Type Shows the file type for the highlighted link in the Links list.

Update Shows the setting for updating the link selected on the Links list, which can be either manual or automatic. Automatic is the default.

Open Source Launches the original program for the linked data selected in the Links list and opens the file containing the linked data.

NOTE *If you click the Open Source button and the native program for the linked data is not available on your computer, Visio 2000 displays an error message telling you that the link is not working.*

Change Source Opens the Change Source dialog box, which looks very similar to the Browse dialog box shown earlier in Figure 6-6. The Change Source dialog box allows you to reset the path for the link selected in the Links list.

Break Link Removes the link between the linked data's original document and the Visio 2000 drawing page. This turns the linked data into embedded data. When you select to break a link, Visio 2000 displays a dialog box telling you that this action will disconnect the linked data from its source and asks if you want to continue. Click Yes and the link is broken.

Update Now Forces a manual update of the linked data selected in the Links list.

You can also open the source file by selecting the linked data and then choosing Edit | Linked Object | Open.

When you're done updating the information for your linked data, click Close. Visio 2000 applies the new settings to the data. Remember to save the diagram after changing any linked data settings.

Linking to a Visio 2000 Diagram from Another Program

Just as you can insert linked data into a Visio 2000 diagram, you can insert Visio 2000 data into the files of another program. First, however, you must make sure that both documents have been saved. Because linking involves setting up a relationship between the documents based on their relative paths, the documents must have full path names to have a linking relationship.

Once the documents are saved, select the data you want on the Visio 2000 drawing page and then choose Edit | Copy Drawing. This copies all the data from the page to the clipboard.

In the document where you want to link to the Visio 2000 data, choose Edit | Paste Special. Make sure the diagram is placed as a Visio 2000 Drawing Object, then choose to paste the data as a link.

 You can only paste the page that is displayed in Visio 2000 when you choose Edit | Copy. If you want to paste more than one page, you need to repeat this process for each page.

Once the linked data has been pasted to the new document, remember to save it.

Troubleshooting Linking and Embedding Problems

Because embedded data requires two programs working together, problems sometimes occur that would not happen if just one program were used to create a document. No matter if you're inserting other program data into Visio 2000, or Visio 2000 data into another program, editing that data can be problematic.

The most common error message you'll see is one indicating you cannot edit the data; the message might not give a reason for the error. This message appears when the source file for the data or source program containing the document can't be opened for some reason.

Here are some reasons you might encounter an error while editing (and some ways to resolve such problems):

■ The program used to create the document is not loaded on your computer.

Make sure the program you're using with Visio 2000 has been installed on your computer before you attempt to edit embedded data from that program. If for some reason you cannot load the program, you may be able to convert the data into a file format you can use with a program you already have loaded. You may be able to convert the data by selecting the embedded object and then selecting Convert.

■ Your computer cannot open both Visio 2000 and the new program at the same time.

Make sure you have enough memory free to run both programs at once. You can free up memory by closing other programs that are running or by closing all programs, restarting your computer, and then attempting to run both programs simultaneously.

■ The program that created the data is not responding.

The most common cause of this is to have an open dialog box in the program set to edit the data. With both programs running you may have minimized one, and when you cannot see both programs, you may have unintentionally left a dialog box open in the minimized program. If the program is running, check to make sure it is not held up by an open dialog box.

■ The data is already being edited.

For linked and embedded data, it's possible to have a copy of the data open either in Visio 2000 (for a linked file) or in an edit window (for an embedded object). Make sure you have all other copies of the data closed before you try to edit it. For linked data, this means you must make sure no one else has a copy of the source file open.

■ The filename has changed on the linked file.

Because linked files create a bond between the data in one document and the embedded data in another, if you change the filename of the document used to create the data, it breaks the link. To reestablish the link, select the linked data and then choose Edit | Links and edit the link information using the Change Source button.

Using Visio 2000 with Microsoft Products

Visio 2000 is designed to work seamlessly with Microsoft products, especially the products in the Microsoft Office Suite. You can include a Visio 2000 drawing page in your Microsoft Binder projects and import Microsoft Excel data and create a flowchart, and you can include Visio 2000 diagrams in your Microsoft PowerPoint presentations. You can even create new Microsoft Exchange routing slips from inside Visio 2000. This section discusses some of the most common uses of Visio 2000 with Microsoft Office.

Adding Visio 2000 Hyperlinks to Office Documents

In Chapter 7, "Linking and the Internet," you'll learn how to add hyperlinks to your Visio 2000 shapes. Office documents can also have hyperlinks, and you can paste a hyperlinked Visio 2000 shape into one of these documents.

To paste a hyperlinked Visio 2000 shape into your Microsoft Office document, first set the hyperlink for the shape in Visio 2000. Then select the hyperlinked shape in Visio 2000 and copy the shape by choosing Edit | Copy. This copies the shape to the clipboard.

After the hyperlinked shape is on the clipboard, open the Office document where you would like to include it. Then, to paste the entire shape and its hyperlink, choose Edit | Paste. If you just want to include the hyperlink alone onto a different object, choose Edit | Paste as Hyperlink.

| NOTE | *Versions of Microsoft programs older than Microsoft Office 97 do not support the Paste as Hyperlink feature.* |

Adding Graphics to Microsoft Word

Using Visio 2000 graphics in Microsoft Word can really enhance your Word documents. There are three standard ways to include a Visio 2000 diagram in Microsoft Word:

- Saving the diagram as an image
- Embedding the diagram
- Linking to the diagram from Word

Saving the Diagram as an Image

This process allows you to place your diagram into your Microsoft Word document as you would a piece of clip art, moving and resizing as you need. Also, the copy of the diagram is saved with the Word document. Unfortunately, you may loose resolution when you save the diagram as an image, and you loose the ability to continue to change the diagram. For more information about how to save Visio 2000 diagrams as images, see Chapter 2, "Creating Your First Diagram."

Embedding the Visio 2000 Diagram

Embedding allows you to continue to edit the diagram as a Visio 2000 document and saves the image data with the document. You can also move embedded images around on the drawing page, but Microsoft Word can be a little picky about how text wraps around embedded documents. If necessary, you can also convert embedded data into standard images. For more information about embedding Visio 2000 documents, see the section "Embedding" earlier in this chapter.

Linking to the Diagram from Microsoft Word

Linking allows you to continue editing your diagram no matter where you change it, and both your Microsoft Word document and your Visio 2000 diagram will reflect the change. Unfortunately, the relationship between the files must stay the same or the link breaks. For more information about linking to Visio 2000 documents, see the section "Linking" earlier in this chapter.

Importing and Exporting Data from Microsoft Excel and Microsoft Access

Several different Visio 2000 macros and templates are designed to import and export data to and from Microsoft Excel and Microsoft Access. This section briefly discusses the most commonly used features.

Importing or Exporting Flowchart Information

The Organizational Wizard and the Import Flowchart Data Wizard can use data from Microsoft Excel and Microsoft Access to create an organizational chart. Both templates can also export data based on the charts you create to these formats. For more information, see Chapter 5, "Creating Flowcharts."

Updating Automatically from Databases

Several Visio 2000 macros have been created to help you keep a Visio 2000 diagram and Microsoft databases in sync. The Database Wizard can help you set up the relationship; open it by choosing Tools | Macros | Database Wizard. The Macros menu also includes database export, refresh, settings, and update tools.

Creating Presentations Using Visio 2000 Diagrams in Microsoft PowerPoint

Visio 2000 and PowerPoint work so well together, it's as if they were made for each other. Microsoft PowerPoint enables you to use your Visio 2000 diagrams to make your point and to strengthen your presentations.

Because PowerPoint is an OLE-compatible program, you can link and embed your Visio 2000 diagram if you choose, or even create a whole new Visio 2000 diagram right in PowerPoint. You can also copy and paste your Visio 2000 diagram into PowerPoint. You can even just drag all or part of a Visio 2000 diagram into an open presentation in PowerPoint, and it is incorporated quickly and easily.

One feature that helps Visio 2000 and PowerPoint work well together is *color schemes*. The color schemes you set in Visio 2000 are the same as those that come with PowerPoint, allowing you to choose a color scheme for your PowerPoint presentation and then apply it to all parts of your Visio 2000 diagram that you wish to include.

If you want, you can even include PowerPoint clip art in Visio 2000 diagrams, helping you to create a cohesive theme within diagrams, just as you would throughout a presentation.

Displaying Diagrams in Microsoft Internet Explorer

Microsoft Internet Explorer and Visio 2000 also work very well together. To open a Visio 2000 diagram within Internet Explorer, choose File | Open. In the Open dialog box, click Browse. Then select the All Files file type and locate the Visio 2000 diagram.

When you open a Visio 2000 diagram, the Visio 2000 menus, toolbars, and stencils appear. You're able to edit your Visio 2000 diagram in Internet Explorer just as you can in the main Visio 2000 window. You can also use the Internet Explorer navigation buttons and menus (such as the Forward and Back buttons) to move between Visio 2000 diagrams, Office documents, and World Wide Web pages.

Sending a Diagram as an E-Mail Message with Microsoft Exchange

E-mail has become a major tool for conducting business, and Visio 2000 diagrams often need to be sent through e-mail. Visio 2000 has included three options to make this process easier, all of which can be accessed by choosing File | Send To. The options are as follows:

Mail Recipient   Opens your Microsoft mail program, starts a new message, and adds the current Visio 2000 drawing as an attachment.

Routing Receipt   Opens Microsoft Exchange and creates a routing slip with the current Visio 2000 drawing attached. You select the address for the document to be routed to, the order in which it is routed, and you can track the status of the diagram at any time. You can also add message text to the routing slip and send it, or you can continue to edit the drawing and send it later.

Save to Exchange Folder   Allows you to save your Visio 2000 drawing as an embedded object in a Microsoft Exchange folder you select.

Summary

In this chapter, you learned how to include Office documents in your Visio 2000 diagrams and how to include Visio 2000 diagrams in your Office documents. You also learned how to link the two documents together to create automatic updates, as well as finding out the most common ways Microsoft Office software can be used with Visio 2000.

In the next chapter, you'll learn how to use Visio 2000 to hyperlink to other documents and how to save Visio 2000 drawings for use on the World Wide Web.

6

CHAPTER 7

Linking and the Internet

In the last chapter, you learned how to make Visio 2000 and Microsoft Office programs work together.

In this chapter, you'll learn how to add hyperlinks to your Visio 2000 diagrams. You'll learn how you can create internal links within Visio 2000 diagrams and external links to other documents. You'll also learn how to save Visio 2000 diagrams so they can be viewed on the World Wide Web.

Linking in Visio

With the prevalence of the Web, hyperlinks have become a part of everyday life for many people. As you may already know, hyperlinks typically appear as underlined text on Web pages. When you click a hyperlink, you jump from one page to another (or from one part of a page to another part). Likewise, in Visio 2000, you can use hyperlinks to jump from one diagram to another, or to different parts of the same diagram. You can also use hyperlinks to jump from a Visio 2000 diagram to a completely different type of document.

Hyperlinks are links between a *host document*—the place where you click—and a *linked document*—the place where you are taken. Hyperlinks can be included in any Visio 2000 diagram and can be especially helpful when you have large diagrams that span several pages. For example, if you have an organization chart that spans many pages, you could link the managers' shapes to pages that discuss the performance of the departments they oversee. Each manager shape would be a host, and the departmental pages would be the linked pages. If you clicked the link on a manager's shape, Visio 2000 would automatically display the departmental page.

 Visio 2000 includes advanced hyperlinking features that are not available in earlier versions of Visio.

Understanding Visio 2000 Hyperlinks

Visio 2000 hyperlinks fall into two categories: internal and external. These two types of hyperlinks have much in common. Both kinds of links can open other documents when clicked, and both are set using the same dialog boxes. They differ, however, in the types of documents they link, so the process for setting internal and external links is slightly different—and the results can be dramatically different depending on the type of link you create.

Internal Links

An *internal link* is a link to a Visio 2000 drawing. Often, internal links are links to different pages within the same Visio 2000 drawing. Linking within a single drawing can provide easy access to information when the drawing spans many pages. Linking within the same drawing can also add new meaning; the link between two objects can indicate a relationship that may be difficult to illustrate in any other way.

External Links

An *external link* is a link to any file other than a Visio drawing. With Visio 2000, you can create hyperlinks to virtually any kind of document or file. When someone clicks the link in a Visio 2000 drawing, Visio 2000 opens the linked file using the default program set to open that file type.

7

> **TIP** *To find out which program opens a particular file type, open any Windows folder and select View | Options | File Types. On the File Types tab, select a file type to see the program that opens it.*

Setting Links

Setting Visio 2000 links involves several steps. First, create the drawing to contain the links, or open an existing drawing. To create hyperlinks, you need to already have shapes on the page. Second, make sure to always save the document that will host the links before you start adding hyperlinks. (This only takes a few moments and can save a lot of grief later.) Third, open the Web toolbar by going to the View menu of the main Visio 2000 window and selecting Toolbars | Web. The Web toolbar makes accessing hyperlink features quick and easy. Table 7-1 describes the buttons on the Web toolbar. Once you have taken these three steps, you're ready to add hyperlinks.

Adding Hyperlinks

With Visio 2000, you can add links to any shape or group of shapes, as well as to backgrounds and text. You can also add a hyperlink to an entire page. When you add a link to a single shape, the link only exists on that shape. The ramifications of linking to groups, backgrounds, and pages are not as intuitive. For example, if you add a link to an entire page (by displaying a page without selecting any shapes),

Button	Name	Function
	Insert Hyperlink	Creates a hyperlink on the selected shape or shapes.
	Back	Takes you back to the last hyperlink you clicked. Enabled only after you have clicked a link.
	Forward	Takes you forward to the next link. Enabled only after you have gone back to a link.
	Visio 2000 on the Web	Opens the default Web browser to the Visio home page.

TABLE 7-1   The Hyperlink Toolbar Buttons

the link exists wherever there's no shape on the drawing page. Or, if you add a link to a group of shapes, all the shapes in the group have that link; however, if you add a link to one of the individual shapes in the group, the new link takes precedence, even though the group link still exists. Also, links to backgrounds affect all pages that use the background.

Once you've selected the object (that is, the shape, group, background, or page) to which you want to add a hyperlink, click the Insert Hyperlink button, or select Hyperlink from the Insert menu. The Hyperlinks window opens, as shown in Figure 7-1. The following paragraphs explain the different parts of the Hyperlinks window.

Address   Shows the location of the linked document. Links to documents on the local hard drive are listed as file paths. Links to documents on the World Wide Web are listed as URLs. The next section, "Browsing for Addresses and Sub-addresses," explains how to add a file path or URL to this field.

Sub-address   Specifies an exact place within the linked document. Sub-addresses can only be used for internal hyperlinks (that is, links to Visio 2000 documents). Often, the sub-address creates a link to a particular page in the linked document, but it can also be used to create a link to an individual shape.

Browse   Allows you to browse through files to locate the address and sub-address of the linked document. These buttons are explained in more detail in the following section, "Browsing for Addresses and Sub-addresses."

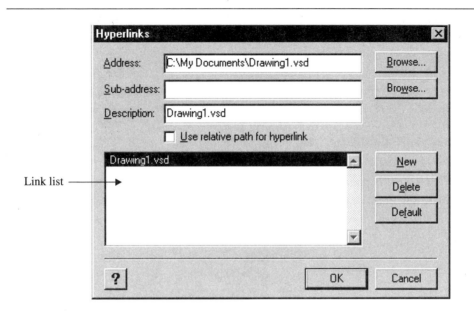

Link list

FIGURE 7-1 The Hyperlinks window

Description Shows the text that displays for the link. The default is the filename for the document. The description also displays as pop-up text when the mouse pointer is hovered over the link in an HTML file.

Use relative path for hyperlink Defines how the link is saved to the system. When the box is checked, Visio 2000 lists the link in relation to the location of the current Visio 2000 document or the "hyperlink base." The *hyperlink base* is a custom file path you can set by selecting File | Properties | Summary and entering a path in the Hyperlink Base field. When the "Use relative path for hyperlink" checkbox is unchecked, Visio 2000 lists the complete address for the link. For local links this is the complete path name. For Web links, this is the complete URL.

Link list The Link list shows all the links that have been set for the selected object. The first link in the list is the *default link*; this may be the only active link if the host document is saved in HTML format.

New Allows you to add a new hyperlink after one has already been set.

Delete   Removes the link selected in the Link list.

Default   Sets the selected link as the default link. That link moves to the top of the Link list.

You can access the Hyperlinks window for an object (that is, for a shape, group, page, or background) by selecting the object and clicking the Insert Hyperlink button.

Browsing for Addresses and Sub-addresses

When you set an address or sub-address in the Hyperlinks window, you can browse to find the file or page you need.

To browse to the address for a link, click the Browse button next to the Address field. A drop-down menu appears, as shown in Figure 7-2.

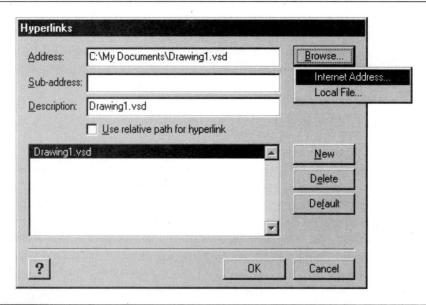

FIGURE 7-2   The Browse button's drop-down menu

Internet Address   Launches the default Web browser so you can find the URL. Visio 2000 follows your Web-browsing and automatically places the current URL in the Address field.

Local File   Opens the Link to File dialog box, which is shown in Figure 7-3. Browse to the file, select it, and then click Open. The Link to File dialog box closes, and the Address box is updated with the file path.

NOTE   *Before clicking the Browse button for the Address field, make sure you're connected to the Internet or to the server that holds the file to which you're creating a link.*

7

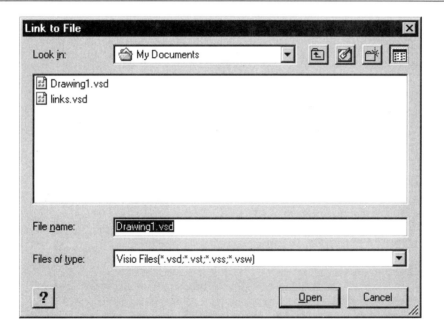

FIGURE 7-3   The Link to File dialog box

If the address of the linked document is a local file path to a Visio 2000 file, you can set a sub-address for the link. Sub-addresses allow you to link to a particular page or shape in the linked document. You can do this by manually entering text in the Sub-address field, but usually it's easier to use the Browse button for the Sub-address field. Click the Browse button next to the Sub-address field to open a Hyperlink dialog box shown here:

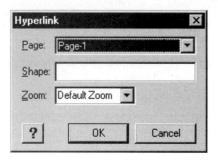

Page   Specifies a particular page in the linked document. By default, the first page of the document appears in this field.

Shape   Specifies a particular shape in the linked document by entering the shape's name. To find the name of an individual shape, right-click on the shape and select Format | Special. The name is listed in the Name field.

If you set the Shape field incorrectly for a sub-address, when you select the link, Visio 2000 takes you to the end of the document and displays an error message.

Zoom   Sets the page view used when Visio 2000 opens the linked document. By default, this is set as the default zoom for the page. You may set it for any of the standard page views available in Visio, but not to a custom zoom setting.

If you select a shape as the sub-address, make sure the Page field in the Hyperlink dialog box shows the page that the shape is on.

When you're finished setting the sub-address for the link, click OK. The Hyperlink dialog box closes, but the Hyperlinks window remains open. Click OK again to close the Hyperlinks window.

Accessing Links

Once you've set a link for a shape, you can view its hyperlinks by right-clicking on the shape. If there's more than one hyperlink, the default hyperlink is listed at the top. When you select a hyperlink from the list, Visio 2000 automatically jumps to the link's destination, centering on the sub-link if one has been set.

NOTE *If a hyperlink has been set for a shape, the mouse pointer displays a hyperlink symbol when you move the pointer over the shape.*

You can also access links if you are in full-screen view by simply clicking the shape or page to activate the hyperlink. Visio 2000 opens the document using its native program. To move between hyperlinks in full-screen view, use the right and left arrows on the Web toolbar or left-click with the mouse. This takes you backward and forward through the links.

NOTE *When you click a link in full-screen view, Visio 2000 doesn't open the new document in full-screen view. Instead, Visio 2000 opens the document in a normal window for the program.*

As you move back and forth between your Visio 2000 diagram and linked documents, remember that you'll need to have the native program loaded on your computer to see the linked documents. Also, there are some limitations on how you can move between documents. You can only move back and forth between Visio 2000 drawings and Microsoft Office documents (Office 97 or later). Other programs don't have the capacity to switch back and forth with Visio. If you want to go to and from other document types, such as text files, you must host the files in Internet Explorer (version 3.01 or later).

Adding Special Hyperlink Shapes

Visio 2000 includes several shapes as hyperlinking shapes that can be used as buttons on finished Visio 2000 HTML pages. They are located at the bottom of the Borders and Tiles stencil, which opens with Visio 2000's Basic Drawing template. If you use another template, you can open the Borders and Tiles stencil by clicking on the Open Stencil button and choosing the Borders and Tiles stencil from the Visio 2000 Extras folder.

There are three hyperlinking master shapes on the stencil: Hyperlink Button, Hyperlink Circle 1, and Hyperlink Circle 2. Each of these is actually a set of shapes, and you must choose a specific shape after you drag the master shape to the drawing. When you drag one of these master shapes to the drawing page, Visio 2000 opens the Custom Properties dialog box, asking you which of the individual shapes you'd like, as shown here:

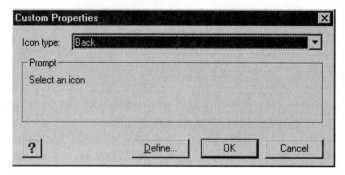

Icon Type   Sets the icon that appears on the page. Choose between Back, Directory, Down, Forward, Help, Home, Info, Mail, None, Photo, Search, and Up. Each choice creates a different shape on the drawing page. You can change the shape at any time by right-clicking on it and selecting Change Icon. This opens the Custom Properties dialog box.

Once you've selected the type of shape, Visio 2000 displays the Hyperlinks window, shown earlier in Figure 7-1. Fill in the data for the link, and then click OK.

 Before you use these shapes, it's best to plan your Web site so you can set the right links.

Changing Hyperlinks

There are many reasons you may need to change a hyperlink after it has been set. For example, you may need to add more than one link to a shape, or you may wish to remove links you previously added. You may also need to change the path or filenames for links when the documents they reference have moved or changed. Also, if during the process of creating your Visio 2000 diagram, you added links simply for your own use (ones that won't be part of the finished document), you'll need to delete all those links.

Whatever your reason for needing to alter a link, make sure you always save your Visio 2000 document before you begin this process.

Adding More Than One Link to a Shape

To add another hyperlink to an object that already has one, simply follow the procedures for adding the first hyperlink, with one small difference:

1. Select the shape, group, or page.

2. Click the Insert Hyperlink button. This opens the Hyperlinks window.

3. Click the New button to access the fields where you enter information for the new link.

4. Fill in the Address and Sub-address fields.

5. Add a description.

6. Click OK when done.

When you add more than one hyperlink to a shape, the first hyperlink added is set as the default.

Changing the Default Link

To change the default link:

1. Select the shape, group, or page.

2. Click the Insert Hyperlink button. This opens the Hyperlinks window.

3. Select the link you want as the default link from the Link list.

4. Click Default.

5. Click OK when done.

The default link is sometimes the only link recognized when you save files as HTML. For more information about HTML files, see the section "Saving as HTML" later in this chapter.

7

Changing Hyperlink Information

To change any information other than the default link, proceed as if adding or deleting a link:

1. Select the shape, group, or page.

2. Click the Insert Hyperlink button. This opens the Hyperlinks window, shown earlier in Figure 7-1.

3. Select the link you need to change.

4. Change the information, including address, sub-address, and description.

5. Click OK when done.

Deleting Hyperlinks

To remove a hyperlink from any Visio 2000 object, first select the object. If the link is on the page, select the page by deselecting everything else, so that no green control squares appear anywhere on the page. If the link is on a shape, select the shape. Then click the Insert Hyperlink button on the Web toolbar. The Hyperlinks window opens. In the Link list, select the hyperlink you want to remove and click Delete. When you've deleted all the hyperlinks you want to remove, click OK to close the Hyperlinks window.

Creating Web Pages in Visio

The Internet has become a cornerstone of business and is quickly becoming a part of our everyday lives. Web pages have become vital to a company's communication with the outside world and how it operates. Intranet sites have become primary distribution points for company information. Both of these modes of communication require HTML and graphics to get your point across, and Visio 2000 is a powerful tool for creating graphical Web content.

 Visio 2000 was developed with Microsoft's Internet Explorer 5.0. All HTML content is optimized for this browser.

Visio 2000 has ways to help you integrate your diagrams into both intranet and Internet sites. You can save your files in any of a number of Web-friendly formats, or you can create individual pages for your diagrams with the HTML code already included.

This section assumes you know something about how HTML works and how to create Web sites. If you need information about using the Web for business, or a primer on how to create Web pages, see Appendix C, "Resources," for more information.

Designing Your Site

The first step in any Web-page creation process must always be to plan out your pages. Since links between pages require an idea of what directory the file is located in, you must have a clear idea of what files you need and how they interrelate before you start.

If you're creating Web pages that are to fit inside a design framework already in place, you need to know the file-naming conventions, the folder structure, and the computer where the pages will eventually reside. If you're creating a completely new site, you need to plan out beforehand how it'll look and what your file structure will be. Make sure you have all this information before you begin to save your diagrams as HTML.

Visio 2000 is a great tool for Web-site design. Use the shapes and connections to create a visual representation of your Web site before you begin. Later, you can use the design diagram on a Web page as a site map.

Using Visio 2000 Images on the World Wide Web

Once you've created your diagrams, including hyperlinks, you're ready to start thinking about using your images on the Web. Visio 2000 includes an option called Save As HTML. However, there are several issues about using your Visio 2000 diagrams on Web pages you must consider before making your final choices.

Web Issues

When it comes to the Web, there are often as many issues as there are options. The ability for infinite information distribution and the flexibility for clients and servers leads to lots of choices you need to make up front.

BROWSER VERSIONS Most content on the Web is viewed using a Web browser (for example, Netscape Navigator or Microsoft Internet Explorer), and each browser has several different versions. Consequently, the first thing to consider is how users will view your pages. Because the different versions, let alone the different products, all have unique sets of standards, it can be quite difficult to plan a site that looks good in all browsers.

Fortunately, the entire browser issue gets much less complicated if you know who'll be looking at the pages you create. It's easier to make decisions regarding browser-compliance if your Web pages will be used in a limited context—for example, at a company meeting or on an intranet where everyone uses the same browser.

Visio 2000 was developed with the Internet Explorer version 5.0 standards in mind, meaning that HTML files produced in Visio 2000 are optimized for that browser. Some of the newer features available for exporting to HTML may not be usable on earlier versions of the browser, and some may not work at all.

> **TIP** *Always test your HTML files in a few different versions of both the Netscape and Microsoft browsers if you plan to put the files on the Web.*

IMAGE TYPES No matter which browser you choose, in the end, Visio 2000 exports your diagrams as images. These images can have special properties—such as different links for different parts of the image and the ability to zoom in—or they can just be flat images you place inside other HTML documents. The choice of which type of image you need is partially based on the browser version you think is mostly likely to be used to view your pages. Newer browsers are capable of more sophisticated image-handling; older browsers aren't.

But the choice of browser is not the only consideration when you decide on image types. The more complex the image, the larger the file will be. Since the size of the file determines how long it takes to load, large image files might hinder people from visiting your site. This is especially important if you plan to have your images up on the Web, where bandwidth and download times are major issues.

There are two basic kinds of images for Web pages: flat images and image maps. *Flat images* are simply pictures that have no special features. Like any image, however, flat images can have links if you create the links in the Web page's HTML code. *Image maps* are graphics with different links or features in different regions. They have attached HTML files that give the browser all the information it needs to process the different regions.

Flat images can be small and are often added to pages with text to give them a nicer look and feel. Visio 2000 can save images in both of the standard Web image formats: Graphic Interchange Format (.gif) and JPEG format (.jpg). Images saved in one of these formats can be included in any Web page and can be displayed by any browser. As long as they are a reasonable size, they pose no problems with download time or bandwidth.

Image maps are more complicated. They come in two types: client-side image maps, and server-side image maps. *Client-side image maps* are the most common and are more widely accepted. They allow different regions of one image to have different "hot spots" or links, and they also allow different parts of the image to behave independently from other parts. Client-side image maps are supported in most browsers. By default, when you save drawings with links as HTML pages, the drawing is converted into a client-side image map. *Server-side image maps* require a program on the Web server to examine map data to make the different regions of the image work independently. Server-side image maps also require that you move all your images and HTML code to the server before they work. Since client-side image maps are the default in Visio, they're the only type of image map covered in this book.

7

NOTE   *For more information about server-side image maps, see Appendix C, "Resources."*

VISIO 2000's HTML TEMPLATE   After you choose the browser you'll design for and make decisions about the types of images you'll include, the next consideration is how your pages will look.

Visio 2000 includes a template for formatting HTML files. You open this template when you choose to save files as HTML. If you choose to create pages yourself, you need to create some sort of template of your own so you know where your images belong and what general size they need to be.

Visio 2000's template is a text page with standard HTML tags and special codes that correspond to elements from the drawing, such as page number, graphics, and links (or anchors) to other HTML pages or files. When you save your diagram as HTML, drawing elements are substituted for the codes.

You can get the best of both worlds by creating a custom template for saving and formatting HTML pages by modifying the Visio 2000 default template. This allows you to include standard substitution codes with your own HTML tags and formatting. When you save a drawing as an HTML file, you can choose which template you want to use, so you can even create more than one custom template. To learn how to customize the Visio 2000 HTML template, see Chapter 11.

Visio 2000's HTML Export Feature vs. Standard Web Image Formats

Deciding whether to use Visio 2000's HTML export feature or to use your own HTML and save diagrams as standard Web images can be confusing. Here's a quick reference for when it's best to use each type of solution.

It's best to save drawings with Visio 2000's HTML export feature when:

- You want to create a Web-ready version using several pages of a multiple-page drawing.

- Your drawing includes shapes with links you'd like to preserve by creating an image map.

- You have several linked Visio 2000 diagrams you'd like to stay linked after exporting.

- You have a very complicated Visio 2000 diagram that clients may need to zoom in on.

It's best to export drawings in standard Web image formats when:

- You know clients with older browsers may look at your Web pages.

- You already have an HTML-coded page in which you want to insert a Visio 2000 drawing.

- You want to export only a portion of a Visio 2000 diagram.

Creating a File System

No matter how you decide to export your pages, you must have some sort of file system framework created before you begin creating HTML pages or Web-ready images. If you don't create a file system first, you'll be forced to rename all your files and may loose functional links. Therefore, you need to make sure you know how files will be stored; in other words, you need a file system before you begin setting links.

Creating a file system also means deciding how your files will link together. There are two types of links in HTML: relative and absolute.

A *relative link* lists the location of the linked file in relation to the host file. These links are useful because you don't need to know where the entire Web site will eventually reside to create them. However, you must move the entire site together, or else you'll break the links.

Absolute links list the location of the linked file with a complete file path. If done correctly, it's impossible to break these links, since they give a global reference to a file. However, they require that you know the absolute path to your files before you begin adding links.

Relative links are often the safest for small Web sites that have few outside links or dependencies. Absolute links can be more time-consuming to create, but they're impossible to break once they've been set up.

 To set the absolute path for relative links, go to the File menu of the main Visio 2000 window and select Properties. In the Properties dialog box, set the Hyperlink Base field on the Summary tab.

Saving as HTML

Once you've created diagrams and dealt with all the issues surrounding Web page-creation, you're ready to start saving your diagrams for use on Web pages. This section details how to use Visio 2000's Save As HTML feature. Saving diagrams as images is covered in the next section.

 Always save your diagram in standard Visio 2000 format (.vsd) before you save it as HTML. If there's a problem with the conversion and you haven't saved a Visio 2000 version of the diagram, you may loose your data.

Using Save As HTML

To save your file as HTML, select Save As from the File menu. In the Save As dialog box, shown in Figure 7-4, you'll find HTML listed among the file types. Enter the name and location you want Visio 2000 to save to, select "HTML Files (*.htm, *.html)" from the Save As Type list, and then click Save. The Save As window closes and the Save As HTML dialog box appears, as shown in Figure 7-5.

The following paragraphs describe the different parts of the Save As HTML dialog box.

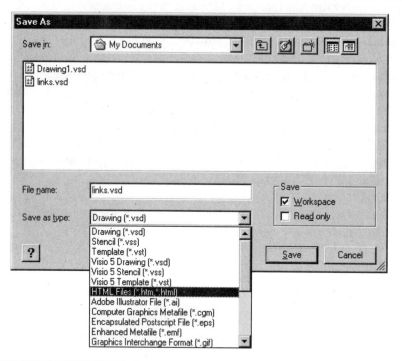

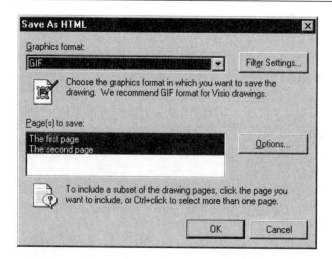

Graphics format   Sets the format for the graphics your diagrams are translated into. For more information, see "Selecting Graphic Types" a little later in this chapter.

Page(s) to save   Lists all the pages in the document. By default, they're all selected to export. Choose to export one page only by selecting it from the list. Choose to export more than one page by holding down CTRL while you select the pages in the list.

Filter Settings   Opens the Filter Settings dialog box. See the section "Using Filter Settings" later in this chapter for more information.

Options   Opens the Export Options window. See the section entitled "Setting the Export Options" later in this chapter for more information.

7

NOTE   *There are many options to be set in the Save As HTML dialog box and related dialog boxes. Make sure your pages are generated correctly by setting the correct options and filter settings.*

Once you've set all the HTML options, select OK on the Save As HTML dialog box (Figure 7-5). Visio 2000 displays a progress bar to let you know it's generating files, then it displays a message telling you it's finished and asks if you'd like to view the pages. Clicking Yes launches your default Web browser and opens the HTML version of your Visio 2000 diagram.

Selecting Graphic Types

Visio 2000's Export As HTML feature comes with four types of image filters. You can export in these formats:

- Graphic Interchange Format (.gif)

- Joint Photographic Experts Group Format (.jpg)

- Portable Network Graphics Format (.png)

- Vector-Based Markup Language (.vml)

Visio 2000 uses the GIF format as the default, and that's probably the best. Unless you need your HTML pages to include graphics in another format, use GIF or JPEG formats. They're the most widely used formats on the Web. Ideally, GIFs and JPEGs are small, making them the obvious choice for the Web.

Unfortunately, except for the VML filter, these image filters were not created by Visio. They can sometimes give unpredictable results.

Using VML

VML is a special graphic format available in Visio for the first time. VML is a special implementation of XML, the new Web standard currently under development. VML stands for Vector-Based Markup Language—a new format developed by Microsoft, Visio, Autodesk, and Hewlett-Packard to display vector-based drawings. Until now, vector-based drawings were converted into one of several types of bitmaps for use on the Web. Consequently, they lost the scalability and preciseness available in vector diagrams. VML allows the browser to zoom in on the page without loosing graphic quality, making it a very valuable tool, even for complex Visio 2000 diagrams.

 Only Internet Explorer, version 5.0 and later, can handle VML files. If you translate to VML files, you need to choose an alternate graphic for all other browsers.

If you select VML from the list of graphic types on the Save As HTML dialog box (refer to Figure 7-5), the Filter Settings button opens a different dialog box than for other image types. The VML Settings dialog box is shown here:

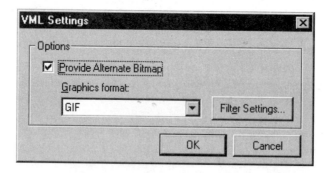

Provide Alternate Bitmap   Determines whether or not Visio 2000 creates an alternate bitmap when it creates the VML image. The alternate bitmap is required to view the page in any browser other than Internet Explorer version 5.0 or later.

 Always include an alternate bitmap. You can never be absolutely sure which browser will be used to view a Web page.

Graphics format   Sets the graphic format for the alternate bitmap. This is the same list as on the main Save As HTML dialog box, excluding the option for VML.

Filter Settings   Opens the standard Filter Settings dialog box for the graphics type set in the Graphics Format field. An example of this dialog box is shown in the following section.

Using Filter Settings

Filters are small applications that translate Visio 2000 diagrams into other types of images. Since they're small programs in and of themselves, you can set parameters for them and how they'll translate your images.

If you need to change the filter settings for your graphics, click the Filter Settings button. This displays a Filter Settings dialog box similar to the one shown here:

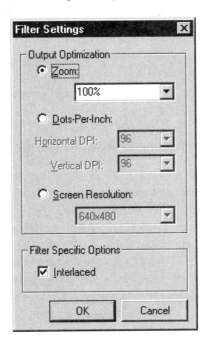

The Filter Settings dialog box changes depending on the type of image selected in the Graphics Format field. The dialog box shown above is an example of the filter settings for a GIF image. Most options in the dialog box are the same for all image types, with additional filter-specific options for GIFs and JPEGs.

You can choose one of three ways to define the output size: Zoom, Dots-Per-Inch, or Screen Resolution.

Zoom   Sets the size of the image that Visio 2000 exports. The settings refer to the size of the exported image in relation to the original diagram. You can choose zoom levels of 25, 50, 75, 100, 200, and 400 percent.

Dots-Per-Inch   Sets the resolution of the exported image. Image size plus the dots per inch results in the total pixel size of your completed image. The higher the dots per inch, the better the resolution and the greater the file size.

Screen Resolution   Bases the image's size on the screen resolution you select. This can result in huge file sizes, because Visio 2000 attempts to make the sharpest image possible.

Filter Specific Options   Determine image quality. For GIFs, the filter-specific option determines whether or not the image is interlaced. *Interlaced* GIF images provide greater resolution for their size. The only other image type with filter-specific options is JPEG. You select the JPEG quality by choosing from a list of different percentages.

Setting the Export Options

As you set the filter settings and choose the image typed for HTML files, there are a few more options to set. These options relate to how the image will be used, and they're set in the Export Options dialog box. In the Save As HTML dialog box (refer to Figure 7-5), click the Options button to open the Export Options dialog box shown here:

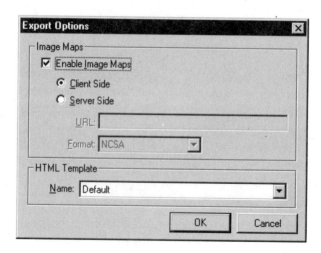

Enable Image Maps   Allows Visio 2000 to export your diagram as an image map. If you don't leave this box unchecked, Visio 2000 creates HTML files and removes all links the diagrams may have.

Client Side   Creates an image map that doesn't require any server intervention to work. A client-side image map can be handled completely by the browser. This is the most common kind of image map.

Server Side   Creates an image map that requires server intervention to work. If you select this option, you're asked for the URL and format of the server so Visio 2000 can include that information in the HTML files it creates. Only select this option if your system administrator has enabled server-side image mapping on your Web server. Hyperlinks for server-side image maps aren't active until you move the MAP files from your local folder to the CGI folder on the Web server.

HTML Template   Shows the template that Visio 2000 uses to translate files. Visio 2000 ships with one default translator. However, you can create your own. See Chapter 11, "Using Advanced Visio 2000 Features," for more information.

Understanding the Pages Produced by the Save As HTML Feature

The pages produced by Visio 2000's Save As HTML feature can be difficult to sort out. Visio 2000 places all the files in the directory you select, and it uses the name provided for the first part of every filename.

The number and type depend on two basic things: the image type you have selected and the number of pages in the document. Table 7-2 describes what the various files contain. In filenames listed in Table 7-2, the word *name* is a variable standing for the filename you have specified in the Save As dialog box.

For a drawing with more than one page, Visio 2000 generates at least five files for the drawing, plus two files for every page. If you need to change their location, you need to move all these files together, and they must all stay within one directory. If you nest any of the files in a directory, the links within the files will break, and you won't be able to display the pages properly.

TIP   *Before you start, create a folder to contain all your Save As HTML files together. That way, you can move them as one compact group without worrying about breaking links.*

Filename	Function
*name*_ie_body.htm, *name*_ns_body.htm	The body documents for the options bar at the bottom of the page formatted for both Internet Explorer (ie) and Netscape (ns).
*name*_ie_frame.htm, *name*_ns_frame.htm	The frame formatting information formatted for both Internet Explorer (ie) and Netscape (ns).
name#_raster.htm	The image map information. One is generated for each page, and Visio 2000 replaces # with a page number.
name#_raster.***	This is the actual image. Instead of ***, you'll see the appropriate extension for the image format; instead of #, you'll see a page number corresponding to the *name*#_raster.htm page.
*name*_util.js	The JavaScript that runs the HTML pages.
name#_vml.vml	If you choose to use VML, this file is included. It is the VML formatting file for the image.

TABLE 7-2   List of Generated HTML Pages

Saving as an Image

There are times when you don't want Visio 2000 to translate your files into image maps, or when you don't want Visio 2000's Save As HTML feature to create HTML pages for you. If you simply want a Web-ready version of your Visio 2000 diagram, you need to save the diagram as a standard Web image.

 All links in your diagram are lost when you translate them as images.

Saving a Visio 2000 diagram as an image follows the same basic pattern. First, you create the diagram, and then you select the part you wish to export as an image. If you wish to export the entire page, click on the page where there are no shapes to make sure no individual shape is selected.

Once you have the correct part of the diagram selected, choose Save As from the File menu. A Save As dialog box appears. Choose either GIF or JPG from the "Save as type" drop-down list and click OK. One of the dialog boxes shown in Figures 7-6 and 7-7 appears. The type of dialog box depends on the type of image you select.

For a GIF image, you can decide how your image is translated, including setting the image's resolution and size. For a JPEG image, you also need to decide how

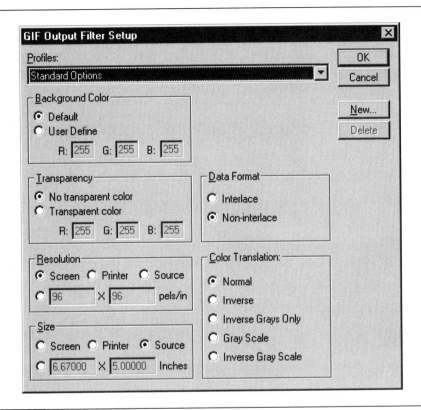

FIGURE 7-6   GIF Output Filter Setup

your image is translated. You can set options including color format and image quality. For both GIF and JPEG images, Visio 2000 has a standard set of protocols you can use to export your images. You only need to change the options manually if you have specific needs or if the standard translations don't work well on your system.

When you've finished with the filter settings, click OK. Visio 2000 displays a progress bar to let you know it's translating the files. The progress bar vanishes after your files have been translated.

You can insert your images into HTML documents by using the tags set aside for images. For more information about using images in HTML documents, see the HTML resources listed in Appendix C.

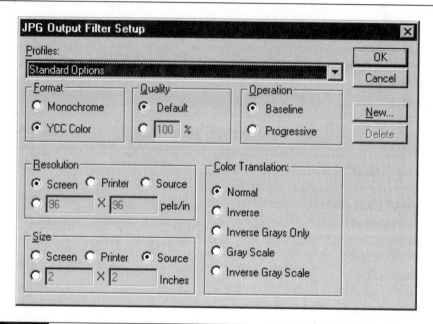

FIGURE 7-7 JPG Output Filter Setup

Summary

In this chapter, you learned how to work with Visio 2000 to create HTML files and Web-ready images of your diagrams.

In the next chapter, you'll learn how to use project-scheduling templates to create time lines and calendars. You'll also learn how to work with the Office Layout template, using it to create diagrams of your office space and to generate inventory and ownership reports.

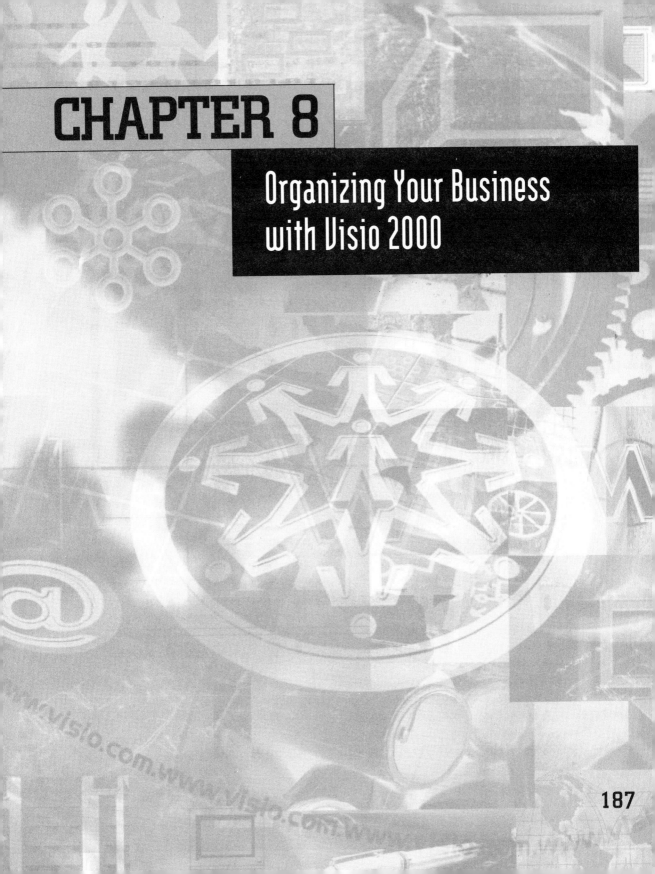

CHAPTER 8

Organizing Your Business with Visio 2000

In the last chapter, you learned about HTML and how to create HTML files with Visio. You also learned how to set hyperlinks between Visio 2000 diagrams and how to hyperlink to documents outside Visio 2000.

In this chapter, you'll learn how to use the project scheduling templates in Visio 2000, as well as how to work with these templates to manage your business. You'll also learn how to work with the Office Layout template, using it to create office diagrams and to generate inventory and ownership reports.

Scheduling with Visio 2000

Schedules are an integral part of any business. Visio 2000 has made scheduling easy with four different ways to create and display schedules using Visio 2000 templates. All four of the Visio 2000 scheduling solutions are stored in the Project Scheduling folder. They are:

- Calendar template
- Timeline template
- PERT template
- Gantt template

Using the Calendar Template

Of the project scheduling solutions, the Calendar template is the easiest to use. It creates complete one-month and one-year calendars on which you can note important dates and project information. The calendars produced by this template are meant to look like most standard commercial calendars. Each day of the week has its own box. Figure 8-1 shows an example of a monthly calendar created by the Calendar template.

To create a calendar with the Calendar template, first open the Calendar template by choosing that template when you open a new Visio 2000 document. The Calendar template appears with the Calendar Shapes stencil open and the drawing page set to landscape, as shown in Figure 8-2.

There are three kinds of calendar shapes on the Calendar Shapes stencil. The Large Month shape is the most commonly used one. However, the Yearly shape and the Small Month shape are also very useful. The following sections discuss each type of calendar shape in more detail.

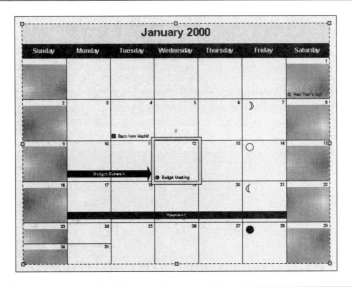

FIGURE 8-1   A monthly calendar created with Visio 2000

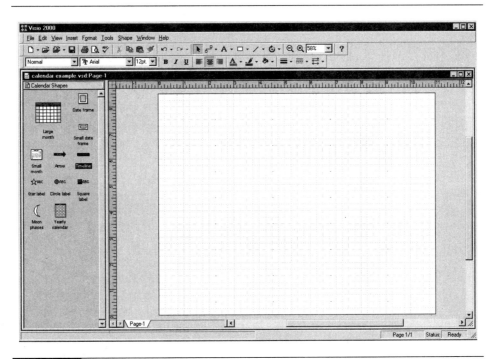

FIGURE 8-2   The Calendar template

All the calendar shapes on the stencil can be resized proportionally, so you can make them as large or as small as you like.

Using the Large Month Shape

To create a single, large monthly calendar, drag the Large Month shape to the drawing page. A Custom Properties dialog box automatically appears, as shown here:

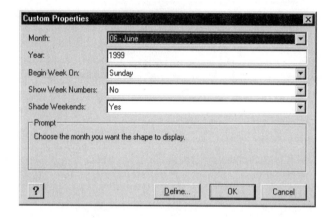

Month   Lists all the months in the year, with the current month set as the default. To set the month for your calendar, select it from the list.

Year   Lists the current year. If you need to create a calendar for another year, fill in the year (using all four digits).

Begin Week On   Allows you to choose to start your week on either Monday or Sunday. (Sunday is the default.) If you need your week to start on a different day, click the Define button and change the options.

Show Week Numbers   Toggles week numbering on and off. The default is No.

Shade Weekends   Controls whether the boxes for the weekend days (Saturday and Sunday) are shaded. The default is Yes.

If the Custom Properties dialog box contains all the options you need, set those options and then click OK.

Occasionally, you will find that the options in the Custom Properties dialog box are not exactly what you need. To modify the fields in the Custom Properties dialog box, click the Define button. When you click Define, you'll see the Define Custom Properties dialog box, shown here:

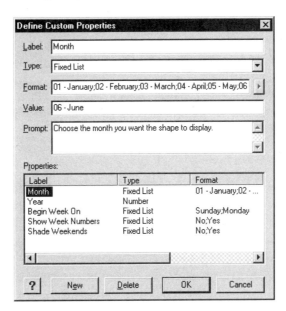

The custom properties fields are listed at the bottom. To modify a custom property field, select that field in the Properties area of the Define Custom Properties dialog box. Then update the field's label, type, format, value, or prompt, as needed. After you've made the necessary changes, click OK. For more information about defining custom properties, see Chapter 11, "Using Advanced Visio 2000 Features."

For all calendar shapes, the drawing page has a landscape orientation by default. Check the printer settings to make sure your printer is ready to print pages with landscape orientation.

Modifying a Monthly Calendar

After you drag the Large Month shape to the drawing page, you may want to make some modifications to the calendar.

To add text to the calendar's squares, click on a square where you'd like to add text and start typing. Visio 2000 zooms the view to 100 percent as you enter the text. When you're finished, click the Pointer tool.

To add arrows or timelines, drag them from the stencil and add them to the calendar. Using the green control handles, resize the shapes until they cover the number of days you need. Be sure to snap them in place.

To add labels, drag them from the stencil, and then type the text to create the label.

To add moon phases, drag the Moon Phases shape from the stencil and place it on the correct date. Then right-click on the moon phase and select the correct phase from the menu. Visio 2000 includes four phases for the calendar moon: First Quarter, Full, Last Quarter, and New Moon.

To include either the small or normal data frames, drag them from the stencil and place them around the date or label. They will snap to the date box or label shape.

Using the Small Month and the Yearly Calendar Shapes

The Small Month and the Yearly Calendar shapes can be used individually on a page or they can be grouped together to show more than one month or year per page. For example, two Yearly Calendar shapes can be grouped so that two years appear on one landscape legal-sized page. Five Small Month calendar shapes fit side-to-side on the drawing page when the printer page orientation is set to portrait.

TIP	*None of the labels or other shapes on the Calendar Shapes stencil fit on the smaller calendar shapes. If you need to use labels, frames, and so forth, you can resize them, or you can simply use the Large Month calendar shape and size it down when you're done.*

When you drag the Small Month shape or the Yearly Calendar shape from the stencil to the drawing page, you'll see a dialog box asking for the dates to use. This dialog box looks much like the Custom Properties dialog box shown earlier; however, for these shapes, the dialog box has fewer fields. For the Small Month calendar, it asks for the month. For the Yearly Calendar shape, it asks for the year and the first day of the week.

Timelines

Timelines are a good way to visually convey information about scheduling. They can provide a lot of information in a way that is both interesting to look at and easy to grasp. Figure 8-3 shows an example of a timeline diagram.

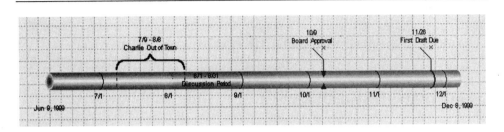

FIGURE 8-3   A timeline diagram

To create a timeline, open the Timeline template as you would any other of the Visio 2000 templates, by selecting that template when you open a new Visio 2000 document. The Timeline template is located in the Project Scheduling Solutions folder. When you open the template, the main Visio 2000 window appears with three stencils open, as shown in Figure 8-4. The three stencils are the Backgrounds

8

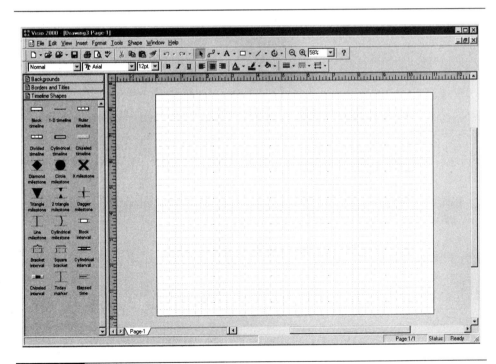

FIGURE 8-4   The Timeline template

stencil, the Borders and Titles stencil, and the Timeline Shapes stencil. Both the Background and Border and Titles stencil are standard business stencils. The Timeline stencil holds all the shapes needed to make timelines.

Using Timeline Backbones

There are six timeline shapes to use as the backbone of your timeline. The first part of making a timeline is deciding which of these shapes you'll use, since all the markers you later drag to the timeline depend on the type of backbone you choose. The six backbones are:

Block timeline   A simple rectangle with start and end dates. All added dates display outside the rectangle.

1-D timeline   A line with start and end dates, including several date markers or "ticks" in the middle of the timeline.

Ruler timeline   A rectangle with several date markers or "ticks" in the center, and all dates listed inside the rectangle.

Divided timeline   A rectangle with several separate sections created by lines that go from one side to the other. This is a good timeline backbone for projects with very distinct parts.

Cylindrical timeline   A three-dimensional cylinder with all dates placed either above or below the line. This is a very useful shape for multimedia.

Chiseled timeline   A three-dimensional rectangle that has divided sections. This backbone is best used on a colored background so you can see the chiseled effect.

TIP	*You may want to use different timeline backbones for your printed and projected versions.*

When you've decided which of the timeline backbones to use, drag it to the drawing page. The Configure Timeline dialog box opens, as shown here:

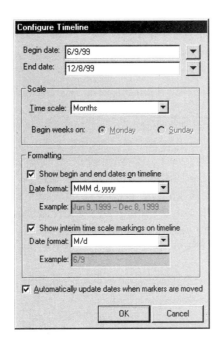

Begin date   Specifies the start date for the timeline backbone. This date displays by default on the far left below the backbone. The default is the current date.

End date   Specifies the end date for the timeline backbone. This date displays by default on the far right below the backbone. The default is six months from the current date.

Scale   Sets the timescale as well as the date a week begins on (if week is selected). Months is the default.

Formatting – Show begin and end dates on timeline   Specifies how the begin and end dates are displayed and allows you to select if they are shown on the timeline at all.

Formatting – Show interim time scale markings on timeline   Specifies the date format for all the dates listed on the timeline, as well as whether any date scale markings are shown on the timeline backbone.

Automatically update dates when markers are moved   Specifies if and when Visio 2000 automatically updates the dates you set on the timeline as you move the marker shapes. There's very little reason to uncheck this box.

Adding Milestones and Intervals

When you've configured and set the timeline backbone, you're ready to place milestones and intervals.

Milestones and intervals are the information carriers of your timeline. All timelines should have enough milestone and interval information to make them worth the reader's time, but not so much as to overwhelm them with information. If you find you're crowding the page with too much information, use the arrow at the end of the timeline backbone to separate your timeline into more than one page.

To add milestones to the timeline, select the milestone that matches your timeline backbone. Eight different milestones come with the Timeline Shapes stencil, each different in shape, meaning, and associated timeline backbone. Once you've selected the correct milestone, drag the milestone to the timeline backbone. The Configure Milestone dialog box appears, as shown here:

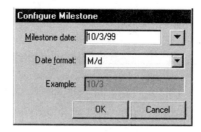

This dialog box sets the date for the milestone as well as the display format for the date. The down arrow to the right of the date displays a small calendar from which you can choose a date for the milestone. Once you're satisfied with the date information, click OK.

 To access the Configure Milestone dialog box again, right-click on the milestone and choose Configure Milestone.

To add an interval, pick one of the five interval shapes, making sure it coordinates with the timeline backbone you chose, then move the interval to the timeline backbone on the page. The Configure Interval dialog box appears, much like the Configure Milestone dialog box. The dialog box specifies beginning and ending dates, set by default when you dropped the interval to the backbone. The dialog box also displays the default format for displaying the date. You can also access the Configure Interval dialog box by right-clicking on the interval and selecting Configure Interval.

To change, expand, or move an interval, select the interval with the Pointer tool and move it along the timeline backbone or use the green control handles to change the shape of the interval. As long as the "Automatically update dates when markers are moved" box is checked on the Configure Timeline dialog box, Visio 2000 revises the dates to reflect the new length and location of the interval.

To add text to intervals or milestones, click on the shape and type in the new text.

> **NOTE** *If you change the width or length of the timeline backbone, the milestone and interval shapes may not fit and will need to be resized.*

When you're pleased with the look of your timeline, save it to the format you need to display. Make sure, if you are printing the timeline, that it fits on your drawing page and looks good with the page orientation.

PERT Diagrams

8

PERT diagrams were developed by the U.S. Department of Defense to help manage large and complex military projects. PERT stands for "Program Evaluation and Review Technique." This graphical way of organizing and managing projects became very popular with research and educational organizations and is now in use wherever large projects are managed.

PERT diagrams are used to create a high-level project management chart—usually at the start of the project at the brainstorming stage—to help everyone involved understand the project's timetable and dependencies. The planning and brainstorming advantages afforded by PERT diagrams makes them invaluable when managing large projects.

Each rectangular shape in a PERT diagram represents a task, and each arrow represents a dependency. The dates are shown in sets of beginning and end dates. The use of dependency arrows in PERT diagrams is especially handy for showing which steps must precede others. Figure 8-5 shows an example PERT diagram.

Visio 2000 makes it easy to create these powerful charts by including PERT shapes, which can be dragged onto the drawing page. PERT charts are usually created during meetings where brainstorming about a new project is taking place. You can use Visio 2000 to convert meeting notes into a form that can be used in documentation and presentations.

To create a PERT chart with Visio 2000, first you need to open the PERT Chart template by choosing that template when you open a new document. The PERT Chart template opens three stencils: PERT Chart Shapes, Borders and Titles, and Backgrounds. The PERT Chart Shapes stencil has nine shapes, including two types

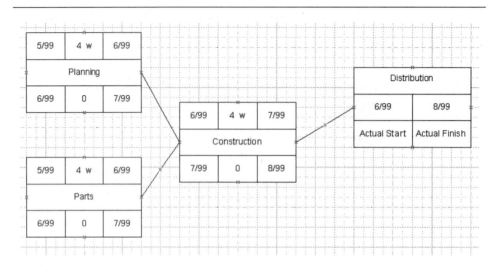

FIGURE 8-5   A PERT diagram

of PERT task boxes. To start your diagram, drag one of the PERT task box shapes to the drawing page. Usually, PERT diagrams start with either a PERT 1 or PERT 2 shape, as shown in Figure 8-6.

PERT 1 shapes are task boxes that include not only the name of the task, but its duration, projected start and end dates, possible late start and end dates, and the difference between the projected and late dates. PERT 2 shapes are task boxes that only track start and end dates, both projected and actual. For most projects, the information in the Task Name box is the first to be filled in. Then duration is filled in. The start and end dates are added after the place the task holds in the project is

Early Start	Duration	Early Finish
Task Name		
Late Start	Slack	Late Finish

PERT 1 shape

Task Name	
Scheduled Start	Scheduled Finish
Actual Start	Actual Finish

PERT 2 shape

FIGURE 8-6   PERT 1 and PERT 2 shapes

free. For PERT 2 shapes the bottom row of boxes, those pertaining to the actual start and end dates, is left blank until the project is actually underway.

Once you've added all the PERT 1 and 2 shapes you need for your diagram, you're ready to start adding connections between the tasks. Connections between tasks in PERT diagrams indicate a dependency. The dependency can be due to supply issues, human resource issues, or even simply timing issues. It's best to make sure you have some understanding of the likely dependencies before you begin to connect your PERT 1 and PERT 2 shapes.

After all your connections have been made, you may wish to add callouts to your shapes to explain the dependencies or to give more information about the tasks. You may also find you need one of the "summarization structures." Summarization structures give information about a shape. They have a special gluing function: by pulling the extra control handle in the middle of the Summarization Structures shape to the control point of any other shape, Visio 2000 automatically connects the two shapes with a dynamic connector.

After all the shapes and connections have been completed, drag the Legend shape to the drawing page and fill in the information with the Text tool. When you've labeled the diagram with a Legend shape, you've completed your PERT diagram. Remember to save your diagram before you exit Visio 2000.

Gantt Diagrams and Microsoft Project

You may recognize Gantt charts if you've used project management software such as Microsoft Project. Gantt charts illustrate the time each part of a project takes and where in the project flow each step happens, giving everyone in a project a visual cue to how the flow from step to step takes place. Powerful visual reminders are an important part of helping a project succeed, making these charts among the most popular charts in business. Figure 8-7 shows an example of a Gantt chart.

ID	Task Name	Start	End	Duration	Jul 1999
1	Planning	7/7/99	7/12/99	3d 4h	
2	**Completion**	**7/8/99**	**7/19/99**	**7d 4h**	
3	Outlining	7/8/99	7/12/99	3d	
4	Construction	7/9/99	7/14/99	3d 4h	
5	Documenting	7/14/99	7/19/99	3d 4h	

FIGURE 8-7   A Gantt chart

Visio 2000 includes a template to help you quickly and easily create Gantt charts on your own. Visio 2000 also includes a set of filters allowing you to import and export data for Gantt charts to and from Microsoft Project.

Making Gantt Chart Diagrams

Typically, the first step in creating Gantt charts is to create a PERT diagram. Often the brainstorming that goes into a PERT diagram is too valuable to lose, so the tasks and dependencies that make up a PERT diagram are reworked into the more visually powerful Gantt charts. However, even if you haven't created a PERT diagram, brainstorming about the ways your project might proceed is a vital first step before you begin a Gantt chart.

After you've conceptualized your project, open the Gantt Chart template as you would any other—by opening a new document and selecting the Gantt Chart template. After Visio 2000 loads the template, a dialog box asking for information about your Gantt chart pops us, as shown here:

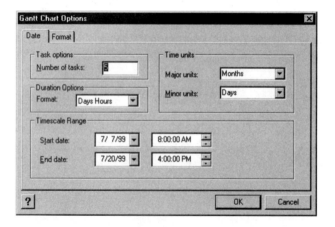

NOTE *The Gantt Chart Options dialog box also opens when you select Options from the Gantt Chart menu.*

Number of Tasks The number or rows in your Gantt chart. This cannot be altered from this dialog box later. However, you can add and remove rows as you need them with other tools.

Duration Options, Format Sets the default timescale for the chart. Task bars display with units set here.

Start and End Dates   Sets the start and end dates for the project. All tasks are set by default to start on the start date.

Time Units   Sets the upper (major) and lower (minor) labels for the column holding the task timeline bars.

TIP   *Don't worry about setting these options perfectly the first time. You can easily change them later.*

The Format tab of this dialog box contains information about the shapes Visio 2000 uses to indicate the start, end, and milestone dates for the project. Typically, you won't need to change the defaults. However, if the project becomes very complicated, you may wish to. The Format tab is also where information about the default titles for the columns can be changed. Again, you need not do that because you're able to manually change these labels after you've finished setting the options.

When you've completed setting the Gantt chart options, click OK. Visio 2000 automatically creates a Gantt chart in the drawing page based on the options. The basic chart Visio 2000 creates with the option information is almost blank, formatted only by the number of tasks you specified and the start and end dates. All project-specific information needs to be set by changing the Gantt chart information.

8

Changing Gantt Charts

Whether you've just created a new chart or you need to alter an existing chart, most of the work with these charts falls under the category of changing Gantt chart information. There are four basic types of information to change on your Gantt charts: task length and labels, text formatting, column labels and formatting, and overall chart options.

TASKS   The rows of your Gantt chart represent the individual parts of your project. To add a task, select the task preceding the new task and choose Insert Task. To remove a task, select it and then choose Delete Task. There can be more than one level of tasks in Visio 2000 Gantt charts, allowing for tasks to have subtasks to help you refine your planning. To create a subtask, first make sure it's directly under the task that will be its superior, then select the subtask and choose Demote Task. To remove a task's place as a subtask but keep it as part of the chart, select it and choose Promote Task.

COLUMNS   The columns of your Gantt chart hold individual information about each task in your chart. Adding columns means adding information about each task. To add a column, select the preceding column and choose Insert Column. The Insert Column dialog box appears, asking for the column title. Choose a name from the drop-down list and click OK. To label a column, select the rectangle containing the title text with the Text tool and edit the text. To delete a column, select it and choose Delete Column.

LINKS   Tasks can also be linked together to show a dependency in a project. To link tasks, select both tasks, and then choose Link Task. To remove a dependency relationship, select either task and choose Unlink Task.

CHART SETTINGS   These options are important not only to the look of your chart but to the calculations needed to plan your project. Some of the chart settings are decided as you open the Gantt chart; others can only be changed once you start your Gantt chart. Settings for your entire chart are set in either the Gantt Chart Options dialog box, or the Configure Working Times dialog box. The Configure Working Times dialog box allows you to set the days and times your team is likely to work, assisting Visio 2000 in calculating the number of days a project or task is likely to take.

| TIP | *With all this information to sort out, planning your Gantt chart before you start is very important.* |

With all these different types of information to change, Visio 2000 provides four ways to modify the content and appearance of a Gantt chart.

RIGHT-CLICK   Most information on your Gantt chart can be reached by right-clicking on the relevant area and choosing a selection from the menu. This is the quickest and easiest way to access the basic information about your Gantt chart.

GANTT CHART MENU   The Gantt Chart template includes an addition to your standard menu bar: The Gantt Chart menu. Inside this menu you can access the configuration for the tasks and columns in your chart, as well as the Gantt Chart Options menu and all of the other dialog boxes needed to change your Gantt chart.

GANTT CHART SHAPES STENCIL   The Gantt Chart Shapes stencil opens automatically with the Gantt Chart template. It allows you to drag and drop columns, rows, labels, links, titles, and other chart tools into your Gantt chart, or have them float on the page outside your chart.

GANTT CHART TOOLBAR   The Gantt Chart template comes with its own toolbar allowing you access to several content-altering processes with the click of a button. Table 8-1 describes the function of each button in the Gantt toolbar.

Button	Name	Function
	Link Tasks	Creates a new link between tasks
	Unlink Tasks	Breaks an already-established link between tasks
	Promote Task	Turns a subtask into a full task
	Demote Task	Turns a full task into a subtask
	Add Row	Inserts a blank row without an attached task
	Delete Row	Removes a row without an assigned task
	Go to Start	Scrolls the task timelines to the start date for the project
	Go to Previous	Takes you to the previous linked task
	Go to Next	Takes you to the next linked task
	Go to End	Scrolls the task timelines to the end date for the project
	Find Task	Displays a dialog box that allows you to locate a task based on text you input

TABLE 8-1   Gantt Chart Toolbar Buttons

Using Microsoft Project and Visio 2000

After you've finished creating your Gantt chart, you may wish to export the information into a Microsoft Project file. Or, instead of creating a Gantt chart from scratch, you may want to create the chart from a Microsoft Project file where the project has already been planned.

Visio 2000 makes it easy to exchange data between Gantt chart diagrams and Microsoft Project. See Chapter 6, "Using Visio 2000 with Microsoft Office," for more information.

> **TIP** *Visio 2000 provides import and export commands so you can exchange data with Microsoft Project and other project management tools that use the MPX file format. You can also enter project information into an Excel workbook or text file, as explained in Chapter 6.*

Designing an Office with Visio 2000

Visio 2000 has a powerful tool for businesses to plan their facilities: the Office Layout template. All businesses go through stages where they need to rearrange facilities, either to move to another building or simply expand. The Office Layout template enables you to create floor plans effortlessly, so the moving or expansion process goes smoothly. The template includes shapes for walls, furniture, computers, even electrical outlets, allowing you to generate a very detailed representation of the office space.

Open the Office Layout template like any template, as a new document. However, before you start your office layout diagram, make sure you:

- Measure the room you want to diagram.

- Measure the objects you want in the office you're planning, and make a complete list.

- Measure the windows, doors, and any other structural members in the room. Remember to note which direction the doors open.

- Make sure you know who might occupy the space and which items of furniture belong to that employee.

Creating an Office Diagram

A Visio 2000 office diagram includes several different parts, from the page size and scale to placing the walls to including the furniture. These steps need to be done in a systematic way, otherwise you may need to completely redo your diagram to take into account a new page size or other fundamental change.

Setting the Scale and Page Size

Before you add any shapes to the page, make sure your drawing is set up correctly. By default, the Office Layout template opens with a drawing scale of 1/4 inch = 1 foot, and a page size of 8.5 × 11 inches with the page orientated to landscape. This allows you to draw a room of up to 30 × 45 feet.

If you need to change any of the drawing settings, you can do so on the Drawing Scale tab in the Page Settings dialog box by choosing File | Page Settings.

When you're determining a drawing scale for an office layout, remember:

- In Visio 2000, drawing units are sizes in the real world. Page units are sizes on the printed page. The ratio of page units to drawing units is the drawing scale.

- The smaller the drawing scale, the larger the area you can represent. A scale such as 1/8 inch = 1 foot allows you to draw an entire floor on one page. A scale such as 1 inch = 1 foot allows you to focus on one cubicle.

- When you drop shapes onto a scaled drawing page, they adjust to the scale you've set. Shapes dynamically resize themselves as you change the drawing scale.

Creating the Walls

When you're satisfied with the size of your drawing page and the size of the room you can create, you're ready to place the walls. There are three ways to place walls on your Visio 2000 drawing page: dropping a whole room, placing each wall individually, and converting a line drawing to walls.

DROPPING ROOMS   Dropping whole rooms allows you to quickly create the basic outline of your space and Visio 2000 has included three room shapes to make it easier. The "T" room, the "L" room, and the square room shapes are all basic outlines for most room shapes and are meant to be dropped onto your drawing page and resized to match the actual dimensions of your room. To use the complete rooms, drag them to the blank drawing page and then resize them to the dimensions of your actual room.

PLACING INDIVIDUAL WALLS   For some room shapes, the only option is to place the walls individually. This is usually the case when one wall in a room is at an angle or has a curved shape, or when the room is of a very unique shape. Individual wall shapes allow you to create a room to the exact specifications of your space.

To create a room with individual walls:

1. Drag guides from the horizontal and vertical rulers to indicate the dimensions of the room on the drawing page. This gives the walls something to glue to.

2. Force the zero point of the drawing to be at the corner of your room by holding down the CTRL key and dragging the zero point from the intersection of the two rulers to one of the corners of the room. Moving the zero point allows you to have a scale that starts at the corner of your room, helping you place other shapes by having a more useful ruler setting.

3. Place a wall shape on one side so the wall thickness is outside the room's perimeter. If necessary, choose an option from the Shape menu to flip or rotate the shape.

4. Repeat Step 3 until you have as many walls as you need for the room. Make sure to snap and glue the walls together. The selection handles turn red when the shapes are glued.

CONVERT SPACE SHAPES INTO WALLS   The Convert Shape function allows you to drag space shapes onto the drawing page, merge them together, and then have Visio 2000 place the walls based on the shape. Here's how:

1. Drag space shapes onto drawing page.

2. Overlap the space shapes to approximate the floor plan shape you want, then select all the space shapes.

3. Right-click the selected shapes, and then choose Union from the shortcut menu.

4. Right-click one of the selected shapes, and then choose Convert to Walls from the shortcut menu.

5. Under Settings, specify the actions you want—Add Dimensions and/or Add Guides.

6. Under Original Geometry, choose an option—Delete, Retain, or Convert to Space Shape.

7. Click OK.

On the drawing page, Visio 2000 creates walls to fit your shapes.

Placing Structural Details

After you've created the walls of your drawing, you're ready to start placing the doors, windows, switches, and electrical outlets.

First, align the window and door shapes on top of the walls. If necessary, flip or rotate window shapes so their endpoints snap to the guides on the inside of the walls and flip or rotate Door shapes so the doors open in the correct direction. Both Window and Door shapes have control handles to help you change their angles and sizes to fit your needs.

Then attach the outlets and switches to the wall, being careful to make sure to glue the wall in place. You may want to group the wall with the outlets once you've have placed them to make sure they aren't accidentally moved out of place.

Placing Furniture

After you've placed the walls and all the pieces that go on them, you're ready to start placing furniture in the room.

All the furniture shapes on the Office Layout Shapes stencil are set to be the same physical size regardless of the drawing scale; the dimensions are based on standard office furniture measurements. The shapes dynamically resize when you use the control handles. However, it's best to resize them only if you're sure your office furniture isn't a standard size.

The shapes on the Office Layout Shapes stencil include just about everything you might need in an office floor-plan: chairs, tables, computers, files, even a sofa has been included. Most of these shapes behave like standard Visio 2000 shapes. However, a few of them have some special properties allowing you to make the most of them when you use them in your office layout. Table 8-2 describes the most common office layout shapes.

Shape	Name	Special Function
	Chair	Extra control handles allow you to rotate the chair.
	Conference table	The chairs can be moved in the group by clicking on them. They behave like standard chairs.
	File	The extra control handle allows you to open the file drawers.
	Bookcase	These have openings on one side. Make sure to place them in the correct direction in relation to the wall.
	Dimension Line	Glues to any shape and dynamically resizes to give you a measurement based on the scale set for the drawing.

TABLE 8-2   Special Functions of Office Layout Shapes

Creating Office Layout Reports

The beauty of creating your office layout diagrams with Visio 2000 is that not only do you have a neatly drawn page to use as a layout chart, but you can also create reports based on the furniture and floor space. Visio 2000 has included the Property Reporting Wizard, a wizard that allows you to create reports based on any part of your Visio 2000 diagram. Office layout diagrams can create anything from an inventory list to a list of each employee's furniture needs. The reports are generated from two types of information: information resident on the master shape, and information you enter for the shape.

Information resident in the master shape is data Visio 2000 keeps with the master shape in the ShapeSheet, including the name of the shape and the dimensions of the shape. Master shape information is useful if, for example, you'd like to know how many tables you have in your office. The Property Reporting Wizard can help you retrieve this information.

Information you enter for the shape is data you manually include on each shape in the Custom Properties fields. Custom property information is useful if, for example, you'd like to know how many pieces of furniture belong to one person, or if you'd like to generate a list of every piece of furniture on a diagram by its inventory number. When you right-click on an office layout shape and ask for properties, Visio 2000 displays a dialog box like the one shown here:

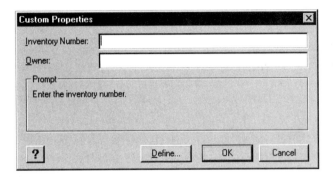

This is the default Custom Properties dialog box for office layout shapes. Inventory Number and Owner are set as default fields for you to enter. If you need to include more than these two fields, you can define your own custom property fields by clicking on the Define button and completing the dialog box. If you need more information about creating new custom property fields, see Chapter 11, "Using Advanced Visio 2000 Features."

 Custom property information can only be included if you enter it. Including custom information about parts of your office layout diagram makes it much more useful.

Generating Inventory Lists with Property Reporting Wizard

The Property Reporting Wizard can export an inventory report based on both types of shape properties. You choose to export data based on all pages in the document, to report on all shapes or selected shapes, to create a report in Excel, Notepad, or Access format, or to include the report as a shape on your drawing page.

 Visio 2000 won't run the Property Reporting Wizard if there are no shapes on the page.

To launch the Property Reporting Wizard, select Property Report from the Tools menu. The opening screen of the Property Repairing Wizard displays, informing you that it helps you create reports based on shapes as well as complete inventories. Click Next to start creating the report. The second screen of the Property Reporting Wizard displays, as shown in Figure 8-8.

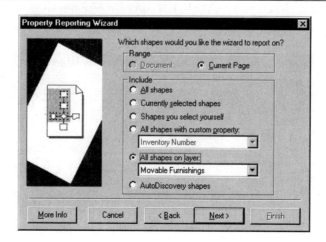

Second screen of the Property Reporting Wizard

This screen gives you several radio buttons to select the type of information you'd like to create your report from. The options are as follows:

All Shapes   Creates a report including every shape on the page.

Currently Selected Shapes   Creates a report based only on the shapes currently selected on the drawing page.

Shapes You Select Yourself   Allows you to select the shapes to create the report. This option also creates a layer for these shapes, making it easier to run the same report again later.

All Shapes with Custom Property   Creates a report based on only the shapes that have custom property information entered. You select the type of information that must be present for the shape to be included in the report.

All Shapes on Layer   Creates a report based on layers set in the Define Layers dialog box.

AutoDiscovery Shapes   Creates a report using only AutoDiscovery shapes.

TIP   *Reports using the "All Shapes on a Layer" option are usually the most useful, since Visio 2000 automatically assigns different types of shapes (i.e., furniture, walls, etc.) to their own layers.*

After you've selected the type of shapes to use to create your report, click Next. The third screen of the Property Reporting Wizard opens, as shown in Figure 8-9. This screen allows you to select the information that is included about the shapes in your report. The following is a list of the information available when the "All Shapes on Layer" option is selected and the layer is set as Movable Furnishings.

NOTE *The wizard automatically includes column headings for Page Name, Shape Name, and Shape Text in the spreadsheet for a numeric report, whether or not you choose those properties on this screen. The information in these columns is necessary for identifying the shapes.*

The options in the third screen of the Property Reporting Wizard are:

Height   Lists the height of the shape as set by the size on the screen and the drawing scale settings.

Master   Lists the actual name Visio 2000 uses to track the name on the page. For example, chair.18 would be the 18th shape taken from the Visio 2000 stencil. There's only one of each master on the page at a time.

Name   Shows the name of the shape type. For example, all chairs on your drawing page have the same name.

NameID   Is a unique identifier for each shape on the drawing page. Similar to Master.

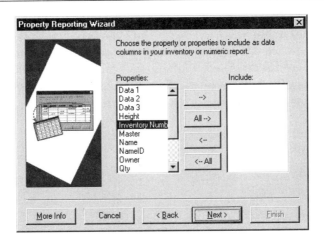

FIGURE 8-9   Third screen of the Property Reporting Wizard

Owner   Contains the custom information you entered about who owns the piece of furniture. If you don't enter this custom information, the column in the report will be blank.

Qty   Lists the quantity of duplicate items. For example, the number of chairs on the drawing page.

Text   Shows any text that has been added to each shape.

Type   Lists the shape type for each shape in the report.

Width   Shows the width of the shape, as set by the size on the screen and the drawing scale settings.

X and Y   Shows the exact position of the shape in the coordinate system of the drawing page.

 For an inventory of furniture and its owners, use Name and Owner. For an inventory list of all the shapes on the page, use Name and Qty.

When you're satisfied with the information you've selected to report for each shape, click Next. The fourth screen of the Property Reporting Wizard displays, asking you to define which type of report you want. Make sure to select Basic Inventory at the bottom of the window and to check the Total Identical Items box, then click Next. Visio 2000 shows a progress bar indicating that it is starting to build the database, then the fifth screen of the Property Reporting Wizard displays, as shown in Figure 8-10.

The fifth screen shows the data in a spreadsheet format. This is how your data looks if you export it into Microsoft Excel. You can save your data from the window by clicking the disk icon in the upper-left corner of the window. Once you're satisfied with the rows and columns, click Next. The sixth screen of the Property Reporting Wizard appears, as shown in Figure 8-11.

NOTE *If you have more than eleven rows, before you go to the next screen Visio 2000 displays a message telling you it can include only the first eleven rows in your report.*

The sixth screen asks for the title of your report and on which page you'd like Visio 2000 to include the report. Screen six also allows you to choose to display the column headings, or column titles, with the report. Fill in the title and select a page from the drop-down list, then click Next. The seventh screen of the Property Reporting Wizard appears as shown in Figure 8-12.

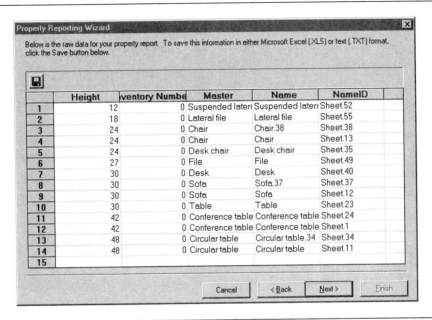

FIGURE 8-10   Fifth screen of the Property Reporting Wizard

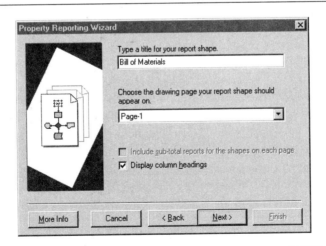

FIGURE 8-11   Sixth screen of the Property Reporting Wizard

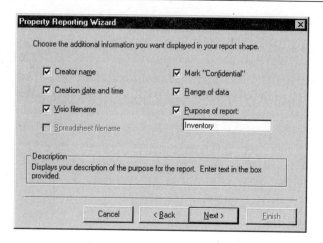

FIGURE 8-12   Seventh screen of the Property Reporting Wizard

The seventh screen lists all the extra information you can include with your report. Select items from the list by checking them. When you're satisfied with the list, click Next. The Eighth screen of the Property Reporting Wizard appears, telling you Visio 2000 is ready to complete the report. If you're satisfied with all the information you've entered, click Finish to create the report.

Visio 2000 shows a progress bar as it creates the report shape to drop onto your drawing page. Once it has built the report, it appears on the lower half of your drawing page. You can move and resize the report as you would any shape on the drawing page. However, if you delete the report, you'll need to go back through the wizard again to recreate it.

Summary

In this chapter, you learned about the Project Scheduling templates in Visio 2000, as well as how to work with the Office Layout template.

In the next chapter, you'll learn how to use Visio 2000 to communicate graphically in meetings or on paper. You'll learn how to create charts, forms, and graphs, as well as how to add maps and geographic shapes to your diagrams. You'll also learn how to create a slide show in Visio 2000 and how to add comments to shapes.

CHAPTER 9

Getting Your Point Across Graphically

In the last chapter, you learned how Visio 2000 can help you organize your business using the office layout and project scheduling templates.

In this chapter, you'll learn how to use Visio 2000 to convey information graphically in presentations and on paper. You'll learn how to create charts, forms, and graphs, as well as how to add maps and geographic shapes to your diagrams. You'll also learn how to create a slide show in Visio 2000, how to use color schemes, and how to add comments to shapes.

Creating Charts and Forms

When you give a presentation, it's often useful to present information graphically. Charts, forms, and graphs are the most common visual aids. Visio 2000 is first and foremost a program to help you create business diagrams, including graphical ways to display business information.

There are three templates designed specifically for creating charts, forms, and graphs. These templates are collected in the Forms and Charts solutions folder. The templates are:

- Charts and Graphs
- Form Design
- Marketing Charts and Diagrams

Understanding the Charts and Graphs Template

The Charts and Graphs template contains shapes for several types of reports and presentations. The chart tools in this template can be used in many types of reports such as financial reports and market projections—and even in complex documents like annual reports. Figure 9-1 shows the main Visio 2000 window with the Charts and Graphs template open and an example of a chart.

The Charts and Graphs template includes two standard Visio stencils (the Borders and Titles stencil and the Backgrounds stencil) as well as the Charting Shapes stencil. The Charting Shapes stencil has all the shapes you need to create many types of business charts, including 2-D and 3-D bar graphs, pie charts, process charts, and line graphs. Although this section describes how to create 2-D and 3-D bar graphs, the procedure for creating other types of charts is very similar. All charts created with the Charting Shapes stencil follow the same basic pattern.

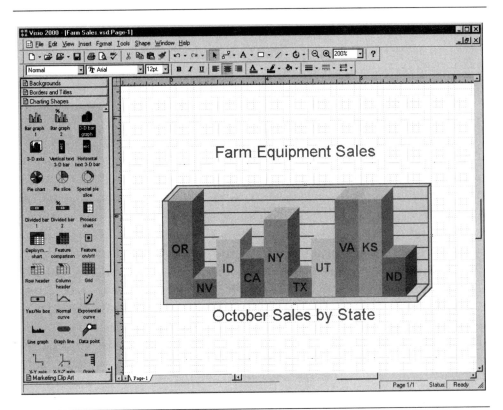

FIGURE 9-1   A chart created with Visio 2000

Creating 2-D Bar Graphs

2-D bar graphs are the simplest type of business chart. Visio 2000 has two different kinds of 2-D bar graph shapes. Bar Graph 1 formats the bars based on numerical values; Bar Graph 2 formats the bars based on percentage values.

To create a 2-D bar graph:

1. Open the Charts and Graphs template.

2. Drag either the Bar Graph 1 or Bar Graph 2 shape from the Charting Shapes stencil. The Custom Properties dialog box appears, as shown in Figure 9-2.

3. In the Custom Properties dialog box, select the number of bars you would like in your graph, and then click OK.

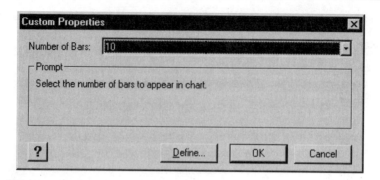

FIGURE 9-2   Custom Properties dialog box for a 2-D bar graph

TIP   *If you need to add another bar later you can access the Custom Properties dialog box by right-clicking on the bars and choosing Custom Properties, or by selecting the bars and choosing Shape | Action | Set Number of Bars.*

4. Set the size to ten segments (Bar Graph 1) or 100 percent (Bar Graph 2) by resizing the "phantom" bar just to the left of the locked group of bars. The height of the locked group is set at 100 units.

5. Change the text in each bar of the graph. Visio 2000 adjusts the size of the bars based on the text in them.

CAUTION   *Make sure to add the percent sign (%) after the number for Bar Graph 2; otherwise, the bars will be formatted incorrectly.*

6. Change the colors of each bar by selecting it and using the Fill button to choose a new color.

7. Add a Graph Scale shape to provide a sense of scale. When you drag the Graph Scale shape to the drawing page, a Custom Properties dialog box appears (similar to the one shown in Figure 9-2), asking you to set the number of divisions for the graph's scale.

8. Finally, add a title to the graph by selecting the entire graph and starting to type, or by using the Text tool.

When you've finished creating the bar graph, remember to save it.

Creating 3-D Bar Graphs

The procedure for creating 3-D bar graphs is slightly more complicated than for 2-D bar graphs, but 3-D bar graphs can provide a more interesting graphic representation—making the extra work worth the effort.

To create a 3-D bar graph:

1. Open the Charts and Graphs template.

2. Drag one of the 3-D Bar Graph shapes from the Charting Shapes stencil. The Custom Properties dialog box appears, as shown in Figure 9-3.

3. In the Custom Properties dialog box, set the number of bars, the color of each bar, and the value of each bar.

NOTE   *The Range field sets the total height of the graph. This should be what you expect the largest number in the graph to be. Visio 2000 resizes all the bars in the graph based on the range.*

9

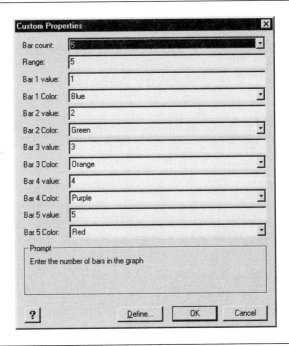

FIGURE 9-3   Custom Properties Window for 3-D bar graph

4. When you've set the custom properties for each bar, click OK. If you need to change the value or other settings for a bar, you need to do so in the Custom Properties dialog box. 3-D bars don't dynamically resize based on their text the way 2-D bars do.

5. Choose Shape | Action to hide or reveal the numbers and lines for the bars. You can also use menu commands to change the number of bars, the value of bars, and the color of bars.

6. Add a 3-D axis shape to provide a sense of scale. When you drag a 3-D axis shape to the drawing page it may appear on top of the bar graph. If so, select the axis shape and then choose Shape | Send to Back.

7. Add titles for the axes of your graph by selecting the graph or the axis shape and starting to type, or by selecting the shape and then choosing the Text tool.

When you've finished creating the 3-D bar graph, remember to save it.

Getting to Know the Form Design Template

Sometimes, it's useful to provide a handout with your presentation, such as a form for the audience to fill out or use later. Visio 2000 includes the Form Design template for just this purpose. The template can be used to create forms of all kinds, including order forms, invoices, fax coversheets, certificates, and even rosters—as well as several dozen other types of forms. Figure 9-4 shows the main Visio 2000 window with the Form Design template open and an example of a fax coversheet created using the template.

To make creating forms quick and simple, Visio 2000 includes many types of ready-made form shapes on the Form Shapes stencil, which opens with the Form Design template.

To create a form, the first step is to design the form on a piece of paper. There are so many form shapes on the stencil that it's easy to go a little overboard if you don't have a clear idea of how your form should look before you start.

After you've created a basic concept for the form, drag the appropriate shape from the stencil onto the drawing page. Visio 2000 comes with Fax Cover and Business Card shapes to create these common forms, but there are many other

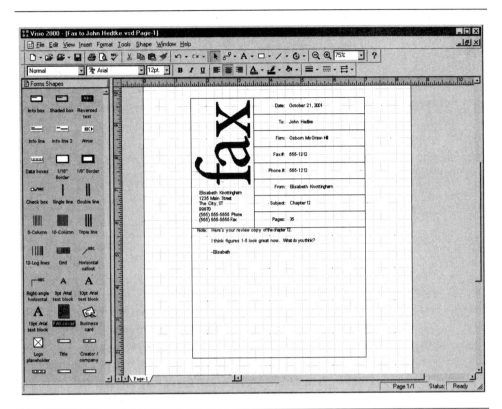

FIGURE 9-4   A fax coversheet created with the Form Design template

standard form shapes to choose from as well. Table 9-1 gives a quick overview of some of the more popular shapes on the Form Shapes stencil and their behaviors.

When you've finished creating a form, be sure to save it.

Exploring the Marketing Charts and Diagrams Template

Selling a product or service requires a certain flair. Graphics and charts can help, but a sales pitch also needs to be visually impressive. To meet this demand, Visio 2000 includes a special template, the Marketing Charts and Diagrams template, which has everything you need to create eye-popping marketing

Shape	Use	Behavior
Info Box, Shaded Box, Reversed Text	Fill-in boxes for building forms	Creates a standard size rectangle for adding text.
Info Line, Info Line 2	Labels for sections of a form	Creates a text box with a line underneath for labels.
Data Boxes	Fill-in box for one-character-at-a-time data	Creates a series of small boxes; increasing the width of the shape adds more boxes.
Check Box	Small checkbox with text	Creates a small box and accompanying text; to uncheck the box, right-click and choose Uncheck Box.
Lines—including Single, Double, 5-Column, 10-Column, Triple, and 10-Log	Borders for columns or rows in a form	Creates a fixed number of lines. The number of lines in the shape cannot be altered, and the width of the shape determines the distance between each line. However, you can overlap several column or line shapes to show more columns. You can also rotate the line shapes to create rows instead of columns.
Grid	Borders for lists of options, names, and so forth; can include checkboxes	Has control handles to change the size of the box and lines. Changing the size of the shape adds more lines or boxes.
Date, Time, Page, and Filename	File information that can be added to a form	Inserts information about the Visio 2000 file. The file information is updated automatically.

TABLE 9-1   Shapes on the Form Shapes stencil

materials. Figure 9-5 shows the main Visio 2000 window with the Marketing Charts and Diagrams template open and an example of a marketing diagram.

Five stencils open up automatically with the Marketing Charts and Diagrams template:

- Backgrounds stencil
- Borders and Titles stencil
- Marketing Clip Art stencil
- Marketing Diagrams stencil
- Charting Shapes stencil

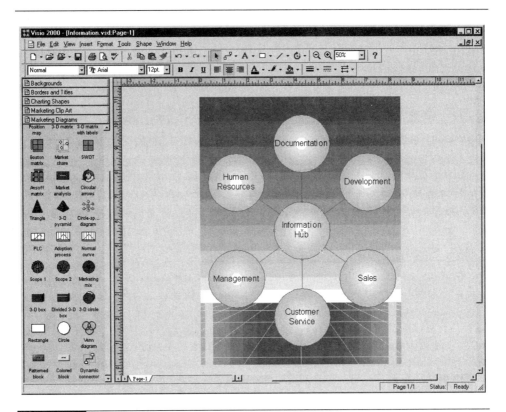

FIGURE 9-5   A marketing diagram created with Visio 2000

The Charting Shapes stencil is described earlier in this chapter in the section "Understanding the Charts and Graphs Template." The other four templates are explained here.

TIP   *To add color to your marketing diagrams, see the section "Using Color Schemes" later in this chapter.*

Using the Backgrounds Stencil

The Backgrounds stencil includes 18 backgrounds meant to fit any of the standard drawing page sizes. The backgrounds coordinate with color schemes and themes to help you create an overall look for your diagrams.

When you drag a background onto the drawing page, Visio 2000 automatically rotates it to fit the drawing page and locks it down. If you later rotate or change the size of your page, the background rotates or resizes with the page. Backgrounds also automatically cover all the drawing page, no matter where you drop the shape.

TIP	*If a background covers other shapes, select it and choose Shape | Send to Back.*

Backgrounds from this stencil are set to fill with any color you choose. When you change the color of a background, it fills with the color in a way that suits the background's image.

Using the Borders and Titles Stencil

The Borders and Titles stencil contains dozens of shapes to enhance the look of Visio 2000 diagrams. For the most part, the shapes on this stencil are not intended to be used as stand-alone diagram elements, but instead are designed to accent text and other shapes.

Included in the Borders and Titles stencil are fifteen border shapes that resize and change orientation to fit the drawing page. The stencil also includes 14 title shapes that resize to fit the text inside. There are also six note box shapes on the stencil. In addition, there are three hyperlink shapes for use on HTML pages created in Visio 2000.

Using the Marketing Clip Art Stencil

Marketing Clip Art is a special subset of Visio 2000 clip art. This clip art has been specially formatted to enhance m marketing diagrams. Included in this stencil are stretchable shapes that replicated themselves instead of resizing. For example, the stretchable dollars shape adds more dollar icons as you increase the width of the shape.

Also included in this stencil are shapes with special control handles and special resizing capabilities. For example, the Variable Stack and Variable Smoke Factory shapes allow you to increase the size of the three-stack or smoke shapes without altering the rest of the image. If you hover the curser over one of the shapes on the drawing page, a tool tip appears explaining how the shape behaves.

Shapes on this stencil often have special functions when you resize them. If you're not sure how a shape will behave, save your diagram before you start resizing marketing clip art.

The Marketing Clip Art stencil also includes useful shapes for reports and other marketing projects. Shapes like standard credit card images, global currency shapes, and award shapes allow you to convey information with professional-looking graphics.

Using the Marketing Diagrams Stencil

Marketing diagrams often include shapes for illustrating processes, path-routing, and cost projections. The Marketing Diagrams stencil includes shapes that look stunning and convey information clearly. Most of the shapes on the Marketing Diagrams stencil are colored, and many are three-dimensional.

 You may find it useful to open the Blocks Raised stencil when you're are creating a marketing diagram. The Blocks Raised stencil includes many more three-dimensional shapes. It's located in the Block Diagram folder.

9

When you drag some shapes from the Marketing Diagrams stencil to the drawing page, a dialog box like the one shown in Figure 9-2 may appear. Use the Custom Properties dialog box to set the number of shapes in the group or the number of subdivisions. If you need to change these properties after you've set them, you can access the dialog box again by selecting the shape and choosing Shape | Action.

Making and Using a Slide Show

Slide shows allow you to view multiple-page diagrams as a succession of full-page images. You can also use a slide show to preview how your diagrams will look when you add them to a document in another program. Figure 9-6 shows an example of one screen of a Visio 2000 slide show.

 Other programs can be used to create slide shows on the computer, but Visio 2000 diagrams may not display as well in those programs as they do in Visio 2000.

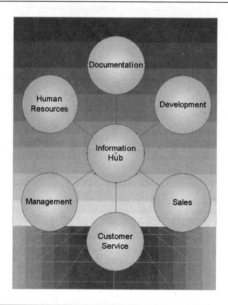

FIGURE 9-6   A Visio 2000 slide show screen

You should use slide shows *after* you have completed your diagrams. When you create a slide show, you can't change the shapes on the drawing page. The slide show is simply a way to view the diagrams.

The first step to using a slide show is to display the diagram in Full Screen view. To see a diagram in Full Screen view, choose View | Full Screen. To leave Full Screen view, right-click and choose Close from the shortcut menu. You can also press ESC to leave Full Screen view.

The slide show starts on the page currently displayed in the Visio 2000 main window.

Navigating Between Images in a Slide Show

When you have your multiple-page diagram in Full Screen view, you need to navigate between the pages differently than you do in the main Visio 2000 window. To go forward in the page order, use the RIGHT ARROW key. To go backward in the page order, use the LEFT ARROW key.

You can also use more sophisticated navigation by right-clicking and using the shortcut menu. Right-click anywhere on the page and a shortcut menu appears, as shown here:

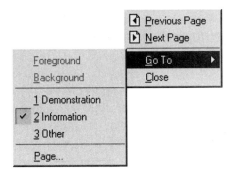

The options are as follows:

Previous Page   Takes you to the page preceding the displayed page. This option disappears on the first page of the slide show.

Next Page   Takes you to the page following the displayed page. This option disappears on the last page of the slide show.

Go To   Displays a list of pages, the option to open a window with a list of pages (Page...), and the option to view the foreground or background of the displayed page.

Close   Ends the slide show and takes you back to the main Visio 2000 window.

NOTE   *Page order is set in the Visio 2000 main window and cannot be changed in Full Screen view.*

Using Hyperlinks in a Slide Show

Hyperlinks set in a diagram work in Visio 2000's slide show. You can tell where a hyperlink has been set because the mouse pointer changes from an arrow to a pointing finger when you move the pointer over the link. Activate a hyperlink by clicking on it. Then Visio 2000 opens up the hyperlinked document. If there's

9

more than one link on a particular shape, a drop-down menu appears, and you can choose the link from the list.

 Visio 2000 is unable to open other documents (including other Visio 2000 documents) in Full Page view. Instead, they are opened in the native program and are displayed in the same view they had when they were last saved.

In order to not interrupt your slide show, documents you link to are opened up in a new program window. Even Visio 2000 documents operate this way, creating the situation where two copies of Visio 2000 are running at the same time.

 Comments do not display in Full Screen view.

Using Color Schemes

Creating an overall set of colors for your presentation can be difficult and time-consuming. Visio 2000 includes *color schemes* to make the process of choosing colors faster. This allows you to add an extra touch to your documents without taking time away from working on the content.

 Color schemes in Visio 2000 are almost identical to color schemes in many Microsoft Office programs—for example, Microsoft PowerPoint. To learn more, see Chapter 6, "Using Visio 2000 with Microsoft Office."

Color schemes can be added at any time during the creation of your Visio 2000 diagram. To set a color scheme for your document, choose Tools | Macros and then select a color scheme from the Visio 2000 Extras folder. The Color Schemes dialog box appears, as shown in Figure 9-7.

The options in the Color Schemes dialog box are as follows:

Choose a Color Scheme   Lists the 17 color schemes that come with Visio 2000 as well as any schemes you've created.

New   Allows you to add a new color scheme based on settings you choose. Clicking this button displays a dialog box like the one shown in Figure 9-8.

Edit   Allows you to edit the selected existing scheme. Clicking this button displays a dialog box like the one shown in Figure 9-8.

Delete   Removes the currently selected scheme.

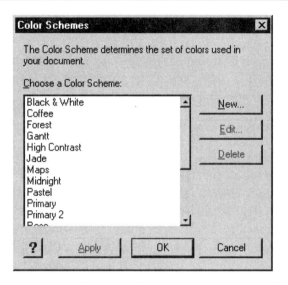

FIGURE 9-7   Color Schemes dialog box

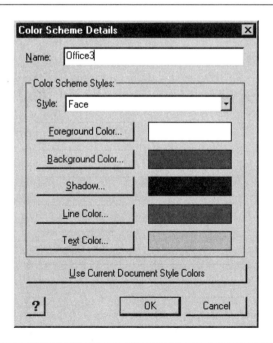

FIGURE 9-8   Color Scheme Details dialog box

You cannot edit or delete one of the standard schemes. Only schemes you create can be edited or deleted.

When you add a new color scheme by clicking on the New button shown in Figure 9-7, the Color Scheme Details dialog box appears, as shown in Figure 9-8. The Color Scheme Details dialog box also appears when you edit a color scheme you've created previously.

The options in the Color Scheme Details dialog box are:

Name   Sets the name for the color scheme.

Style   Sets the style for the color scheme.

Color-setting buttons   These five buttons set the colors for the foreground, background, shadow, line, and text. The boxes directly to their right show the currently set color. Click on the button for the setting you want to change to display in the Color Selection window.

Use Current Document Style Colors   Uses the settings for the current document to create a new color scheme. Styles and colors are taken from the settings in the displayed window of the current document. This is the fastest way to create a new scheme.

 You cannot undo applying a color scheme you've already applied. To return to the default black-and-white color scheme, choose Black & White in the Color Schemes window and click Apply.

Adding Maps

There are times when you need to include geographical representations of the physical world in your diagrams. Demographics and sales regions can best be shown by using maps. And certain other projects may require a detailed map—complete with roads, bodies of water, and landmarks. Visio 2000 has the Maps templates for presentations and projects that require these special types of supporting materials.

There are two types of maps in Visio 2000, and both can be found in the Map solutions folder.

- Geographical maps
- Directional maps

Adding Geographical Maps

The Geographical Maps template contains all the world's land masses, continents, countries, islands, and regions for all your mapping needs. Designed for charts, atlases, and geographical tracking data, geographical maps have added features allowing you to create all or part of a global map with ease. Figure 9-9 shows the main Visio 2000 window with the Geographical Maps template open and an example of a sales distribution map.

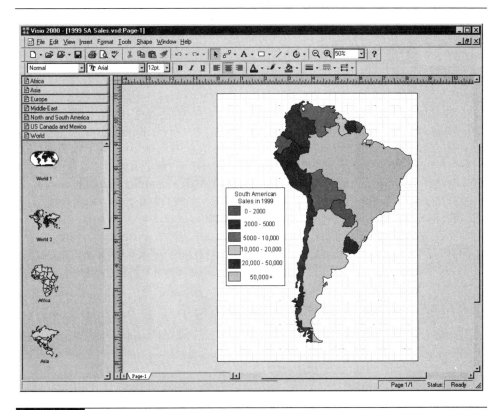

FIGURE 9-9   A geographical map

The sales map shown in Figure 9-9 was created using one of myriad geographical shapes that come with the Geographical Maps template. Seven stencils open automatically with the template. The Geographical Maps template stencils include shapes for every country, region, major body of water, and continent in the world, as well as two global shapes.

The larger shapes in this template, namely the world and continent shapes, are made up of many smaller geographic shapes. Make sure you have enough computer resources available before you move or alter these shapes, because the files are quite large.

Exploring the Geographical Maps Stencils

The seven stencils that come with the Geographical Maps template contain hundreds of shapes. All the shapes in the geographical stencils have been designed to work together. All shape stencils have the same dimension as other similar shapes. For example, all the country shapes, no matter the stencil, can be constructed into a world map without changing any dimensions, because they're are all at the same scale. The same is true of the state shapes. The body of water shapes are sized to fit with the country shapes, and the countries on the global shapes are the same size as the other country shapes.

Visio 2000 has named the stencils very well. However, it can still be a little confusing trying to find the shape you're looking for. Here's a list to help you figure out which shapes are on which stencils and give you an idea of the special properties of some of the shapes:

Africa stencil   Contains all the countries in Africa in alphabetical order. After the country shapes there are seven of the major lakes on the continent and twelve of the major rivers or major river sections.

Asia stencil   Contains all the countries of Asia and the Pacific Rim in alphabetical order. After the country shapes there are seven major bodies of water and almost two dozen major rivers.

Europe stencil   Contains all the countries in Europe, both western and eastern, and all the countries in the northern part of the Asian continent. After the country shapes there are three major lakes and seven major rivers.

Middle-East stencil   Contains the thirteen countries of the Middle East as well as five major rivers.

North and South America stencil   Contains shapes for all the countries of North and South America, as well as sixteen major bodies of water and four dozen major rivers.

US Canada and Mexico stencil   Contains state and province shapes for the United States, Mexico, and Canada. The shapes are listed in alphabetical order within the country, and the countries are listed with the United States first, Canada second, and Mexico last.

World stencil   Contains two global shapes, as well as the continent shapes, on the World stencil are made up of the country shapes from the other stencils. You can ungroup any of these shapes and have all or part of a continent by selecting and moving groups of countries. You can also select each country without removing it from the group and alter its individual fill color or other settings.

> **TIP**   *For a complete list of the shape on each stencil, see Appendix A, "Stencils and Templates."*

Understanding Custom Properties and Layers in Geographical Maps

Each shape on the Geographical Maps stencils has a custom property containing its name. The names of countries are their common names, as are the names of the bodies of water. The use of custom properties makes it easy to identify a country or other shape when it's on the drawing page.

> **TIP**   *When you're placing a lot of geographical shapes, open the Custom Properties window so you don't have to keep right-clicking on shapes and choosing Shape | Custom Properties. You can open the Custom Properties window by choosing View | Windows | Custom Properties.*

There are also three layers that come with the Geographical Maps template: Land, Rivers, and Lakes. All shapes on the stencils are set to be on one of the layers by type. The first time any type shape is dragged to the desktop, Visio 2000 adds the layer to the layer list.

The different layers allow you to display just one type of geographical shape at a time. For example, you could just display the rivers for your map of Africa. Don't be afraid to add layers of your own and to assign shapes to those layers. For more information about layers, see Chapter 3, "Going Further."

Using the Arrange to Shape and Arrange to Page Commands

All the shapes in the Geographical Maps template include two special actions: Arrange to Shape and Arrange to Page. These two actions help you create regional maps from country, state, or province shapes. They're especially useful with the state and province shapes, because there are no country shapes that are divided into states to get the state regions like there are the continent shapes for creating country regions.

Arrange to Shape moves your selected shape to a logical point in reference to another shape. To arrange a set of shapes, first move them all to the drawing page and then right-click on each shape. Choose Arrange to Shape from the shortcut menu. A dialog box appears asking you to choose the shape you'd like to arrange to. Select the shape you want to build the set of shapes around and click OK. Visio 2000 moves the shape to a location relative to the shape you selected.

Arrange to Page moves several shapes into a geographical group centered on the page. It works much like Arrange to Shape. However, instead of moving the shapes relative to one particular shape, the shapes are arranged in relation to the drawing page.

Creating Directional Maps

Sometimes merely providing directions to a meeting or event isn't enough—you need a map. Visio 2000 includes the Directional Maps template for creating maps that can be used to give directions. Not only can directional maps be used to show how to get somewhere, they can also be used to list resources in a particular area. Figure 9-10 shows the main Visio 2000 window with the Directional Maps template open and an example directional map.

The Directional Maps template includes shapes for highways, parkways, traffic, road and street signs, routes, railroad tracks, transit terminals, rivers, and interstates. They also have added styles and layers to help you create and print the part of the map you need. These shapes are on the five stencils that come with the template. Here's a quick overview of each stencil:

Transportation Shapes stencil   Contains street signs, traffic signals, transportation shapes, and direction signs.

Road Shapes stencil   Contains roads, bridges, interstate and other highway signs.

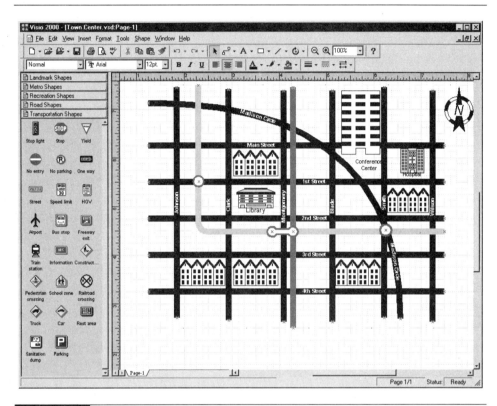

FIGURE 9-10   A directional map

Recreation Shapes stencil   Contains informational signs for recreation centers.

Metro Shapes stencil   Contains mass transportation shapes for metros, including transfer and station shapes.

Landmark Shapes stencil   Contains buildings, and other physical shapes, as well as compass, text callout, and city shapes.

TIP   *For a complete list of the shape on each stencil, see Appendix A, "Stencils and Templates."*

Many of the shapes included in the Directional Maps template have special control handles. They also have other special functions you can access by right-clicking and choosing options from the shortcut menu. Here's an overview of some of the special functions:

- All the shapes in the Recreation Shapes stencil, and some of the shapes on the Transportation Shapes stencil, have an extra control handle you can use by right-clicking and choosing Show Control Handle from the shortcut menu. The extra control handle sets where text added to the shape appears in relation to the shape.

- The tree shape, on the Landmark Shapes stencil, has a right-click option that turns the tree from Deciduous to Coniferous and back again.

- Roads and metro lines can be any of three default widths, or you can choose to make them a custom thickness. If you choose to make a road or metro line a custom thickness, an extra control handle appears in the lower left-hand corner of the shape, allowing you to dynamically change the thickness of the line.

Adding Comments

Comments are small text references you can place in documents as notes that won't appear in the finished diagram. Adding comments helps in the creation process by allowing you and others who work on a document to annotate the actual diagram. Figure 9-11 shows an example of a comment.

Comments are viewed by placing the mouse pointer over the shape. Visio 2000 displays the comment in a text box, as shown in Figure 9-11. Comments are only displayed in the Normal view and are not available in Full Screen view or to print out.

To insert a comment, you need to first place the shape. Comments, like hyperlinks, are added to already-existing shapes. With the shape on the drawing page, select it and make sure nothing else is selected. Then choose Insert | Comment. The Comment window opens, as shown here:

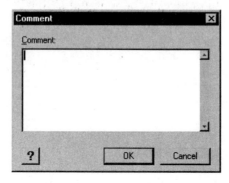

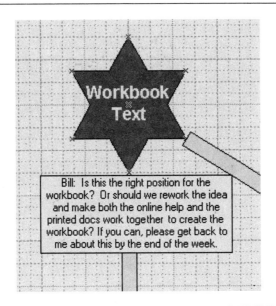

FIGURE 9-11   A comment

Fill in the text you want displayed in the comment. The text can only be in plain text and can have no formatting at all. Click OK to close the window. Visio 2000 adds the comment to the shape. Make sure to test the comment by hovering the mouse pointer over the shape and waiting for the comment to appear.

> **NOTE**   *Only the first five or six lines of your comment display on the screen when you hover the pointer over the shape. The rest of the text can be seen when you edit the comment.*

To edit a comment, select the shape and then choose Insert | Edit Comment. The Comment window appears, as shown earlier, with the full text of the comment. Change the comment text and then click OK.

When you've finished inserting or editing a comment, remember to save the Visio 2000 document.

Summary

In this chapter, you learned how to use Visio 2000 to convey information graphically in meetings or on paper. You learned how to create charts, forms, and graphs, as well as how to add maps and geographic shapes to your diagrams. You also learned how to create a slide show in Visio 2000 and how to add comments to shapes.

In the next chapter, you will learn about the added features in Visio 2000 Technical Edition.

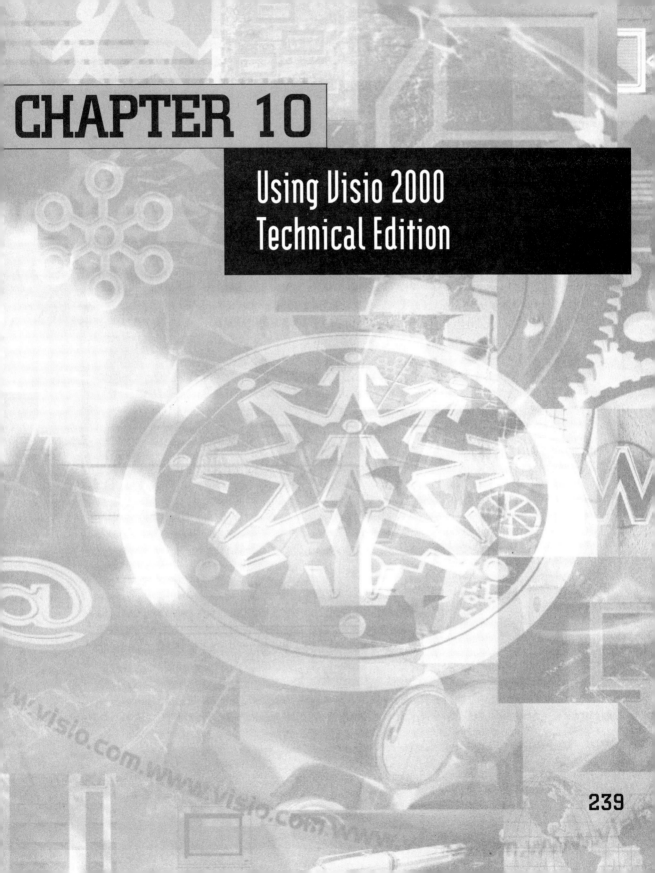

CHAPTER 10

Using Visio 2000 Technical Edition

In the last chapter, you learned how to convey information graphically with Visio 2000. You learned how to create charts, forms, and graphs, as well as how to add maps and geographic shapes to your diagrams.

In this chapter, you'll learn about Visio 2000 Technical Edition. You'll learn how to make the most of the precision drawing tools, how to work with CAD drawings, and how to create engineering drawings. You'll also learn about the facilities management tools that come with Visio 2000 Technical Edition.

Understanding Visio 2000 Technical Edition

Visio Corporation created Visio 2000 Technical Edition for engineering, architectural, and drafting users. This edition includes all the stencils and templates that come with Visio 2000 Standard Edition as well as new templates and stencils geared for the technical worker. Included in Visio 2000 Technical Edition are seven additional solution folders with more than twenty templates to help technical professionals do their jobs more quickly and easily. For example, an architect can quickly lay out the framework of a building core, including dimensions and form. Floor plans can be used as backgrounds for the mechanical drawings, or they can be converted into CAD drawings for use in other programs.

Visio 2000 Technical Edition also includes easy-to-use tools for the general business user to create detailed floor plans even if they don't know anything about architecture or space planning. For example, you could use Visio 2000 Technical Edition to design new shelves for your garage. With Visio 2000 Technical Edition you could quickly lay out the garage space, add new cabinets, drop in a car shape and see how much space is left over for golf clubs or a lawn mower.

The following table lists the additional solution folders and templates in Visio 2000 Technical Edition.

Solution Folder	Templates
Building Architecture	Floor Plans, Home Plans, Plant Layout, Reflected Ceiling Plans, Site Plans
Building Services	Electric & Telcom Plans, Fire & Security Systems, HVAC Control Logic Diagrams, HVAC Plans, Plumbing & Piping Plans
Electrical Engineering	EE – Circuit & Logic, EE – General, EE – Industrial Control Systems, EE – Systems
Facilities Management	Facilities Plan

Solution Folder	Templates
Fluid Power	Fluid Power
Mechanical Engineering	Part & Assembly Drawing
Process Engineering	Process Engineering

The beauty of Visio 2000 Technical Edition is that you can move from a rough concept for a space to a fully scaled floor plan in a few quick steps. Simply drag and drop space shapes onto the drawing page or sketch out areas freehand using any of the built-in drawing tools. Visio 2000 Technical Edition automatically displays the square footage for each space shape. You can join overlapping areas together using the Union command (see Chapter 11, "Using Advanced Visio 2000 Features"), and Visio 2000 Technical Edition instantly recalculates the square footage for the combined space. After roughing out a space, you can right-click and choose the Convert to Walls command from the shortcut menu to instantly build a fully scaled, measured drawing. Visio 2000 Technical Edition cleans up wall corners, and adds guides and dimension lines. When you drop doors, windows, furniture, and other shapes on the finished floor plan, these items automatically orient themselves and snap to the walls. If you change the measured drawings by dragging or rotating the guidelines, Visio 2000 Technical Edition recalculates the size and dimensions.

Exploring Precision Drawing Tools

The precision drawing tools are included in Visio 2000 Standard Edition; however, they are used to their fullest with the Visio 2000 Technical Edition. Often, engineering and architectural drawings require accurate, precise measurements. Visio 2000 Technical Edition provides drawing and positioning tools that are easy and powerful for the most complex drawing types.

Understanding Drawing Scale and Diagram Size

In drawings that depict abstract concepts (for example, in flowcharts and organization charts), the scale of the drawings rarely comes into play. Plan shapes, on the other hand, represent real-world objects, which can rarely be depicted at full size.

The drawing scale and dimensioning tools can help set up your Visio 2000 drawings with the drawing scale and units to create a wide range of engineering and architectural drawings. All Visio 2000 Editions use two ways to establish scale: drawing units and page units. *Drawing units* are measurements in the real world, while *page units* are measurements on the printed page. Scale is the ratio of the page units to the drawing units.

 Scale is represented by two numbers in comparison with one another; for example 1/4" to 1' means a quarter inch on the drawing page equals one foot in real life.

All templates in Visio 2000 open with a default scale. For example, the Floor Plans template opens with an architectural scale of 1:96. Some schematic drawings, such as electrical schematics, have a scale of 1:1. The drawing scale can be changed at any time, and each page can have its own scale.

To change the scale of a drawing, first make sure the page you want to change the scale of is open. When the page is ready, choose File | Page Setup, and then choose the Drawing Scale tab, as shown in Figure 10-1.

You can choose three types of scale on the Drawing Scale tab:

No Scale   Sets the scale as 1:1.

Pre-Defined Scale   Lists standard scales. Choose one of the types of scale from the first box, and then choose one of the different settings for that type.

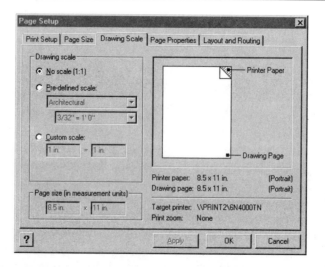

FIGURE 10-1   Drawing Scale tab of the Page Setup dialog box

Custom Scale   Allows you to set any scale you choose. The first box represents the size on the page; the second box represents the size in real life.

> | TIP | *You can change the units for the page on the Page Properties tab. Doing this also affects how the ruler displays.*

When you're done setting the drawing scale, click OK. Visio 2000 automatically updates the drawing page and resizes all the shapes that have a preset real size.

Locating Shapes Precisely

In Chapter 3, "Going Further," you were introduced to the concept of grid lines, guidelines, and guides, as well as the tools for snapping and gluing. In Visio 2000 Technical Edition, these tools become even more valuable, and they have additional functions that can help you create drawings faster and with greater ease.

Using Exact Coordinates to Position Shapes

Sometimes you need to know the exact coordinates of a shape. Every shape has a pin through its reference point that anchors the shape on the drawing page. The location of this pin is listed as a set of X and Y coordinate values, giving the location of the shape relative to the page coordinate system. For example, the pin point of a chair could be the center point, and where the center point is located is the X, Y coordinate pair.

To locate or move a shape by using exact coordinates, first drag or move the shape to the approximate location on the drawing page. Then choose View | Windows | Size & Position. This displays a set of values for the shape, including the coordinates, as shown in Figure 10-2. To move a shape to an exact location, enter values for the new location in the X and Y boxes. Click OK when you're satisfied with the values, and Visio 2000 positions the shape.

Because the location for the shape is set by the reference point, you may need to change where the reference point for a shape is. The Pin Pos box on the Size & Position window allows you to alter the position to one of several preselected places on the shape. Simply click on the Pin Pos box, and choose from the drop-down list.

A new feature in Visio 2000 is the ability to move shapes using the arrow keys. This feature is commonly known as *nudging*. Nudging allows you to select a shape and then change its position by very small increments using the arrow keys on the

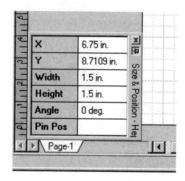

FIGURE 10-2   Size & Position window

keyboard. Visio 2000 also give you the ability to nudge objects one pixel at a time by holding down SHIFT as you use the arrow keys.

If you need to move a shape a specific distance, use the Move command. This command allows you to specify the distance along the X and Y axes, or the distance and the angle to move a shape.

NOTE   *The Move command only exists in Visio 2000 Technical Edition.*

To move a shape a specified distance:

1. Select the shape to move.

2. Choose Tools | Macros | Visio Extras | Move. The Move dialog box appears, as shown here:

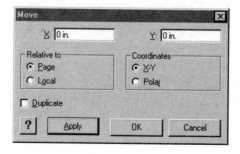

3. Under Relative To, click Page.

4. Under Coordinates, click X-Y.

5. Specify the horizontal (X) and vertical (Y) distances you want to move the shape.

6. Click OK to move the shape.

 Clicking the Apply button allows you to see the impact of the move before you close the dialog box.

Snapping to Points on Shapes

Snapping can be enhanced by deciding where and how you snap. You can snap to geometric points on shapes—such as endpoints, tangents, and intersections—for more accurate designs. This is very useful when you want to place a shape on another shape without knowing the exact coordinates of either one.

NOTE *Snapping to geometric points in Visio 2000 Technical Edition is similar to the object snaps used in CAD packages.*

To set snap settings, choose Tools | Snap & Glue. Under Currently Active, make sure that Snap is checked. Under Snap To, check Shape Handles, Shape Vertices, and Connection Points, and then click OK.

Using Advanced Snapping

When drawing in Visio 2000, it's sometimes necessary to specify additional snap-to points. Visio 2000 includes shape extensions to give you maximum control over how your shapes snap. Extension lines appear when your pointer is positioned near the target point of the shape, allowing you to span to it there instead of just at a control point. You can draw shapes with exacting precision using shape extension lines, since they provide visual feedback about shape angles, tangents, and other useful geometric relationships.

To turn on shape extensions, choose Tools | Snap & Glue. On the General tab of the Snap & Glue dialog box, make sure Shape Extensions is checked under Snap To. On the Advanced tab, choose the geometric options you want under

"Shape extension options." The following illustration shows the Advanced tab for the Snap & Glue dialog box:

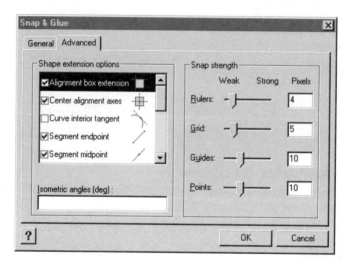

The shape extension options are:

Alignment box extension   Draws a line extended from the shape's alignment box.

Center alignment axes   Draws a line extended from the center of the shape's alignment box.

Curve interior tangent   Illustrates the curve's tangent at the midpoint of the arc segment when you move the cursor over an arc segment.

Segment endpoint   Highlights the endpoint when you move the cursor over a line segment or arc segment. A line segment can include line shapes and lines used to create the sides of a polygon.

Linear extension   Draws a line segment from the nearest endpoint when you move the cursor over a line segment. A line segment can include line shapes and lines used to create the sides of a polygon.

Curved extension   Illustrates how an arc would look as an ellipse when you move the cursor over an arc segment. For freeform shapes, it extends the curve at the endpoint that you're near.

Endpoint perpendicular   Draws a line perpendicular to the nearest endpoint when you move the cursor over a line segment or arc segment. A line segment can include line shapes and lines used to create the sides of a polygon.

Midpoint perpendicular   Draws a line illustrating a perpendicular line on the line segment or arc's midpoint. A line segment can include any edge of a polygon.

Horz line at endpoint   Draws a line illustrating a horizontal line on the nearest endpoint when you move the cursor over a line or arc segment. The line is horizontal to the screen, not the page, so it's not affected by page rotation. A line segment can include line shapes and lines used to create the sides of a polygon.

Vert line at endpoint   Draws a vertical line on the nearest endpoint when you move the cursor over a line or arc segment. The line is vertical to the screen, not the page, so it is not affected by page rotation. A line segment can include line shapes and lines used to create the sides of a polygon.

Ellipse center point   Highlights the ellipse's center point when you move the cursor over an ellipse.

Isometric angle lines   Draws a line extended at the angles specified in the Isometric Angles (Deg.) box. You can enter up to 10 angles in degrees, separated by commas. This option is most useful if you're creating an isometric drawing.

While drawing, move the cursor toward or along a shape to see a shape extension. Shape extensions work with the Line, Arc, Freeform, Pencil, Ellipse, Rectangle and Connection tools.

10

Using the Dynamic Grid

The Dynamic Grid gives you the ability to align a single shape with any horizontal or vertical edge. The Dynamic Grid provides visual cues onscreen and intelligent object-snapping to automatically place shapes in an evenly distributed and aligned order. To do this as you place shapes, Visio 2000 gives you extra guides to move the shapes around, as shown in Figure 10-3.

To dynamically align a shape with other shape edges, first start to drag the shape as normal. Then tell Visio 2000 that you want to consider another of the shape's edges for alignment by pausing over the target shape for about two to three seconds. Once paused, the target shape's geometry is examined for horizontal and vertical lines. Visio 2000 places a dotted line on the shapes, allowing you to position and align shapes quickly and accurately.

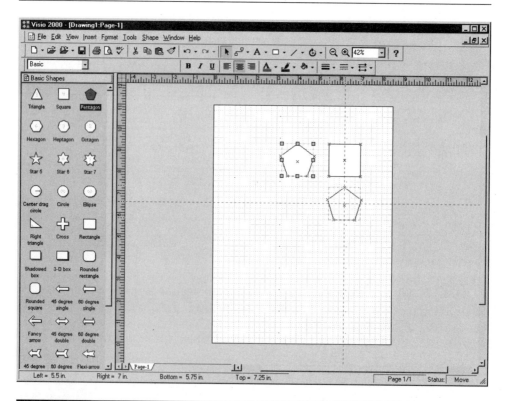

FIGURE 10-3   Dynamic Grid example

A dotted line will show you the most desirable position of a shape in relation to the nearest shape. The dotted lines show the center points of the shapes. For example, if you were locating a PC shape on a desk, the Dynamic Grid will show you the center of the two shapes when they're aligned.

Using Pan & Zoom

Many of the drawings created in Visio 2000 Technical Edition are large and contain hundreds of shapes, and moving around the diagram can get very confusing where there are so many shapes on the page.

Visio 2000 provides a tool that lets you easily navigate around a diagram: the Pan & Zoom window. To open the Pan & Zoom window, choose View | Windows | Pan & Zoom. Figure 10-4 shows an example of a Pan & Zoom window for a large facilities management drawing.

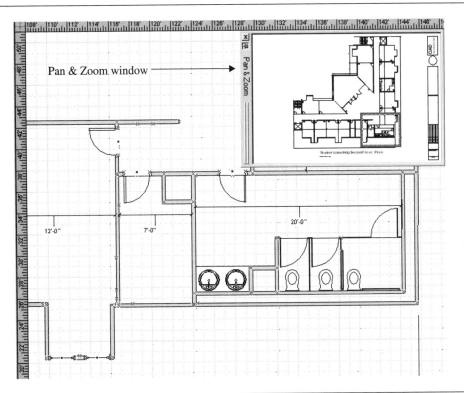

FIGURE 10-4 Architectural drawing with Pan & Zoom window

Pan & Zoom shows a miniaturized overview of the current page. Manipulate the red rectangle to zoom and pan in the drawing. The window stays open, allowing you to maintain a bird's-eye view of your drawing no matter how closely zoomed in you are.

You can customize how the Pan & Zoom window works, as follows:

- To hide the Pan & Zoom window, right-click the window, and then choose AutoHide. You can also add sounds for the window as it opens and closes. When the Pan & Zoom window is hidden, move your pointer over its title bar, and the window will reappear.

- To make the Pan & Zoom window float, right-click inside the Pan & Zoom window, and then choose Float Window. Or you can click the Pan & Zoom window's title bar and drag it away from its docked position.

- To dock the Pan & Zoom window, right-click inside the Pan & Zoom window, and then choose Anchor Window.

> **TIP** *You can drag the Pan & Zoom window to the location you want.*

Working with CAD Drawings

Visio 2000 delivers CAD compatibility for those who need to work with DWG and DGN drawings. You can open CAD drawings in Visio 2000 to use as background images, enlarged plans, or as details. When you open CAD files as backgrounds, shapes will automatically snap to the underlying CAD geometry for faster and more accurate placement. For example, furniture shapes, equipment shapes, electrical outlets, and HVAC ducts automatically rotate and snap into place. You can pan and zoom drawings with background CAD files as quickly as you can move your mouse.

Working with CAD Legacy Data in Visio 2000

Visio 2000 Technical Edition provides the capability to open CAD drawings in Visio 2000 to be used as a background page or a reference layer. After opening the CAD file, you can drag shapes onto it, add notes, and control the way the layers display. Visio 2000 shapes will snap to objects that reside on the CAD drawing.

> **TIP** *A CAD drawing inserted into a Visio 2000 document is a copy of the original CAD drawing. Changes made to the drawing within Visio 2000 do not alter the original.*

When you use Visio 2000 Technical Edition or Visio 2000 Enterprise Edition, you have the additional capability to convert CAD entities into Visio 2000 shapes.

To open a CAD drawing as a background image in Visio 2000, first start Visio 2000, and choose to Open Existing File and click OK. The Open dialog box is shown in Figure 10-5.

Under Files of Type, use the drop-down list to select a CAD drawing file format—AutoCAD Drawing (.dwg, .dxf) or MicroStation drawing (.dgn). Then browse to the file location and click Open. Visio 2000 opens the document.

The CAD Drawing Properties dialog box is used for sizing and scaling the CAD drawing on the Visio 2000 page as well as setting up the drawing page. The window on the right graphically illustrates how the CAD drawing will fit on the Visio 2000 page. Visio 2000 fits the CAD drawing onto the page and gives them

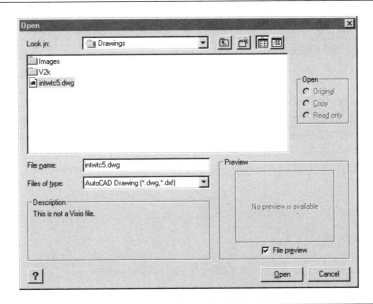

FIGURE 10-5 The Open dialog box with AutoCAD Drawing set as the file type

10

both the same scale. You can then drag Visio 2000 shapes onto the drawing, hide layers or levels, redline drawings, and add comments. Visio 2000 shapes will snap to objects on the background CAD drawing.

Whenever possible, you should work with opened CAD drawings. Working "over" opened CAD drawings is faster and generally gives better visual results. In particular, if you work with CAD drawings that are frequently updated, you should open the CAD drawings so that they can be easily updated with newer versions.

Locking the CAD Layer

In order to facilitate selecting and moving the shapes you drag onto a CAD drawing, you should lock the Visio 2000 layer that contains the CAD drawing. This guarantees that you do not accidentally select and move the CAD drawing instead of the Visio 2000 shapes.

To lock the Visio 2000 layer, first open the CAD drawing. Then right-click on the CAD drawing and choose View | Layer Properties. Click Lock Column for the CAD Drawing layer, and then click OK.

You may need to rotate the drawing page for your CAD drawing. To do so, choose File | Page Setup. On the Print Setup tab, set the orientation of the page to either portrait or landscape. On the Page Size tab, select the "Same as printer page size" radio button.

Controlling the Display of Layers

Controlling the display of CAD layers has always been at the mercy of the CAD operator. Visio 2000 provides a tool for accomplishing this, and no prior CAD experience is required. For example, you might want to turn off all the layers containing office furniture so that you can drag HVAC ducts onto a floor plan.

To control the display of layers:

1. Right-click an inserted CAD drawing and choose CAD Drawing Object | Properties.

2. Click the Layer tab or the Level tab.

3. To hide a layer or level, uncheck it in the Visible column.

4. Click OK to accept your changes.

 You can click Apply instead of OK to keep the dialog box open as you see how the changes affect the drawing. Then click OK to close the dialog box.

Snapping to CAD Geometry

Drag a shape from the template and drop it onto the Visio 2000 drawing. As you position the shape near something on the background CAD drawing your cursor will display "Snap to Geometry." This functionality allows shapes to automatically rotate, align, and snap to each other intelligently for faster layout. Shapes will automatically snap to the underlying DWG geometry for faster and more accurate placement. For example, electrical outlets, HVAC ducts, and furniture shapes automatically rotate and snap into place.

Saving Visio 2000 Drawings into CAD Format

It's possible to convert Visio 2000 Technical Edition drawings into CAD format by choosing Save As from the File menu. Converting drawings works best when done in only one direction—from CAD format into Visio 2000 format, or from Visio 2000 format into CAD format. It's very hard to maintain data integrity when files are going back and forth. The best and easiest way to maintain that data is to convert only once.

Visio 2000 Technical Edition converts the current Visio 2000 drawing page into CAD format. If you're working with a multiple-page drawing, you must convert each page separately.

To convert a Visio 2000 page, first open the drawing containing the pages you wish to convert. Then choose Save As from the File menu. Select the CAD drawing format from the Save As Type box and then click OK.

Converting CAD Entities into Visio 2000 Shapes

If you need to delete or modify objects in the CAD drawing, you must first convert the layers containing those objects into Visio 2000 shapes. This process provides

10

you with an outline shape that you use with Visio 2000 Technical Edition, and if necessary turn it into a Visio 2000 shape.

To convert CAD objects into Visio 2000 shapes:

1. In Visio 2000, right-click the CAD drawing and choose CAD Drawing Object | Convert. The conversion dialog box appears, as shown here:

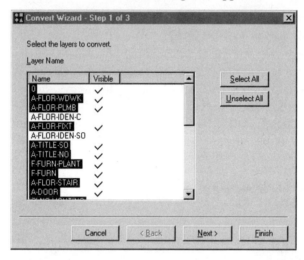

2. When the Convert Wizard opens it assumes that you want to convert all visible layers. Click the Unselect All button; then hold CTRL while you click to select the layers or levels that contain the objects you want to convert. Click Next, and the second box for the Convert Wizard appears, as shown next:

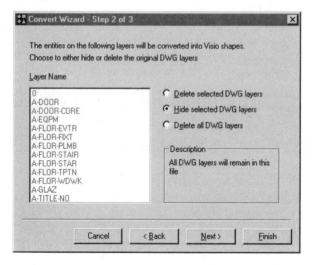

3. Choose whether to delete selected layers or levels, hide the selected layers or levels, or delete all layers or levels. Click Next, and the third box for the Convert Wizard appears:

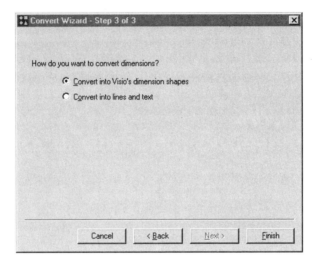

> **NOTE**   *For DGN files, you can't specify to delete only selected layers.*

4. If you're converting DWG files, you need to specify how you want to convert dimensions. Select "Convert into Visio's dimension shapes" to get dimensions that update when you resize the associated Visio 2000 shapes. Select "Convert into lines and text" to preserve the CAD formatting.

> **NOTE**   *For DGN files, you can't specify how dimensions are converted.*

5. Click Finish. Visio 2000 now goes through the process of converting the objects on the selected CAD layers or levels into Visio 2000 shapes.

6. These shapes can now be added to stencils. You can add custom properties—in effect turning them into SmartShapes objects.

For the CAD User

Seasoned CAD users typically look for their favorite CAD commands in Visio 2000. It's fair to say that some CAD commands don't exist, while others will be slightly different and even easier than their CAD equivalents.

The following table lists some favorite CAD commands and their Visio 2000 Technical Edition equivalents.

CAD Command	Visio 2000 Technical Edition
Copy an object	Select the shape, hold the CTRL key while you drag a copy to the new location.
Move an object	With the Pointer tool, select the shape and drag it.
Move an object a specific distance	Select the shape and choose Tools I Macros I Visio Extras I Move.
Add Hatching to an object	Select the shape and choose Format I Fill. The options are Color, Pattern, and Pattern color. You can also create your own patterns.
Create a block/cell	Use the Visio 2000 drawing tools to draw the shape, and then drag the shape to a stencil.
Object Snaps	Choose Tools I Snap & Glue and check Shape Extensions. On the Advanced tab, check the shape extensions you need.
Set drawing scale	Choose File I Page Setup, select the Drawing Scale tab, then select the scale.

Managing Your Facility

Facilities managers have traditionally relied on CAD and proprietary CAFM (computer-aided facilities management) tools to create space plans, track and manage physical assets, and move facilities. These tools often cost thousands of dollars, require extensive training, and make it hard to share data with others. Visio 2000 Technical Edition combines the aspects of CAD and database-oriented tools with core Microsoft technologies.

The Facilities Management solution combines space-planning and asset-tracking capabilities. This offers you two different views of your facility information: a spatial view when using the facilities plan, and an organizational view when using the CAFM Explorer. With the CAFM Explorer, you can:

■ Create and update facility plans based on space requirements, such as head count, office configurations, and so forth

■ Locate and list assets, such as equipment, furniture, and fixtures

■ View office assignments graphically and then quickly update them

In addition to facilities plans, Visio 2000 Technical Edition offers other drawing types, such as floor plans, site plans, HVAC, security systems, and network diagrams that can be used in conjunction with the facilities plans.

With Visio 2000 you can link to and work with the data from any SQL-compliant database for which they have 32-bit ODBC drivers, such as Oracle, SQL Server, dBase, and Access. ODBC (Open Database Connectivity) is a Microsoft standard with which programs can access, view, and modify data from the database.

> **NOTE** *You must have the appropriate ODBC components and database drivers installed on your computer. To find out if your database program is ODBC-compliant, check the program's documentation.*

Creating Facilities Management Drawings

When you first start a facilities plan you must connect your drawing to a facilities database. This database contains the information you want to track for your organization. That way, the drawings you create act as a "visual database" and have asset-tracking capabilities added to them. These capabilities are information about resources and assets, specifically spaces, boundaries, people, furniture, fixtures, and equipment.

Connecting Your Drawings to a Database

Before starting a facilities drawing, you need to configure a data source. The Facilities Management solution needs to know what the data source is and where it's located.

The quickest way to get started is to use the database that is created, by default, when you start a facilities plan. This is a Microsoft Access database that is stored on your computer. It contains commonly used information, and you can add additional tracking information.

You can also configure a data source yourself to track assets. To handle your own database administrations, open your computer's Control Panel (by choosing Settings | Control Panel from the Start menu). In the Control Panel dialog box, open ODBC Data Sources.

> **NOTE** *The Microsoft Repository only supports SQL and Access data sources.*

Creating a Facilities Plan

To create a facilities plan, first open Visio 2000 Technical Edition. Choose to open the Facilities Management drawing type. This opens the first screen of the Facilities Management Setup Wizard telling you what this wizard will accomplish. Click Next and the second screen appears, as shown in Figure 10-6. The second

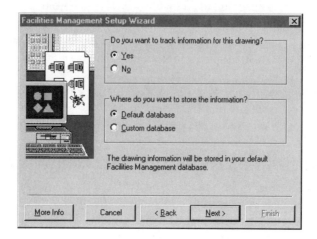

FIGURE 10-6   Second screen of the Facilities Management Setup Wizard

screen asks if you want to track information for the drawing and where you'll store the information. You probably want to store the information in the database you previously configured via the ODBC Data Sources in the Control Panel.

If you haven't configured a data source, the wizard automatically selects Custom Database. When you click Next, if you select the Custom Database, the third screen appears asking you to select the type of database, as shown in Figure 10-7. The third screen is the Site Information screen. Enter a company name, location, building, and

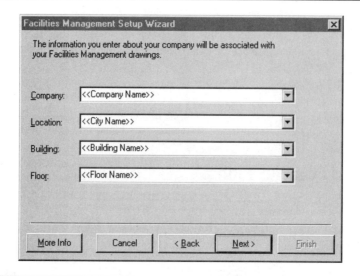

FIGURE 10-7   Third screen of the Facilities Management Setup Wizard

a floor name. Then when the information is complete, click Next. The last screen of the Facilities Management Setup Wizard appears, asking if you'd like to complete the wizard and start your diagram. Click Finish to complete the wizard.

After the drawing is connected to a facilities database, you can begin to draw the building shell for one floor.

Creating a Floor Plan

Each page in your Visio 2000 drawing can represent a floor or a portion of a floor. You cannot represent more than one floor on the same page. The creation of the plan can be accomplished one of three ways:

- Use the shapes on the Walls, Shell and Structure, and Building Core stencils
- Insert a floor plan from a CAD program
- Use an existing plan created in Visio 2000

Sizing Walls in Visio 2000

Visio 2000 Technical Edition has automated the process of dimensioning through the use of room and space shapes. Simply select a group of walls to be dimensioned, right-click and select Add Dimension from the shortcut menu.

With space shapes, convert the space shape to walls. Right-click on the space and select Convert To Walls. The Convert to Walls dialog box appears, as shown here:

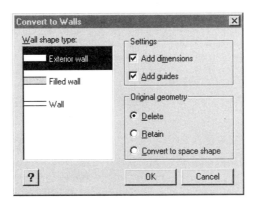

Be sure to select Add Guides and Add Dimensions in the Convert to Walls dialog box, then click OK. Visio 2000 Technical Edition automatically reforms the shape as a space shape with walls, including dimensions and connected wall shapes.

When dimensions are connected to a shape, they'll stay with the shape even as you move or resize it. You can glue the dimension lines to the connection points of shapes or wall shapes. You can choose from a wide variety of dimensioning shapes, including horizontal and vertical baselines, horizontal and vertical outside dimensions, and diameter and radius dimensions.

Tracking Assets

Visio 2000 Technical Edition has the ability to help you not only create spaces but keep track of how those spaces are used. You can assign information to your facilities management diagrams, allowing you to run reports to show how the space is allocated. The ability to track assets is part of all facilities management diagrams.

After you complete the floor plan, you can start assigning information for spaces, areas, or departments. You can assign people to the spaces and calculate the square footage each person takes up or that has been allocated to each department.

Tracking Assets requires several steps:

1. Designating spaces

2. Designating boundaries

3. Assigning people to spaces

4. Assigning assets to spaces

5. Designating categories

6. Assigning a category to a shape

7. Working with databases to retrieve and update data

Each step is important, and all are outlined in detail in this section.

Designating Spaces

If you have created a floor plan by using either the Building Architecture or Office Layout solution, it might already contain space shapes. In that case, you can begin assigning assets to spaces. Otherwise, you need to drag shapes to the drawing page before you can assign them to a person or department.

> **TIP**
>
> *If you drag walls to the drawing page and create a room out of them, Visio 2000 Technical Edition will automatically size a space shape to them. First you need to make sure your room is closed by gluing all the walls together, then drop the space shape on them.*

To specify information (properties) for a space, right-click on the shape and choose Properties from the menu. In the Properties window, fill in the appropriate information in the Value column. Values in the Properties dialog box are saved as soon as you change them.

Designating Boundaries

In addition to designating spaces, you can also designate areas or departments by using the Boundary shape on the Resources stencil. This shape creates a boundary around an area. This is used only for square-footage totals; you can't associate people or assets to a boundary.

To create a Boundary, drag the Boundary shape from the Resources stencil onto the drawing page near a collection of offices. Size the shape so that it encompasses all the offices you wish. Then right-click on the Boundary shape and select Properties. The Boundary window appears. Fill in the required values in the Boundary window. Then click OK.

> **TIP**
>
> *For irregular shapes, you can modify the Boundary shape the same way you modify a Space shape.*

Assigning People to Spaces

You can also assign people to spaces and associate them with that location. You can assign a person to more than one space, and you can assign more than one person to a single space.

To assign a person to a space, drag a Person space from the Resources stencil and place it onto a Space shape. When you want to move a person to a different office or location, simply drag the Person shape onto the new location. When a resource or asset is dragged onto a space shape, it becomes associated with that space. You have to associate resources and assets with Space shapes if you want to use the Find command on the Facilities menu to locate them by their space. To specify information about a person, double-click the Person shape. Fill out the information on the Properties dialog box.

You can use the CAFM Explorer to organize people within departments or areas.

Assigning Assets to Spaces

To associate an asset with a space, drag an asset shape (desk, chair, filing cabinet, etc.) from the stencil onto a Space shape. Right-click on the asset and choose properties from the menu. Fill out the Properties dialog box, making sure to double-check the information before you click OK. Any asset not assigned to a space will be associated with the floor or page.

 Remember to save your drawing frequently so that your drawing and the database are synchronized.

Steelcase Furniture Systems

The Steelcase furniture shapes included with the Facilities Management template are a special kind of asset in Visio 2000 Technical Edition. If you use Steelcase furniture, you can configure the furniture to exact Steelcase specifications by using the Equipment Selector and the shapes on the Steelcase Furniture stencil. When you drag a shape from the stencil onto the drawing page, the Steelcase Furniture window appears as shown in Figure 10-8. You can choose options from the Steelcase database to fit your exact specifications. Choose Facilities | Furniture | Configure to change the specifications of your Steelcase furniture.

Designating Categories

Facilities information is organized into *categories* and *properties*. Categories are groups that shapes belong to. Properties are information you track for a given category.

Many of the shapes in the Facilities Management solution are assigned to a category. Every category has a name, a reference word or number (called *ref*), note properties, and other properties specific to that category.

You can customize the default categories by adding your own properties or by adding your own subcategories and properties. A subcategory is a category based on a default category. When you add a subcategory, it will inherit the properties of the categories it was based on. After you add subcategories, you must assign the subcategory to the appropriate shape.

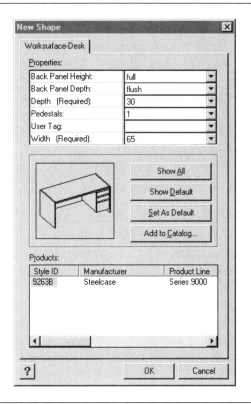

FIGURE 10-8   Steelcase Furniture window

To add new categories and properties, select Categories from the Facilities |
Customize menu. This displays the Categories window. You can add a new
category, edit a category, or delete a category, as well as add a new property or
edit a property.

Assigning a Category to a Shape

You can assign categories to shapes you create, as well as change or assign a
category to any shape. You can also assign a category to one or more shapes.
Remember, if you change the category of a shape on the drawing page, only that
particular shape will have that change. On the other hand, if you change the
category of a shape on a stencil, every time you drag that shape onto the drawing
page it will have the new category.

To assign a category to a shape on a stencil, first make sure nothing is selected on the drawing page, then select Convert Shapes from the Facilities menu. This launches the Convert Shapes Wizard, the first screen of which tells you that it will convert the shape for you. Click Next. The second screen of the Convert Shapes Wizard appears, as shown in Figure 10-9. On the second screen, use the Browse button to search for stencils located elsewhere. Select the stencil, then click Next.

The third screen of the Convert Shapes Wizard appears, as shown in Figure 10-17. On the third screen, uncheck Show Only Unassigned Shapes in order to see all the shapes. From the Categories list, select a category. From the Shapes list, select a shape.

When you're finished with the wizard, click Finish to reassign the shapes. Visio 2000 Technical Edition displays a dialog box asking if you wish to assign more categories. Click No. The shape now assigns itself to the correct category when you drag the shape from the stencil onto the drawing page.

Working with Data from an Existing Database

You can link properties in your facilities plan to fields in existing databases so that you don't need to reenter existing data into your plan. If the external database is updated, your plan will also be updated. To access an external database you must know its name, user name, and (if it's protected) the password. You also need to know enough about the database tables in order to select the data you need.

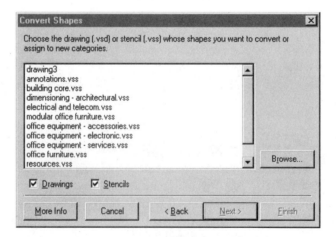

FIGURE 10-9   Second screen of the Convert Shapes Wizard

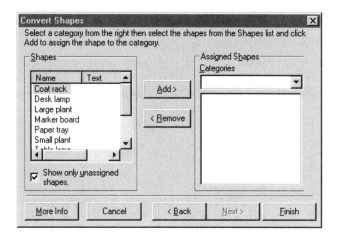

FIGURE 10-10 Third screen of the Convert Shapes Wizard

Here's the process for connecting to a database:

1. Select Facilities | Customize | Get External Data.

2. Click Create to create a new connection or link to an existing database.

3. Type a connection name for the connection. You have to create a unique name for each category you link to a table or view in the external database.

4. Select the data source that points to the existing database, and then click Next.

5. Under Object Types, click the type of database objects you want to view, and then under Database Objects, select the particular table or view you want. Click Next. Use Preview to verify that you have located the correct data.

6. Select one or more columns to use as the primary key to identify each record in the table, and then click Next.

7. Select the Facilities Management category that will use data from the existing database.

8. Select a Facilities Management property and a database field to link together, and then click Add.

9. Click Finish.

After the link has been set up, you can use the data in the plan:

1. Right-click the asset or person shape in your plan and select Properties.

2. In the Properties dialog box, click Use Existing Item.

3. In the Search For box, type text to locate the correct record in the external database.

4. Select the record you want, and then click OK.

At this point, any property that is linked to a database field is automatically filled in. Linked properties are unavailable for editing in the Properties dialog box. Click OK to save the changes and close the Properties dialog box.

Locating Assets in Your Facilities Plan

The CAFM Explorer is a tool for listing people, assets, spaces and boundaries, and then locating them in your facilities plan. It offers a hierarchical view of the facilities data. It is a great holding place for information about resources or assets. By default, the CAFM Explorer displays the facilities information you entered in your facilities plan. Each Facilities Management shape in the plan is represented as an item.

To start the CAFM Explorer, choose Facilities | Explorer | View. This launches the CAFM Explorer, with it docked on the side of the window. Click View Full Screen on the Facilities Explorer toolbar to expand the size of your Explorer window. You can use the Find command on the Edit menu to locate specific shapes.

Creating Engineering Diagrams in Visio 2000 Technical Edition

The key to Visio 2000 Technical Edition's ease of use is SmartShapes technology. Included are intelligent shapes designed to behave like pipes, valves, pumps, and other real-world objects. Engineers can easily assemble drawings by dragging and dropping these industry-standard shapes onto a page. They can even store data in shapes, link them to databases or spreadsheets, and automatically generate detailed reports.

Process Engineering

With Visio 2000 Technical Edition you can create piping and instrumentation diagrams (P&IDs) and process flow diagrams (PFDs) that show how industrial process equipment is interconnected by a system of pipelines. P&ID schematics also show the instruments and valves and monitor and control the flow of materials through the pipelines.

Draw P&IDs and PFDs by dragging process engineering equipment shapes onto the drawing page and connecting them with "smart" pipelines. Then drag components, such as valves and instruments, onto the pipelines. You can add data to components in your diagrams by entering the data specifications you want for a component into its datasheet.

To identify components in your diagram, you can create "intelligent" tags. These are tags that contain information that identify the components. The Tag Builder is used to customize the tags. Intelligent tags are filled in automatically when you drag the shape onto the drawing.

From the data in the datasheets you can generate lists of equipment, pipelines, valves, and instruments. As you modify diagrams, you can generate a new list from the updated datasheets.

By creating projects in the Process Engineering solution, you can manage all your project-related documents. The Project Explorer lets you work in tandem with any project diagram or document.

10

> **TIP** *Visio 2000 Technical Edition includes a sample Process Engineering project. This project includes P&IDs, datasheets, and lists. This is a great way to learn more about the Process Engineering solution. Open the example by choosing Open from the File menu and then browse to Visio | Samples | Process Engineering | Process Engineering Project. Select Sample Project.vsd and click Open.*

Creating a New Project

In the Process Engineering solution, you work in projects and use the Project Explorer to view and open documents in your project. In a project, you create and manage all the diagrams and documents you need for that project—PFDs, P&IDs (datasheets, and lists). When you begin a new project you can base it on an existing one. That way, you can reuse the datasheets, lists, and sheet formats that were created in previous projects.

You can create P&IDs or PFDs that are not part of a project; however, you will not be able to use the intelligent features, such as datasheets and intelligent tags.

You should create a project for each engineering project that you will be working on. You can create as many projects as you like, but remember that you can work on only one project at a time. For ease of use, all files for a single project should be stored in the same folder.

To create a new project:

1. Choose File | New | Process Engineering | Process Engineering.

2. Choose Create a New Project.

3. Under Project File, click Browse and locate the folder where you want to store the project, or, under File Name in the Save Project File dialog box, type the path and name you want to use for the project. Click OK.

4. A new project opens, displaying the Project Explorer window. To begin a new diagram, choose Process Engineering | New Drawing.

5. Type the name you want for your new drawing. In the Name option you type in the name of the new drawing. The Based On option allows you to select a sheet format. If you don't want to use a sheet format, select None.

After you've started and named a project, the Process Engineering menu will appear on the Visio 2000 main menu bar. The commands that you'll need to work with will appear on that menu.

As you work on a project you might need to delete or add drawings to it. To add a drawing to your project, right-click the drawing you want under the Not In Project heading of the Project Explorer, and then choose Add to Project from the shortcut menu.

If you add a diagram that wasn't created in the Process Engineering solution, the shapes in that diagram won't have the intelligence of Process Engineering shapes unless you convert them to Process Engineering shapes.

To remove a diagram from your project, right-click the diagram you want under the Project Name heading in the Project Explorer, then choose Remove From Project from the shortcut menu.

Working with Datasheets

In the Process Engineering solution you can add data directly to shape components without having to call up a separate spreadsheet or database. Each shape has a related datasheet. Datasheets are forms containing fields of data for the components in your drawing. Some datasheet information appears directly on the drawing page through the use of tags. You can view all the datasheets for components in your project in the Components view of the Project Explorer.

To add or edit data for components in a P&ID or PFD, select the shape to which you want to add data, then choose Process Engineering | Edit Datasheet. The Process Engineering datasheet appears, as shown in Figure 10-11. Click a

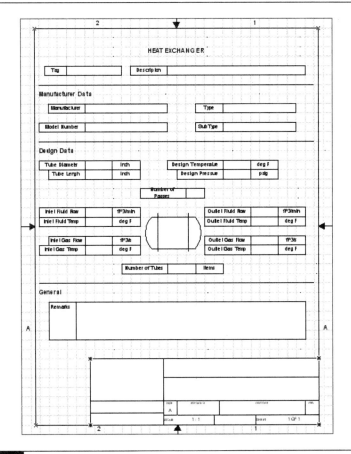

FIGURE 10-11   Process Engineering datasheet

field to add or edit data on the datasheet. Press TAB to move to the next field. The data is saved as soon as you type or select it. When you've finished entering the data, click Close.

You can add or edit data for multiple components in the Datasheet window. To open the Datasheet window, choose Process Engineering | Datasheet Window. Select one or more components in the diagram, then type or select data in the Datasheet window.

You use the datasheet information to generate lists of component information. These lists report specific information about each component, such as the manufacturer's name, a tag or label assigned by the process engineer, or the size, pressure capacity, or heat rating of a component.

Creating Intelligent Tags

By default, intelligent tags are generated automatically when data is entered in the component datasheet. To change this setting, choose Process Engineering | Tags | Tag Settings. In the dialog box, uncheck "Automatically generate intelligent tags."

To create and edit intelligent tags, choose Process Engineering | Tags | Customize Tags. Then select the datasheet category and the datasheet you want to modify, and then click OK. The Custom Tags dialog box opens. For each datasheet field you want to use in the tag, select the field from the Available Fields list, and then click the Add Field button to add it to the tag expression.

As you build your tag expression, you can view how it will appear in the Sample Tag Value box. If you want punctuation marks or text to separate fields, type the punctuation or text directly into the Tag Expression box. For example, you might want to use hyphens to separate fields.

If you want to create a tag with multiple lines, press the ENTER key in the tag expression field at the point where you want to start a new line. If you want to number components that use this datasheet automatically as you drag them onto the drawing page, click the Counter button and set the counter properties. Once you've set the properties, set a starting value and choose the number of digits to show.

Then select the tag fields that determine when to increment the counter. For example, if you have an intelligent tag for valves that shows the line size and material, you could select the Line Size field to number sequentially all valves that have the same line size. Four-inch valves and six-inch valves would be numbered separately. If you were to select both Line Size and Material to control numbering, only valves that have the same line size and material would be numbered sequentially. Four-inch steel valves would be numbered separately from four-inch plastic valves.

If you want intelligent tags to substitute codes for values in a datasheet field, click the Substitutions button and select or create tag substitution tables for each of the fields in your tag expression.

After you've finished setting the options in the Custom Tags dialog box, click OK. When you fill out the datasheet for a component, the tag is automatically updated to show the current values. You can also use the Datasheet window or the Edit Tag Number command to change the datasheet fields and update the tag.

Mechanical Engineering

Visio 2000 Technical Edition supplies shapes that let you create part and assembly drawings to provide information needed for manufacturing a product. Part drawings are created in order to show each individual part that makes up a product. Assembly drawings show how all the parts fit together.

Creating Part and Assembly Drawings

Start by opening the Part and Assembly Drawing solution, located in the Mechanical Drawing solutions folder.

The Part and Assembly Drawing drawing page appears in landscape orientation and has no scale. The ruler and the grid are set to Fine resolution, and the ruler zero point and the grid origin are at the lower-left corner of the drawing page. You can change these settings at any time by using the features described in Chapter 3, "Going Further."

To create a title block, drag shapes from the Title Blocks stencil. Drag shapes from the Drawing Tool Shapes stencil onto the drawing page to draw outlines of objects. You can configure many of the shapes by right-clicking them and choosing the appropriate command from the shortcut menu as well as using the control handles. To display a screen tip explaining what the control handle does, hover the pointer over the control handle.

Drag shapes from the Fasteners 1, Fasteners 2, and Springs and Bearings stencils onto the drawing page. When you drag many of these shapes from these stencils onto the drawing page, you'll be prompted for information about the shape's characteristics. Fill in the appropriate data to configure the shape. You can change custom property data at any time by right-clicking the shape and choosing the appropriate command from the shortcut menu.

In order to complete your drawing, you now need to add the following:

■ Dimensions

■ Datum feature symbols and feature control frames from the Geometric Dimensioning and Tolerancing stencil

■ Welding symbols from the Welding Symbols stencil

■ Callouts and other reference notes from the Annotations stencil

Creating Electrical and Electronic Drawings

With Visio 2000 Technical Edition you can create electrical and electronic schematic diagrams as well as wiring diagrams. You can also generate a netlist file from your drawing that can be used to input information into a circuit analysis program, such as SPICE.

There are a number of different types of electrical or electronic drawings that you can create. The following table lists the drawing type and which stencil to open:

Drawing Type	Visio 2000 Stencil
Integrated circuit and logic circuit schematics	EE – Circuit & Logic
General electrical diagrams (schematics, one-line, and wiring)	EE – General
Control system schematics	EE – Industrial Control Systems
Printed circuit boards	EE – Systems

Generating a Netlist File

A netlist is an industry-standard text file that lists all the components in a circuit, along with the nodes (connection points) to which each component is attached and the value of each component. In Visio 2000 Technical Edition, the Netlist Generator compiles data about electrical circuit diagrams by creating a text file in the standard netlist format.

For the Netlist Generator to work properly, you must draw your diagram using the following criteria:

- The circuit must be a connected drawing. Use the Connector tool, rather than the Line tool, to connect the components on the drawing.

- Components must be 2-D (two-dimensional) shapes. All the electrical and electronic shapes are 2-D. If you create your own shapes, be sure they're 2-D.

The labeling of components must follow these guidelines:

- You must specify the name or designation of the component in the first part of the shape's text. The first letter of the name determines the device type letter, so the name you give each component should begin with the relevant letter. For example, use "R" for a resistor or "C" for a capacitor. (Refer to your SPICE program documentation for more information on the correct letters.) Names should not contain spaces.

■ You must specify the component's value in the second part of the shape's text. Values should not contain spaces.

■ You must separate the name and the value with a space, as in this example: R6 10k.

■ Although there is no character limit, a label usually has fewer than 20 characters.

After you've satisfied all the requirements, you're ready to generate a netlist. In your drawing, select the components that make up the circuit you want to analyze.

Choose Netlist Generator from the Tools | Macros | Electrical Engineering menu. This launches the Netlist Generator. In the Netlist Generator window, specify a prefix for unnamed nodes and a location for the netlist file.

HVAC, Electrical, and Plumbing Drawings

Visio 2000 Technical Edition provides you with shapes to create building services diagrams of HVAC control systems, basic duct layouts, fire and security plans, and lighting and electrical layouts. All these drawing types can be created on a blank drawing page or as a layer in an existing floor plan. The floor plan could have been created with Visio 2000 or brought in from CAD.

Building Services Solution Folder

The templates for creating these drawing types are all found in the Building Services Solution folder. The templates are:

■ Electric & Telcom Plans

■ Fire & Security Systems

■ HVAC Control Logic Diagrams

■ HVAC Plans

■ Plumbing & Piping Plans

Fluid Power Drawings

Visio 2000 Technical Edition provides the tools and shapes for creating hydraulic and pneumatic circuit diagrams. You can use the valve shapes provided with Visio 2000 Technical Edition or create your own valve shapes by using the Valve Builder.

To create a new Fluid Power diagram, open the Fluid Power template, located in the Fluid Power solutions folder. Then drag equipment and valve shapes from the Fluid Power – Equipment, Fluid Power – Valve Assembly, and Fluid Power – Valves stencils onto the drawing page. You can configure many fluid power shapes by right-clicking them and choosing the appropriate command from the shortcut menu.

Now use the Connector tool to connect the components. Remember that there are additional connectors located in the General Connectors stencil in the Annotation folder. Add interest to your drawing by adding text, labels, callouts and other reference notes from the Annotations stencil.

Creating Your Own Valves

You can use the Valve Builder to create a wide range of pneumatic or hydraulic valve shapes. The Valve Builder allows you to create valves that have from one to four positions and from two to five ports. In addition, you can specify the position that the valve is in by selecting different combinations of controls.

To create your own valves, you first need to open the Valve Builder by choosing it from the Tools menu.

> **TIP** *You can also choose Tools | Macro | Fluid Power | Valve Builder.*

Then Drag the Valve Builder shape from the Fluid Power – Valves stencil onto the drawing page. This displays the Valve Builder window, as shown in Figure 10-12.

There are a number of options you can set in the Valve Builder window:

Positions and Ports   Specifies the number of positions and ports you want the valve to have and select a flow path option from the list.

Arrowheads   Specifies the number and direction of arrowheads for the valve.

Fluid Type   Selects a hydraulic or pneumatic fluid type.

Control Location   Specifies the location for the control.

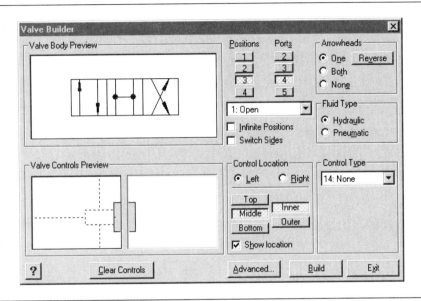

FIGURE 10-12   Valve Builder window

10

Control Type   Selects the type of control you want from the list.

Advanced   Sets the options for building the valve.

Build   Creates the valve.

Summary

In this chapter, you learned about Visio 2000 Technical Edition. You learned how to make the most of the precision drawing tools, how to work with CAD drawings in Visio 2000, and how to create engineering drawings in Visio 2000 Technical Edition. You also learned about the facilities management tools that come with Visio 2000 Technical Edition.

In the next chapter, you'll learn about advanced Visio 2000 features, including how to create your own shapes. You will also learn about the networking template in Visio 2000 Standard Edition.

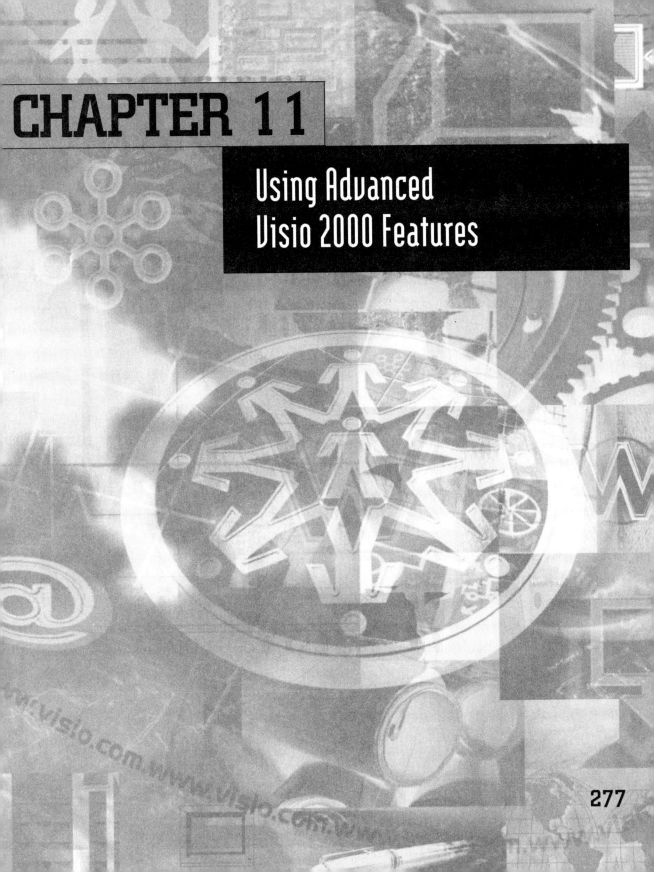

CHAPTER 11

Using Advanced Visio 2000 Features

In the last chapter, you learned about the additional features of Visio 2000 Technical Edition.

In this chapter, you'll learn how to create original shapes, both by modifying existing shapes and by creating new shapes from scratch. You'll also learn how to define custom properties for shapes, how to create networking diagrams, and how to compare organization charts.

Making New Shapes

In Chapter 4, "Using Stencils and Templates," you learned how to move shapes from one stencil to another and how to create new stencils by adding shapes from other stencils. This section explains how to create entirely new shapes for stencils.

Occasionally, the thousands of shapes that come with Visio 2000 may not meet your special needs. You might need a custom shape of some kind. Simple company logos, unique professional shapes, and combined groups of standard shapes are all good candidates for new master shapes. Making a new master shape allows you to create the shape once, and then pull it from a stencil over and over and be assured that the shape will always look and act the same.

There are two ways to create new shapes: modifying shapes that already exist on stencils, and creating new shapes using the drawing tools. Both methods produce fully functional master shapes, complete with custom properties if you wish.

Modifying Existing Shapes

If you find yourself modifying the same shape over and over, you can save time and energy by creating a custom shape. The fastest way to create a new shape is to modify an existing master shape. There are two major benefits of modifying an existing master shape. First, it's quick and easy. Second, the new shape can inherit the custom properties of the original master shape, including resizing and double-click functions.

You can add functionality to a custom shape by using the SmartShape Wizard, and you can use the Pencil tool to touch up or redraw an existing master shape.

SmartShape Wizard

Far and away the easiest way to change an existing master shape is to use the SmartShape Wizard. The SmartShape Wizard helps you add "smarts" to a shape.

The SmartShape Wizard is included with all editions of Visio 2000. It's stored in the Visio 2000 Extras folder. You access the SmartShape Wizard by choosing Tools | Macros and then selecting the wizard. The SmartShape Wizard allows you to customize a shape's behavior. For example, you can add extra control handles, create built-in connectors, protect the shape's attributes, and insert a hidden note.

To customize an existing shape using the SmartShape Wizard, first drag the shape to the drawing page. With the shape selected, choose Tools | Macros | SmartShape Wizard. The wizard opens as shown in Figure 11-1.

NOTE *If you did not install the SmartShape Wizard when you installed Visio 2000, you need to do so before you can use it. See Chapter 1, "Visio 2000 Basics," to learn more about installation.*

There are four different ways you can modify the shape:

Customize shape's text   Alters where the text for the shape appears in relation to the shape by adding an extra control handle indicating the center of the text box.

Create built-in connectors   Adds an extra control handle which allows instant connections to be made between the selected shape and any other shape by dragging the control handle to the new shape. These extra control handles are just like the ones on shapes on the Organization Chart Shapes stencil.

11

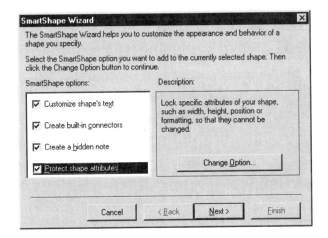

FIGURE 11-1   First screen of the SmartShape Wizard

Create a hidden note   Includes a text note attached to the shape. The information in the note can be custom properties about the shape.

Protect shape attributes   Locks selected attributes of the shape so they can't be modified. This option is an extended version of the dialog box you access by right-clicking a shape and choosing Format | Protection.

Select the options you'd like to change by placing check marks next to those options. As you select each option, you can change how it works by clicking the Change Option button. When you click the Change Option button, a window appears, allowing you to change the settings for that option. Figure 11-2 shows the window that appears when you select "Customize shape's text" and then click the Change Option button.

The Change Option window for the "Customize shape's text" option allows you to set where the extra control handle appears on the shape. Using the control handle, you can extend the text box as far out from that side as you like, but you cannot change the orientation of the text control handle once you've set it.

The Change Option window for the "Create built-in connectors" option allows you to choose how connectors attach to other shapes (see Figure 11-3). The settings in this window also determine how connectors are drawn around other objects not attached to the shape.

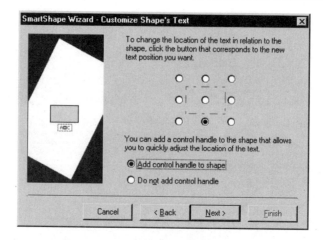

FIGURE 11-2   Change Option window for the "Customize shape's text" option

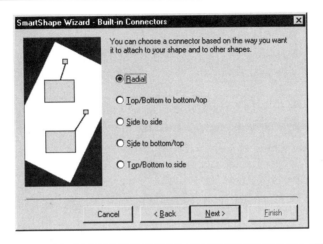

FIGURE 11-3   Change Option window for the "Create built-in connectors" option

The Change Option window for the "Create a hidden note" option allows you to add hidden text next to the shape (see Figure 11-4). The note can be hidden or shown by right-clicking on the shape and making a selection from the shortcut menu. You can also include custom properties in the note. However, the shape must already have custom properties for this option to work.

11

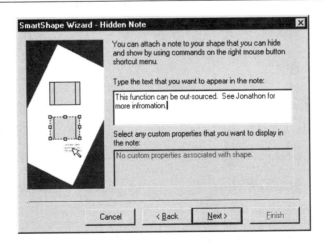

FIGURE 11-4   Change Option window for the "Create a hidden note" option

The Change Option window for the "Protect shape attributes" option lists all the attributes you can protect for the shape (see Figure 11-5). There are 16 attributes that can be locked or otherwise protected. When you hover the mouse pointer over an attribute, a description of that attribute appears at the bottom of the window.

NOTE *When you click the Next button in any of the Change Option windows, Visio 2000 returns you to the screen shown in Figure 11-1.*

After you've set your preferences for the options, you're ready to proceed with the SmartShape Wizard. Click Next on the first screen of the SmartShape Wizard, shown in Figure 11-1. The second main screen of the SmartShape Wizard opens, as shown in Figure 11-6.

The second screen lists the options you've chosen in the first screen and asks if you'd like to modify the existing shape or modify a copy of the existing shape.

CAUTION *If you choose to modify the existing shape, you cannot undo your changes. It's always best to modify a copy of the existing shape.*

When you're ready to apply your changes to the shape (or, as we recommend, to a copy of the shape), click Finish. Visio 2000 displays a small window showing

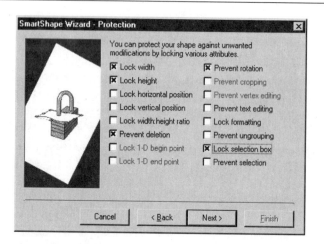

FIGURE 11-5 Change Option window for the "Protect shape attributes" option

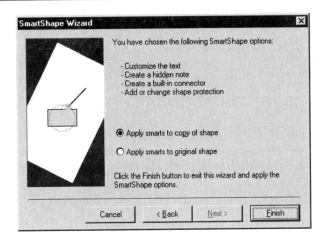

FIGURE 11-6   Second screen of the SmartShape Wizard

you the progress of the wizard. When the wizard is finished, it displays a message telling you the SmartShape creation is complete.

If you want your modified shape to become a master shape that you can use over and over, you need to add it to a stencil. Make sure the stencil is ready to be modified before you drag the shape onto it. If the stencil is in read-only mode, Visio 2000 will ask if you want to open the stencil to edit. For more information about editing stencils, see Chapter 4, "Using Stencils and Templates."

Using the Pencil Tool

If you want to do more than simply add "smarts" to an existing shape—for example, if you want to change the contour of a shape—you need to use something other than the SmartShape Wizard. To alter the geometry of a shape, the best tool is the Pencil tool. With the Pencil tool, you can change the arc of individual lines that make up the shape arc, and you can change the shape's vertices. Figure 11-7 shows a hexagon shape before and after it was modified with the Pencil tool.

In Figure 11-7, you can see how the Pencil tool was used to pull the sides of the hexagon into arcs. For an explanation of how the Pencil tool works, see Chapter 2, "Creating Your First Diagram." For a detailed discussion of altering shapes, see "Understanding Shape Architecture," later in this chapter.

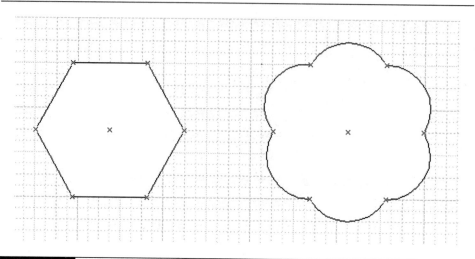

FIGURE 11-7   A hexagon shape modified with the Pencil tool

After you've modified a shape using the Pencil tool, you can convert it into a master shape by adding it to a stencil. To add a shape to a stencil, make sure the stencil is set to be edited, and then drag the modified shape to the stencil. After you've modified the stencil, save it in a folder within the Solutions folder.

   If the stencil isn't set to be edited, Visio 2000 asks if you'd like to open the stencil to edit it. Always make sure to open a copy of the stencil. Don't overwrite the stencils that come with Visio 2000.

Creating an Entirely New Shape

There may be times when simply modifying an existing shape won't give you the results you're looking for. When that's the case, you can create an entirely new shape.

There are two ways to create a new shape. You can combine parts of shapes that already exist, or you can use the drawing tools to create a shape from scratch. Combining shapes uses *shape operations,* which are discussed in detail later in this section. To use the drawing tools, you first need to understand shape architecture—that is, how shapes are defined in Visio 2000.

Understanding Shape Architecture

Shape architecture is how Visio 2000 defines the way shapes look on the drawing page. Visio 2000 defines shapes as sets of vertices and arcs that work together. Figure 11-8 shows a shape that has been selected with the Pencil tool, illustrating its vertices, segments (also called arcs), and control points.

You can edit the vertices and arcs with the Pencil tool, but no matter how a shape is created, it still has vertices and arcs. A shape is defined as closed—and therefore able to be filled—when the last segment ends on the first vertex.

When you create a new shape using a drawing tool, you can modify the shape architecture by using the Pencil tool to alter the location of vertices or the curvature of the shape's segments. The control points, located around the shape, are the mechanism that allows you to alter the curvature of segments.

To change the arc of a segment using the Pencil tool, first select the shape with the Pencil tool. (Figure 11-8 shows an example of a shape that has been selected.) Then move the Pencil tool over a control point until it turns into a cross with arrows on all ends. Click and drag the control point, noticing as you do that the shape changes as you drag the control point. There are also special control points

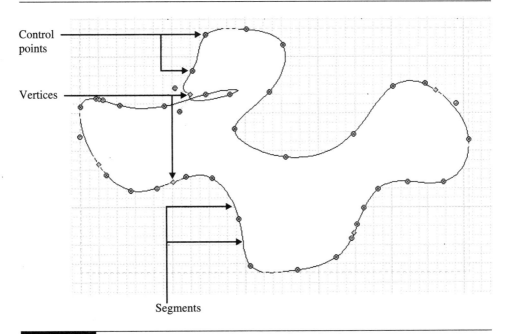

11

Control points

Vertices

Segments

FIGURE 11-8   Vertices, segments, and control points of a shape

that extend from vertices, allowing you to change the angle the arcs use to connect at the vertices. These special control points, called *eccentricity handles*, appear as green, dotted lines.

You can add a vertex anywhere on the outline of the shape by holding down the CTRL key and clicking with the Pencil tool where you want to add the vertex. This adds not only a vertex, but also control points on either side of it. There is always at least one control point between vertices.

You can alter a shape's architecture beyond recognition by using the Pencil tool to move control points. Figure 11-8 demonstrates just the beginning of what you can accomplish by modifying shape architecture.

> **NOTE**   *Some shapes on Visio 2000's stencils are locked, and you cannot alter their shape architecture.*

Using Shape Operations

Visio 2000 has thousands of shapes, including everything from simple shapes for children's drawings to complex shapes for network architecture diagrams. However, sometimes these shapes aren't exactly what you need. You might need to create a shape using parts from several existing shapes. Or you might need to create a complex shape comprised of many individual shapes you've drawn with the Pencil tool. *Shape operations* were created for just these kinds of cases. Figure 11-9 shows a shape from the Basic Shapes stencil that has been modified using shape operations.

There are 12 different shape operations that modify or merge together shapes in various ways. To use shape operations, all the shapes you wish to modify or merge must exist on the drawing page. Most operations require selecting more than one shape. For such operations, the resulting shape will have the formatting of the shape that was selected first.

> **NOTE**   *When you select multiple shapes, the first shape selected has green handles, and all other shapes have blue handles.*

The following 12 shape operations are available by choosing Tools | Operations:

Update Alignment Box   Resizes the box and control handles that surround a shape. Typically, you use this operation *after* you have finished modifying a shape's geometry. When you change the geometry of a shape, the alignment box doesn't automatically resize. You need to use this operation to resize the alignment box.

FIGURE 11-9   Interlaced seven-pointed stars created with shape operations

11

Reverse Ends   Reverses the start and end settings. One-dimensional shapes have two endpoints—a start and an end. Normally, when you rotate a shape, the endpoints stay positioned in the same orientation with respect to one another. Reverse Ends allows you to flip a shape inside its alignment box, switching the start and end. Use the Reverse Ends operation only after you have finished modifying a shape's geometry.

Union   Creates a single shape out of all selected shapes. Figure 11-10 shows three shapes before and after using the Union operation. When you use this operation, the resulting shape is created from the outline of overlapping shapes. If the shapes you select don't overlap, the resulting shape will not look different from the original shapes, but it will behave as a single shape. The Union operation can be used only on 2-D shapes.

Combine   Creates a single shape out of all selected shapes and deletes the area where the original shapes overlap. Figure 11-11 shows three shapes before and after using the Combine operation. You can use the Combine operation on both 1-D and 2-D shapes.

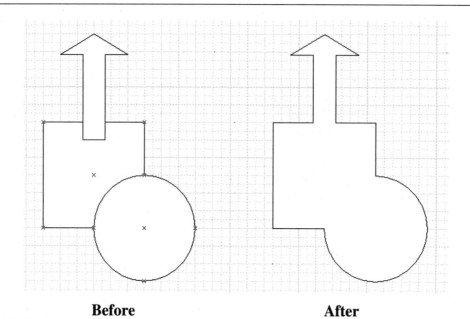

Before   **After**

FIGURE 11-10 Shapes merged using the Union operation

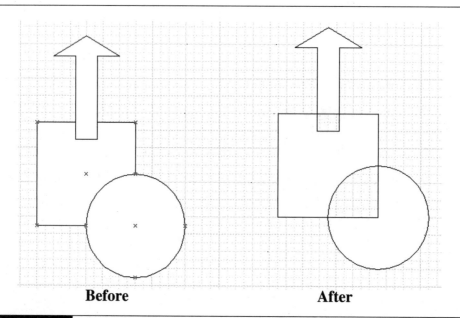

Before   **After**

FIGURE 11-11 Shapes merged using the Combine operation

NOTE *Using the Combine operation is not the same as grouping shapes. When you group shapes, you can still edit the grouped shapes individually. When you use the Combine operation, you create a single shape; the original shapes can no longer be edited separately.*

Fragment Breaks overlapping shapes into their component pieces. Figure 11-12 shows shapes before and after using the Fragment operation. This operation creates new shapes where the original shapes intersect, resulting in smaller pieces of the original shapes. You can then use the pieces individually, or you can use the Union operation to merge some of them together. The Fragment operation is especially useful when you need only part of a shape. You can use the Fragment operation with a standard shape (such as a rectangle) to break off pieces of other shapes. The pieces can then be added to other shapes using the Combine and Union operations.

Intersect Creates a single shape out of the area where two or more shapes intersect. Figure 11-13 shows shapes before and after using the Intersect operation. This operation works only on shapes that intersect. If you try to use the Intersect operation on shapes that don't intersect, the result will be no

11

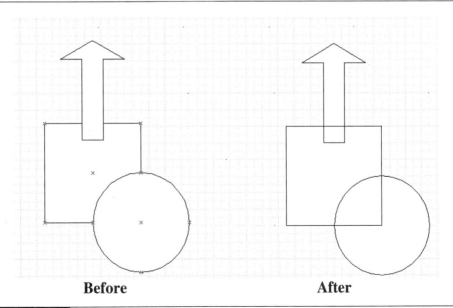

Before   **After**

FIGURE 11-12 Shapes created using the Fragment operation

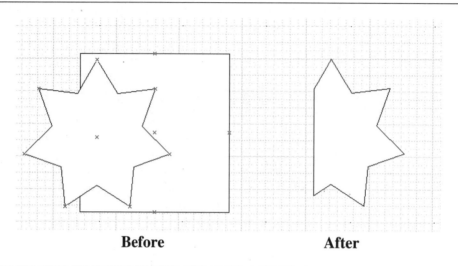

Before   **After**

FIGURE 11-13   A shape created using the Intersect operation

shape at all. This operation also doesn't work on 1-D lines, because it uses combined surface areas and 1-D lines have no surface area.

Subtract   Removes the area where one shape overlaps another. The order in which you select shapes is very important when using the Subtract operation. The shape you select first remains, and the shape you select second—the "cutting shape"—disappears completely. Figure 11-14 shows shapes before and after using the Subtract operation. In the middle example, the square was selected first, and the circle was the cutting shape. In the example on the right, the circle was selected first, and the square was the cutting shape.

Join   Creates a new shape out of straight-line or arc segments. You arrange the segments however you want the shape to look and then use Join to merge them into a single shape. If you place all the segments start to end, the Join operation creates a complete 2-D shape.

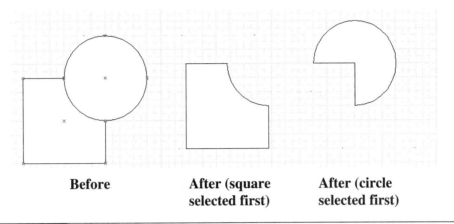

Before   **After (square selected first)**   **After (circle selected first)**

FIGURE 11-14   Shapes created using the Subtract operation

Trim   Turns a 2-D object into connected 1-D objects based on the outline of the selected shape. This means you can no longer fill a trimmed shape, because it no longer functions like a 2-D shape. Instead it behaves as a series of connected 1-D shapes. Trim acts like the opposite of Join, turning shapes into lines instead of the other way around. If you choose to trim two or more shapes that intersect, the result is several line segments outlining the shapes and separated at all points of intersection.

NOTE   *Visio 2000's Trim functions like the AutoCAD function Trim.*

Offset   Creates two or more new shapes at a specified distance from the original shape. When you select a shape and then choose Offset, the Offset dialog box appears, as shown here:

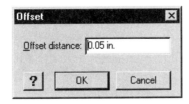

Choose the distance between the original shape and the new shapes, and then click OK. If the original shape is a 1-D line, Visio 2000 creates lines on both sides of the original line at the distance you specify. If the original object is 2-D shape, Visio 2000 creates 1-D lines around the shape in such a way that the new shapes do not intersect with it. No matter what you choose to offset, Visio 2000 creates the resulting lines so the shapes don't intersect. This can produce some odd-looking shapes if you use the Offset operation on complex 2-D shapes.

Fit to Curve   Creates an arc wherever a straight line appears in the selected shape. Figure 11-15 shows a cross shape before and after using the Fit to Curve operation. Fit to Curve turns all straight lines into arcs that have the same vertices as the original line segments. If the shape you start with is a closed 2-D shape, the new shape will also be a closed 2-D shape. Fit to Curve doesn't work on 1-D lines.

Custom Fit   Creates several small spline shapes out of the original shape. Use this operation to edit clip art and other imported images that might not otherwise be editable.

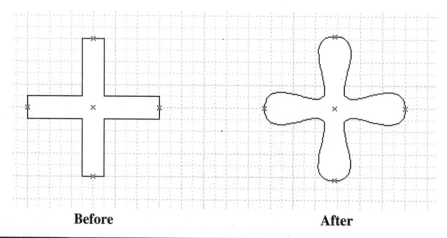

Before   **After**

FIGURE 11-15   A cross shape before and after using the Fit to Curve operation

Introducing ShapeSheets

Visio 2000 keeps track of all shapes using ShapeSheets. Whenever you create a new shape, Visio 2000 uses a ShapeSheet to keep track of it. Likewise, Visio 2000 uses ShapeSheets to keep track of changes to all of the original shapes on the stencils that come with the program. ShapeSheets are how Visio 2000 knows how to draw and move a shape when you drag it to the drawing page.

ShapeSheets are a series of tables that contain all the settings for a shape. Figure 11-16 shows the ShapeSheet for a standard square.

ShapeSheets are generally used by developers when creating new shapes or modifying the behavior of existing shapes. You can view the ShapeSheet for a shape by selecting it and then choosing Window I Show ShapeSheet.

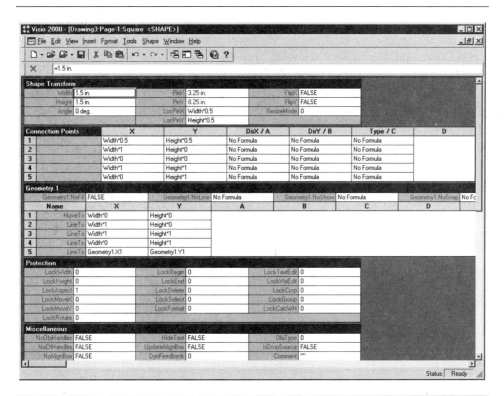

FIGURE 11-16 ShapeSheet for a square

ShapeSheets are made up of tables that describe the shape. For example, the ShapeSheet for a square, shown in Figure 11-16, starts with a Shape Transform table, listing the width and height of the square as well as its current location and the degrees it's been rotated. Then there is a Connection Points table listing all the connection points set for the square, and so on until the end of the ShapeSheet. There is a total of 15 tables on the ShapeSheet describing a basic square. ShapeSheets for more complicated shapes have many more tables.

Inside the cells of some of the tables in a ShapeSheet are formulas. It's often more accurate to describe the movement and relationship of a shape with formulas rather than simply with numbers or text. The formulas are what makes a Visio 2000's shapes "smart," because formulas can handle complex motions and changes and still keep the shape looking the way you expect. ShapeSheet information can be viewed as current values instead of the formula by choosing View | Values.

ShapeSheets are a very advanced topic for most Visio 2000 users. If you need more information about Visio 2000 ShapeSheets, you should install and read the developer's documentation that comes with Visio 2000.

 To close a ShapeSheet, click on the Close button in the upper-right corner of the ShapeSheet window.

Defining Custom Properties

Custom properties are information you can add to a shape that doesn't show on the page but can be exported or used as a selection criteria. In Chapter 8, "Organizing Your Business with Visio 2000," custom property data was added to indicate ownership of different pieces of office furniture.

Some shapes come with custom properties already included; for example, the furniture shapes on the Office Layout Shapes stencil come with an option to include the inventory number and owner. Most shapes in Visio 2000 don't include custom properties by default. However, you can add a custom property to any shape.

Defining custom properties allows you a way to add data to your shape—data that you can use both with Visio 2000 and with other programs when you export the data from the drawing page. Defining custom properties for a shape adds custom property fields that can have data entered later.

To define custom properties for a shape, select the shape and choose Shape | Custom Properties. If a shape already has a custom property defined, the Custom Properties dialog box opens. In the Custom Properties dialog box, click Define to open the Define Custom Properties dialog box, which is shown in Figure 11-17. If a shape doesn't already have a custom property defined, Visio 2000 displays a message telling you the shape has no custom properties and asking if you would like to define some. Choose Yes, and the Define Custom Properties dialog box appears, as shown in Figure 11-17.

Use the Define Custom Properties dialog box to add custom property fields to a shape. There are five pieces of information you need to supply to create a custom property field:

Label Type the name for the custom property into Label. This name appears on the Custom Properties window for the shape. Every custom property for the same shape must have different labels.

Type Use the drop-down list to select the Type. Type sets the kind of information that will be entered into the custom property field. There are eight types of data Visio 2000 can accept: String (plain text), Number, Fixed List (a list of values you define), Variable List (a list you define or for user-entered information), Boolean (either TRUE or FALSE), Currency (displayed using the Regional Settings), Date (includes seconds, minutes, hours, and days), and Duration (elapsed time).

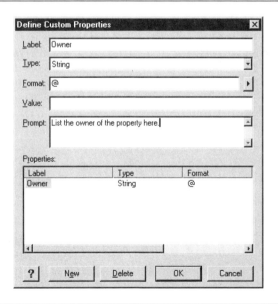

FIGURE 11-17   Define Custom Properties dialog box

Format   Depending on the choice you make in the Type field, Format could be very different. For some Type values, the arrow on the side of the Format field allows you to select a standard format for the added custom property. For the list of values in the Type field, you'll need to include a list in the Format field, a list that becomes the drop-down selection list for the user. For the Boolean Type, the Format field is disabled. For all other Type values choose a Format type from the list.

Value   Enter the starting data into the Value field. The data in the Value field will be over-written by any data entered by the user, even if the Value is protected.

Prompt   Enter the text that you want to display at the bottom of the Custom Properties dialog box when someone adds data to the field.

Use the Properties area of the dialog box to select and edit any of the custom properties already set for a shape. Click the New button to add a new custom property. Click the Delete button to remove the selected custom property from the Properties list.

 If you're in Developer Mode, there will be several more fields to complete on the Define Custom Properties dialog box.

After you've finished adding custom properties to a shape, click OK. If you want to use the custom properties of this shape again when you pull it from the stencil, you need to save the shape as a master shape. To save a shape as a master shape, drag it to a stencil that's set to be edited, and then save the stencil.

Creating Network Diagrams

The Basic Network template is the most advanced template that comes with Visio 2000 Standard Edition. There are several extended networking solutions in other editions of Visio 2000, but this section covers only the Basic Network template in Visio 2000 Standard Edition.

Use the Basic Network template to:

■ Assemble a graphical representation of your network.

■ Track hardware properties, including serial number, location, manufacturer, and description.

- Sort equipment by manufacturers or type.

- Create a networking plan to include in a presentation document.

- Export hardware information from your diagram to a database.

> **TIP** *Before you use the Basic Network template make sure you have a good grasp on the general use of Visio 2000.*

The Basic Network template includes many added features. There are five stencils with more than a hundred shapes, five layers added by default, and most shapes have an extensive list of custom properties already added. Figure 11-18 shows the main Visio 2000 window with the Basic Network template open.

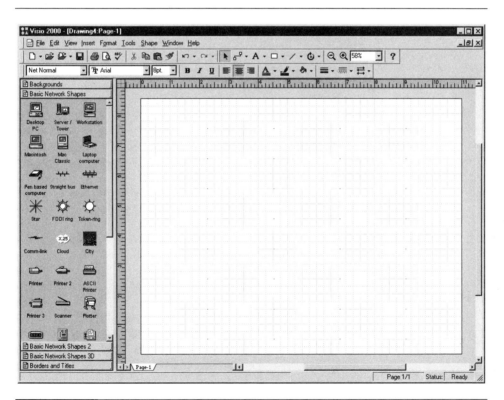

FIGURE 11-18 The Basic Network template

The four basic steps for creating a network diagram are:

1. Create a list of all networking hardware you want to diagram, including owner, manufacturer, product ID, and location.

2. Drag a network ring or network backbone to the drawing page.

3. Add hardware to the ring or backbone by using the extra control handles.

 You can add only eight shapes to a ring.

4. Add custom property information to each piece of hardware on the ring.

After you've added the custom property information, save your diagram. Then you're ready to use it for any purpose you like, including generating reports, adding it to presentations, or even using it to view your network based on hardware type.

To generate a report with your diagram, use the Property Reporting Wizard.

To link your diagram to a database, use the Database Wizard (choose Tools | Macros | Database Wizard). Then use the Database Export, Refresh, Settings, and Update macros to keep the diagram and database working together.

As you work with your network diagram, you may need shapes off stencils that aren't on the network template. Feel free to open any stencils that might help you complete the diagram. For example, the Off Page Reference shape on the Basic Flowchart Shapes template has the option to keep text synchronized across pages, a useful tool when a networking diagram spans several pages.

NOTE *For complete network diagramming solutions, use Visio 2000 Professional Edition.*

Comparing Organization Charts

Visio 2000 includes a wizard to help you compare different organization charts and get a report on the differences. This is a feature of the Organization Chart template, and you need to have the template open to use it.

Launch the Compare Organization Data function by selecting it from the Organization Chart menu. The Compare Organization Data window appears, as shown here:

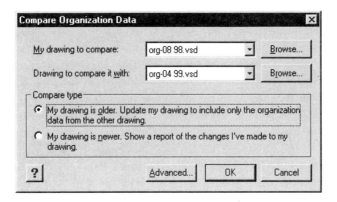

The Compare Organization Data window has fields for two files, your file and the file you wish to compare it to. Browse until you find both files. When both files are listed, indicate which file is older by choosing one of the options in the Compare Type box.

If you want to compare just a few values for the two diagrams, click the Advanced button, which opens the Compare Data Values window, shown here:

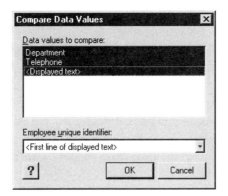

The Compare Data Values window allows you to choose what criteria to compare as well as what the unique identifier is for each employee. After you've finished setting the advanced data, click OK in the Compare Data Values window, and then click OK in the Compare Organization Data window.

Visio 2000 compares the two documents and then generates a report based on the differences. The report is displayed in the Comparison Report window, as shown in Figure 11-19. The Comparison Report window has at least two tabs with two different reports. Each report itemizes the changes based on either the employee or the position. Each difference between the diagrams is noted on both reports. The By Person tab lists

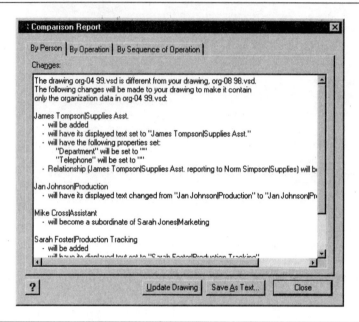

FIGURE 11-19   Comparison Report window

the changes under the name of each employee. The By Operation tab lists the changes in one bulleted list, focusing on the changes in relationships and operations.

Both reports can be saved as text files by using the Save As Text button at the bottom of the window. When you click the Save As Text button, Visio 2000 prompts you for a save location and filename.

If your drawing was older than the one you compared it to, the Comparison Report has another tab, the By Sequence of Operation tab, which outlines the changes that will be made if you choose to update the chart. This also enables the Update Drawing button.

If you choose to update your diagram by clicking the Update Drawing button, only the text of your chart changes, not the relationships and connections between the shapes. Repositioning of shapes and connectors must be done by hand. Also, any employees who aren't included in the newer diagram are removed. If you wish to update your diagram to the newer diagram data, click the Update Drawing button.

Summary

In this chapter, you learned how to create your own shapes both by modifying existing shapes and by creating new shapes from scratch. You also learned how to define custom shape properties, how to create networking diagrams, and the process for comparing organization charts. You are encouraged to use Visio 2000's online help to further explore these topics.

11

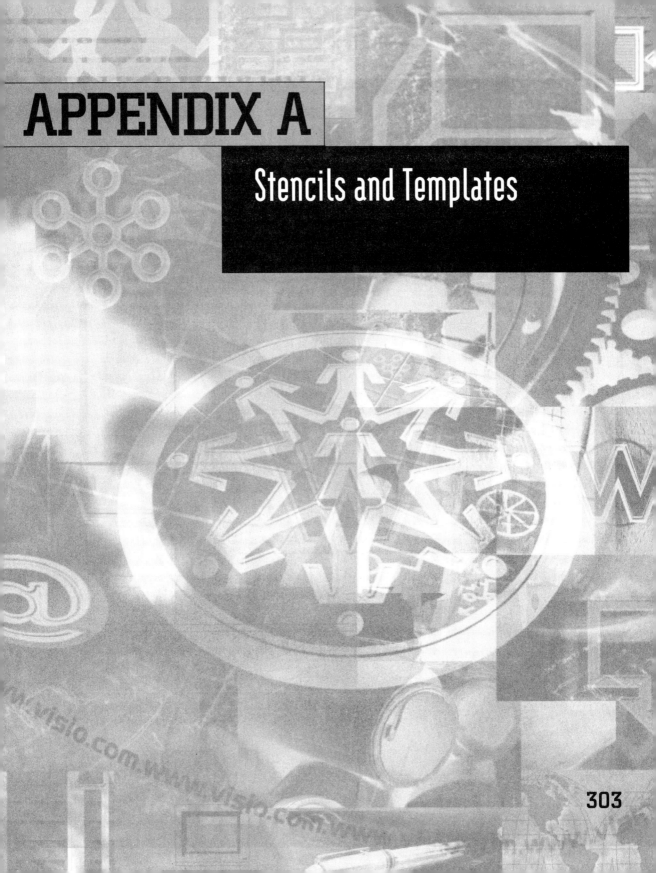

APPENDIX A

Stencils and Templates

This appendix lists all the templates and stencils that come with Visio 2000 Standard Edition, as well as all the shapes that come with each stencil.

Templates

Table A-1 lists all the templates that come with the U.S. version of Visio 2000 Standard Edition.

Template	Stencils Included	Color Schemes? (Yes/No)
_Stencil Report Template.vst	None	No
Audit Diagram.vst	Audit Diagram Shapes.vss	Yes
	Borders and Titles.vss	Yes
	Backgrounds.vss	Yes
Basic Diagram.vst	Basic Shapes.vss	Yes
	Borders and Titles.vss	Yes
	Backgrounds.vss	Yes
Basic Flowchart.vst	Basic Flowchart Shapes.vss	Yes
	Borders and Titles.vss	Yes
	Backgrounds.vss	Yes
Basic Network.vst	Basic Network Shapes 2.vss	Yes
	Basic Network Shapes 3D.vss	No
	Basic Network Shapes.vss	Yes
	Borders and Titles.vss	Yes
	Backgrounds.vss	Yes
Blank Drawing.vst	None	Yes
Block Diagram with Perspective.vst	Blocks with Perspective.vss	Yes

TABLE A-1   Visio 2000 Standard Edition Templates

Template	Stencils Included	Color Schemes? (Yes/No)
Block Diagram.vst	Blocks Raised.vss	Yes
	Blocks.vss	Yes
	Borders and Titles.vss	Yes
	Backgrounds.vss	Yes
Calendar.vst	Calendar Shapes.vss	Yes
Cause and Effect Diagram.vst	Cause and Effect Diagram Shapes.vss	Yes
	Borders and Titles.vss	Yes
	Backgrounds.vss	Yes
Charts and Graphs.vst	Charting Shapes.vss	Yes
	Marketing Clipart.vss	Yes
	Borders and Titles.vss	Yes
	Backgrounds.vss	Yes
Cross-Functional Flowchart.vst	Cross-Functional Flowchart Shapes Vertical.vss	Yes
	Cross-Functional Flowchart Shapes Horizontal.vss	Yes
	Basic Flowchart Shapes.vss	Yes
Data Flow Diagram.vst	Data Flow Diagram Shapes.vss	Yes
	Borders and Titles.vss	Yes
	Backgrounds.vss	Yes
Directional Map.vst	Landmark Shapes.vss	No
	Metro Shapes.vss	No
	Recreation Shapes.vss	No
	Road Shapes.vss	No
	Transportation Shapes.vss	No

A

TABLE A-1   Visio 2000 Standard Edition Templates *(continued)*

Template	Stencils Included	Color Schemes? (Yes/No)
Form Design.vst	Forms Shapes.vss	Yes
Gantt Chart.vst	Gantt Chart Shapes.vss	Yes
	Borders and Titles.vss	Yes
	Backgrounds.vss	Yes
Geographic Maps.vst	Africa.vss	Yes
	Asia.vss	Yes
	Europe.vss	Yes
	North and South America.vss	Yes
	Mid-East.vss	Yes
	US Canada and Mexico.vss	Yes
	World.vss	Yes
IDEF0 Diagram.vst	IDEF0 Diagram Shapes.vss	Yes
Marketing Charts and Diagrams.vst	Marketing Clipart.vss	Yes
	Marketing Diagrams.vss	Yes
	Charting Shapes.vss	Yes
	Borders and Titles.vss	Yes
	Backgrounds.vss	Yes
Mind Mapping Diagram.vst	Mind Mapping Diagram Shapes.vss	Yes
	Borders and Titles.vss	Yes
	Backgrounds.vss	Yes
Office Layout.vst	Office Layout Shapes.vss	No
Organization Chart.vst	Organization Chart Shapes.vss	Yes
	Borders and Titles.vss	Yes
	Backgrounds.vss	Yes

TABLE A-1   Visio 2000 Standard Edition Templates *(continued)*

Template	Stencils Included	Color Schemes? (Yes/No)
Organization Chart Wizard.vst	Organization Chart Shapes.vss	Yes
	Borders and Titles.vss	Yes
	Backgrounds.vss	Yes
PERT Chart.vst	PERT Chart Shapes.vss	Yes
	Borders and Titles.vss	Yes
	Backgrounds.vss	Yes
SDL Diagram.vst	SDL Diagram Shapes.vss	Yes
	Borders and Titles.vss	Yes
	Backgrounds.vss	Yes
Stencil Report Wizard.vst	None	No
Timeline.vst	Timeline Shapes.vss	Yes
	Borders and Titles.vss	Yes
	Backgrounds.vss	Yes
TQM Diagram.vst	TQM Diagram Shapes.vss	Yes
	Borders and Titles.vss	Yes
	Backgrounds.vss	Yes
Work Flow Diagram.vst	Work Flow Diagram Shapes.vss	Yes
	Borders and Titles.vss	Yes
	Backgrounds.vss	Yes
None	Callouts.vss	Yes
	Clipart.vss	No
	Connectors.vss	Yes
	Flags.vss	No
	Symbols.vss	No
	Embellishments.vss	Yes
	Miscellaneous Flowchart Shapes.vss	Yes

A

TABLE A-1   Visio 2000 Standard Edition Templates *(continued)*

Stencils

Table A-2 lists all the stencils that come with the U.S. version of Visio 2000 Standard Edition:

Name	Shapes
Africa.vss	Algeria, Angola, Benin, Botswana, Burkina Faso, Burundi, Cameroon, Central African Republic, Chad, Congo, Djibouti, Egypt, Eritrea, Ethiopia, Gabon, Gambia, Ghana, Guinea, Guinea-Bissau, Ivory Coast, Kenya, Lesotho, Liberia, Libya, Madagascar, Malawi, Mali, Mauritania, Morocco, Mozambique, Namibia, Niger, Nigeria, Rwanda, Senegal, Sierra Leone, Somalia, South Africa, Sudan, Swaziland, Tanzania, United Republic of, Togo, Tunisia, Uganda, Western Sahara, Zaire, Zambia, Zimbabwe, Lake Albert, Lake Chad, Lake Nyasa, Lake Tana, Lake Tanganyika, Lake Turkana, Lake Victoria, Benue, Blue Nile, Chire, Congo R, Lualaba, Lukaga, Niger R, Nile, Orange, Ubangi, White Nile, Zambezi
Asia.vss	Afghanistan, Armenia, Australia, Azerbaijan, Bangladesh, Bhutan, Brunei, Cambodia, China, Georgia.277, India, Indonesia, Japan, Kazakhstan, Kyrgyzstan, Laos, Malaysia, Mongolia, Myanmar, Nepal, New Zealand, North Korea, Pakistan, Papua New Guinea, Philippines, Russia.293, Sri Lanka, South Korea, Taiwan, Tajikistan, Thailand, Turkmenistan, Uzbekistan, Vietnam, Aral Sea, Caspian Sea, Issyk Kul, Koko Nor, Lake Baikal, Lake Balkhash, Lake Urmia, Aldan, Amu Darya, Amur, Angara, Brahmaputra, Darling, Ganges, Huang He, Irtysh, Indus, Irrawaddy, Kama, Kolyma, Lena, Mekong, Murray, Pechora, Ob, Salween, Syr Darya, Tobol, Ural, Vilyuy, Volga, Xi Jiang, Yangtze, Yenisey
Audit Diagram Shapes.vss	I/O, Manual operation, Terminator, Manual file, Display, On-page reference, Off-page reference, Divided process, Multi proc/doc, Lined/Shaded process, Lined document, Multi document, Database, Disk storage, Diskette 1, Diskette 2, Magnetic tape, Data transmission, Manual input, Check 1 (audit), Compare 1, Reference point, Check 2 (audit), Compare 2, Event, Divided event, Title block, Note block, Dynamic connector.101, Line-curve connector.102

TABLE A-2   Visio 2000 Standard Edition Stencils and Shapes

Name	Shapes
Backgrounds.vss	Background steel, Background high-tech, Background stripes, Background web, Background rain, Background leaf, Background orbit, Background horizon, Background world, Background compass, Background clouds, Background city, Background mountains, Background none, Background geometric, Background cosmic, Background expedition, Background tranquil
Basic Flowchart Shapes.vss	Process, Decision, Document, Data, Predefined process, Stored data, Internal storage, Sequential data, Direct data, Manual input.112, Card, Paper tape, Display.115, Manual operation.116, Preparation, Parallel mode, Loop limit, Terminator.120, On-page reference.121, Off-page reference.122, Flowchart shapes, Auto-height box.124, Dynamic connector.126, Line-curve connector.127, Control transfer, Annotation
Basic Network Shapes.vss	Desktop PC, Server / Tower, Workstation.82, Macintosh, Mac Classic, Laptop computer, Pen based computer, Straight bus, Ethernet, Star, FDDI ring, Token-ring, Comm-link.92, Cloud, City.94, Printer.95, Printer 2, ASCII Printer, Printer 3, Scanner.99, Plotter.100, Modem.101, Telephone.102, Fax.103, Bridge.104, MUX / DEMUX, Hub, Floppy drive, Tape drive, Optical drive, Removable storage, Database, Tower box, Monitor, Keyboard.114, Mouse.115, Dynamic connector, Line connector, Line-curve connector
Basic Network Shapes 2.vss	Minicomputer, Processor, Disk array, VAX, Micro VAX, Cray, IBM AS/400, IBM 3174, IBM 37XX, IBM 3262 printer, IBM PS/2, IBM 5294 controller, Repeater.50, Router.51, Comm. hub, Link builder, Terminal server.54, LocalTalk, Oscilloscope, Rack mount, Digitizing pad, Radio tower, Satellite dish.60, Satellite.61, Fiber optic xmitter, 10BASE-T wall plate, Custom equipment, Public switch, PBX / PABX, Punchdown block, Acoustic coupler, Tape, Answering machine, A-B switchbox, Cable, Power strip, Television, Screen, CRT projector, Video, Long card, Short card
Basic Network Shapes 3D.vss	Personal computer, Server, Workstation, Laptop, Mini computer, Mainframe, Printer, Ring network, Bus network, Bottom to top angled, Side to side angled, WAN, Comm-link, Hub / switch, Multiplexer, Router, Bridge, Terminal server, Repeater, PBX / comm. hub, Modem, Telephone, Fax, Comm. tower, Satellite dish, Satellite, City, Town, Keyboard, Mouse, Scanner, Card, Room, PDA, Plotter, Firewall, Color box

A

TABLE A-2   Visio 2000 Standard Edition Stencils and Shapes *(continued)*

Name	Shapes
Basic Shapes.vss	Triangle, Square, Pentagon, Hexagon, Heptagon, Octagon, Star 5, Star 6, Star 7, Center drag circle, Circle, Ellipse, Right triangle, Cross, Rectangle, Shadowed box, 3-D box, Rounded rectangle, Rounded square, 45 degree single, 60 degree single, Fancy arrow, 45 degree double, 60 degree double, 45 degree tail, 60 degree tail, Flexi-arrow 1, Flexi-arrow 2, Flexi-arrow 3, Flexi-arrow 3.30, Dynamic connector, Line-curve connector
Blocks.vss	Auto-height box, Auto-size box, Curved arrow, 1-D single, 2-D single, 2-D double, 1-D single, open, 2-D single, open, 1-D double, 3-D box, Open/closed bar, Arrow box, Button, Concentric layer 1, Concentric layer 2, Concentric layer 3, Concentric center, Partial layer 1, Partial layer 2, Partial layer 3, Partial layer 4, Double tree sloped, Double tree square, Dynamic connector, Multi-tree sloped, Multi-tree square, Line-curve connector, Dotted line, Mid-arrow, Arced arrow, Dot & arrow, Mid-arrow dotted, Single arrowhead, Double arrowhead
Blocks Raised.vss	Up arrow, Right arrow, Up / down arrow, Left arrow, Down arrow, Left / right arrow, Up arrow, open, Right arrow, open, Horizontal bar, Left arrow, open, Down arrow, open, Vertical bar, Elbow 1, Elbow 2, Square block, Elbow 3, Elbow 4, Frame, Circle
Blocks with Perspective.vss	Hole, Shallow block, Block, Arrow, down, Arrow, right, Left / right arrow.25, Arrow, left, Arrow, up, Up / down arrow.28, Elbow 1.29, Elbow 2.30, 1-D Left / right arrow, Elbow 3.32, Elbow 4.33, 1-D Up / down arrow, Wireframe block 1, Wireframe block 2, Circle.37, Vanishing point
Borders and Titles.vss	Border graduated, Border classic, Border classic, Border contemp., Border binder, Border binder, Border elegant, Border elegant, Border retro, Border neon, Border triangles, Border graphic 1, Border graphic 2, Border modern 1, Border modern 2, Border technical 1, Border technical 2, Border small, Title block deco, Title block compass, Title block bold, Title block jagged, Title block contemp., Title block contemp., Title block retro, Title block retro, Title block elegant, Title block elegant, Title block notepad, Title block notepad, Title block classic, Title block classic, Title block corporate 1, Title block corporate 2, Title block horizon, Title block sphere, Title block sphere, Title block geometric, Note box classic, Note box contemp., Note box triangles, Note box deco, Note box neon, Note box file, Hyperlink button, Hyperlink circle 1, Hyperlink circle 2

TABLE A-2   Visio 2000 Standard Edition Stencils and Shapes *(continued)*

Name	Shapes
Calendar Shapes.vss	Large month, Date frame, Small date frame, Small month, Arrow, Timeline, Star label, Circle label, Square label, Moon phases, Yearly calendar
Callouts.vss	Side box callout, Side line callout, Side text callout, Mid box callout, Mid line callout, Mid text callout, Side elbow box, Side line elbow, Side elbow callout, Mid elbow box, Mid line elbow, Mid elbow callout, Annotation, Center text callout, Bend callout, Braces with text, Oval callout, Box callout, Line with text, Partial bracket text, Full bracket text, Side bracket, Side brace, Side parenthesis, File, Yellow note, Tag, 2-D word balloon, Balloon horizontal, Balloon vertical, Button, Angled stamp, Rounded stamp, Window, Blunt starburst, Sharp starburst, Automatic dimension
Cause and Effect Diagram Shapes.vss	Effect, Category 1, Category 2, Fish frame, Primary cause 1, Primary cause 2, Secondary cause 1, Secondary cause 2, Secondary cause 3, Secondary cause 4, Secondary cause 5, Secondary cause 6
Charting Shapes.vss	Bar graph 1, Bar graph 2, 3-D bar graph, 3-D axis, Vertical text 3-D bar, Horizontal text 3-D bar, Pie chart, Pie slice, Special pie slice, Divided bar 1, Divided bar 2, Process chart, Deployment chart, Feature comparison, Feature on/off, Row header, Column header, Grid, Yes/No box, Normal curve, Exponential curve, Line graph, Graph line, Data point, X-Y axis, X-Y-Z axis, Graph scale, X-axis label, Y-axis label, Z-axis label, X axis, Y axis, Z axis, Text block 8pt.288, Text block 10pt, Text block 12pt, 2-D word balloon, 1-D word balloon, Horizontal callout, Annotation
Clipart.vss	Business woman, Man walking, Meeting, Woman with telephone, Presentation, Handshake, Man running, Man with chart, Man with folder, Audience, Politician, Large Macintosh, Small Macintosh, IBM PS/2, Dumb terminal, Workstation, IBM PC AT, Tower, Detailed IBM PS/2, Laptop computer, LaserJet printer, LaserWriter, Dot matrix printer, Facsimile machine, Flatbed scanner, Button.63, CD, Disk, Video cassette, Business telephone, Telephone, 3.5" disk, 5.25" disk, Compact car, City bus, Car pool, Jet, Cruise ship, Luggage, Train symbol, Taxi symbol, Globe 1, Government, Open briefcase, Diamond label, Award circle, Aztec label, Blue ribbon, 1st place, Gold star, Recycle symbol, Coffee cup, Magnifying glass, Target, Clipboard, Notes, Scroll, Date book, Copyright, File cabinet, Alarm clock, Cheers, Globe 2, The big day, Charts and Graphs, Page layout, Chess pieces, Newspaper, Time flies, Paper airplane, Vacationer, Cutting costs, Royal Chair, Tornado, Cards, Brainstorm, Money tree, Celebrate, Surprise, Dance 1, Dance 2, Dynamic globe, Man in the moon, Trophy

A

TABLE A-2   Visio 2000 Standard Edition Stencils and Shapes *(continued)*

Name	Shapes
Connectors.vss	Dynamic connector, Side to side 1, Side to side 2, Sides, Bottom to top 1, Bottom to top 2, Tops or bottoms, Side to side fixed 1, Side to side fixed 2, Top/bottom to side, Bottom to top fixed 1, Bottom to top fixed 2, Side to top/bottom, Bottom to side 1, Bottom to side 2, Bottom to side 3, Side to top, Square loop, Universal connector, Layout connector, Line-arc connector, Line-curve connector, Line connector, Wavy connector 1, Wavy connector 2, Double tree square, Multi-tree square, Double tree sloped, Multi-tree sloped, Curve connect 1, Curve connect 2, Curve connect 3, Directed line 1, Directed line 2, One too many, Angled connector, Flow director 1, Flow director 2, Control transfer, Jumper, Flexi-arrow, 1-D single, 1-D double, 1-D open end, Elbow bus 1, Elbow bus 2, Hollow connect 1, Hollow connect 2, Hollow connect 3, Dotted line, Mid-arrow, Arced arrow, Dot & arrow, Mid-arrow dotted, Single arrowhead, Double arrowhead, Side - side, Side - top/bottom, Bottom - top, Top/bottom - side, 2 lines, 2-line elbow, 4 lines, 4-line elbow, Comm-link 1, Comm-link 2, Bus, Ethernet, Star
Cross-Functional Flowchart Shapes.vss	Separator, Horizontal holder, Functional band
Data Flow Diagram Shapes.vss	Data process, Center to center 1, Center to center 2, Multiple process, Loop on center, Loop on center 2, State, Start state, Stop state, Multi state, External interactor, Stop state 2, Data store, Entity relationship, Object callout, Entity 1, Entity 2, Object, Oval process, Oval process (offset)
Embellishments.vss	Wave section, Wave corner, Braid section, Braid corner, Braid end-cap, Egyptian section, Egyptian corner, Egyptian end-cap, Greek section, Greek corner, Greek border, Cross section, Cross corner, Cross end-cap, Wave section 2, Wave corner 2, Wave corner 3, Roman section, Star section, Triangle section, Chiseled frame, Square frame, Photo frame, Art deco frame, Jewel frame, Classic frame, Fun frame, Art deco circle, Art deco tile, Wave tile, Weave tile, Zigzag tile, Op-art tile, Diamond tile, Graphic tile, Celtic ornament, Button ornament, Arc ornament, Checker section, Single line frame, Multi line frame

TABLE A-2   Visio 2000 Standard Edition Stencils and Shapes *(continued)*

Name	Shapes
Europe.vss	Albania, Austria, Belgium, Bosnia and Herzegovina, Bulgaria, Belarus, Croatia, Cyprus, Czech Republic, Denmark, Estonia, Finland, France, Germany, Greece, Iceland, Ireland, Italy, Hungary, Latvia, Lithuania, Luxembourg, Macedonia, Moldova, Montenegro, Netherlands, Norway, Poland, Portugal, Romania, Russia, Serbia, Slovakia, Slovenia, Spain, Sweden, Switzerland, Turkey.255, Ukraine, United Kingdom, Lake Ladoga, Lake Onega, Lake Vanern, Danube, Dnieper, Don, Gota Alv, Neva, Rhine, Suir
Flags.vss	Albania, Andorra, Argentina, Australia, Austria, Belgium, Bosnia - Herzegovina, Brazil, Bulgaria, Canada, Chile, China, Croatia, Czech Republic, Denmark, Estonia, European Council, Finland, France, Germany, Greece, Greenland, Hong Kong, Hungary, Iceland, India, Indonesia, Ireland, Israel, Italy, Japan, Latvia, Luxembourg, Macedonia, Malaysia, Mexico, Monaco, Netherlands, New Zealand, Norway, Pakistan, Poland, Portugal, Puerto Rico, Qatar, Romania, Russia, Singapore, Slovakia, South Africa, South Korea, Spain, Sweden, Switzerland, Taiwan, Thailand, Turkey, Ukraine, United Arab Emirates, United Kingdom, United States, Vietnam, Yemen, Yugoslavia (Serbia - Montenegro)
Forms Shapes.vss	Info box, Shaded box, Reversed text, Info line, Info line 2, Arrow, Data boxes, 1/16" Border, 1/8" Border, Check box, Single line, Double line, 5-Column, 10-Column, Triple line, 10-Log lines, Grid.311, Horizontal callout.312, Right-angle horizontal, 8pt Arial text block, 10pt Arial text block, 18pt Arial text block, FAX cover, Business card, Logo placeholder, Title, Creator / company, Date / time / page, Filename, Drawing Scale
Gantt Chart Shapes.vss	Gantt Chart frame, Non working time, Column, Row, Task bar, Milestone, Link lines, Title, Legend, Text block 8pt, Text block 10pt, Text block 12pt, Horizontal callout, Right-angle horizontal, Sec scale cell, Text Entry, Row
IDEF0 Diagram Shapes.vss	Activity box, Label, Title block, Text block 8pt, Node, Solid connector, 1 legged connector, IDEF0 connector, Dynamic connector
Landmark Shapes.vss	Building 1, Building 2, Condos, Outdoor mall, Gas station, Airport, Train station, Ferry, River, Lake, Ocean, Scale, Direction, North, Text block 8pt, Text block 10pt, Text block 18pt, Callout, Tree, Cathedral, Skyscraper, Church, Factory, Warehouse, Hospital, Barn, Park, Fire department, School, Motel, Stadium, Convenience store

A

TABLE A-2   Visio 2000 Standard Edition Stencils and Shapes *(continued)*

Name	Shapes
Marketing Clipart.vss	Target, Dart / Pushpin, Thermometer, Globe, Check box, Check / Cross, Stretchable dollars, Stretchable pounds, Sign post, Extend-o hand, People, Scales, Pencil, Growing flower, Oil well, Variable stack, Variable smoke, Variable building, Umbrella, Stack of papers, Cylinder, Cash cow, Dog, Money bag, Star, Question mark, Financial institution, Factory, Wholesaler, Person, Retailer, Consumer, Building block, Rocket, Crystal ball, Sunglasses, Empty box, Full box, Tombstone, Airplane, Train, Train car, Truck, Truck 2, Ship, House, House 2, Wooden barrel, Shopping cart, Shopping cart 2, Oil barrel, Coin, VISA, American Express, MasterCard, Access, Diners Club, Delta, Switch, Eurocard, U.S. dollar, Yen, Pound, Euro, Barbells, Television set, Yin Yang, Puzzle corner, Puzzle side, Puzzle middle 1, Puzzle middle 2, Puzzle middle 3, "NO" sign, Warning sign, Stop sign, Diamond label, Award circle, Aztec label, 1st place, Clipboard, Tree, Copyright
Metro Shapes.vss	Metro line, Rounded metro, Metro curve 1, Metro curve 2, Flexible metro, Station, Transfer station, Stop callout
Mid-East.vss	Israel, Iran, Iraq, Jordan, Kuwait, Lebanon, Oman, Qatar, Saudi Arabia, Syria, Turkey, United Arab Emirates, Yemen, Euphrates, Firat, Murat, Shatt al Arab, Tigris
Mind Mapping Diagram Shapes.vss	Outer branch, First tier line, Second tier line, Third tier line, Fourth tier line, Arrow1, Arrow2, Wavy, Curve, Curvy arrow, Ordering theme, Growing bubble, Big cloud, Small cloud, Question mark, Exclamation, Rounded stamp, Exclamation point, Dollar sign, Stop, Pencil, Bulb, Smiling face, Frowning face, Sun1, Sun2, Star, Lightning, Storm, Coins, Scales, Hourglass, Clock, Food, Drink, City, Factory, Tree, House, Planet, Cross, Apple, Raindrop, Rainbow, Brain, Heart, Moon, Cube, Knight, Auto-size box
Miscellaneous Flowchart Shapes.vss	External entity 2, Transmittal tape, Divided process 2, Rounded process, Create request, Bordered rectangle, Framed rectangle, Open rectangle, Delay, Summing junction, Drum storage, Or, Collate, Extract, Off-line storage, Merge, Sort 2, Deck of cards, File of cards, Microform, Microform recording, Microform processing, Duplicating, Tagged process, Lined/Shaded process, Tagged document, Lined document, Variable start, Variable procedure, Sort, Data store.113, Database, Primitive from call control, Primitive to call control, Message from user, Message to user, Output, Feedback, Check, Check 2, And gate, Or gate, Refinement, Branch: return, XOR (Exclusive Or), Branch: no return, Vertical XOR, Interrupt, Vertical P And, External control, Ellipsis, Dynamic connector.134, Line-curve connector

TABLE A-2   Visio 2000 Standard Edition Stencils and Shapes (*continued*)

Name	Shapes
North and South America.vss	Argentina, Belize, Bolivia, Brazil, Canada, Chile, Colombia, Costa Rica, Cuba, Dominican Republic, Ecuador, El Salvador, French Guiana, Greenland, Guatemala, Guyana, Haiti, Honduras, Jamaica, Mexico.115, Nicaragua, Panama, Paraguay, Peru, Puerto Rico, Suriname, Trinidad, United States, Uruguay, Venezuela, Cedar Lake, Great Bear Lake, Great Lakes, Great Salt Lake, Great Slave Lake, Lake Athabasca, Lake Erie, Lake Manitoba, Lake Nicaragua, Lake Nipigon, Lake Ontario, Lake Titicaca, Lake Winnipeg, Lake Winnipegosis, Nettilling Lake, Reindeer Lake, Araguaia, Arkansas, Amazon, Colorado, Columbia, Dauphin, Great Bear, Guapore, Japura, Koukdjuak, Mackenzie, Madeira, Madre de Dios, Magdalena, Mississippi, Missouri, Nelson, Niagara, Nipigon, Ohio, Orinoco, Parana, Paraguay R, Rio Paranaiba, Peace, Purus, Putamayo, Rio Branco, Rio Grande, North America, Rio Grande, South America, Rio Maranon, Rio Juruena, Rio Negro, Rio Teles Pires, San Francisco, San Juan, Saskatchewan, Slave, Snake, St. Clair, St. Lawrence, Tapajos, Tocantins, Ucayali, Waterhen, Xingu, Yukon
Office Layout Shapes.vss	"T" Room, "L" Room, Room, "T" Space, "L" Space, Space, Table, Conference table, Circular table, Desk chair, Sofa, Chair, Desk, Printer, PC, File, Suspended lateral file, Lateral file, Bookshelf, Plant, Corner surface, Panel, Panel post, 1-post panel, 2-post panel, Corner panel, Curved panel, Work surface, Telephone jack, Switch, 110 volt outlet, Callout, Dimension line, Wall
Organization Chart Shapes.vss	Executive, Manager, Position, Consultant, Vacancy, Assistant, Team frame, MultiStaff, Staff, Title/Date, Title, Dynamic connector
Pert Chart Shapes.vss	PERT 1, PERT 2, Legend, Line connector, Line-curve connector, Dynamic connector, Summarization structure, Horizontal callout, Right-angle horizontal
Recreation Shapes.vss	Restroom, Potable water, Campground, SCUBA diving, Skating, RV, Marina, Snowmobile, Parking, Swimming, Supplies/store, Campfire, Shower, Canoe access, Golf, Fishing, Downhill skiing, Horseback riding, Amphitheater, Boat launch, Cross-country skiing, Hiking, Climbing, Kayaking, Snowboarding, Tennis, Volleyball, Racquetball/handball
Road Shapes.vss	Curve 1, Curve 2, Corner, 3-way, 4-way, Roundabout, Cloverleaf interchange, Diamond interchange, Flexible road, Roadway break, Thin road, Railroad, Rail curve, Interstate, State route, U.S. Route, Canadian highway

A

TABLE A-2   Visio 2000 Standard Edition Stencils and Shapes *(continued)*

Name	Shapes
SDL Diagram Shapes.vss	Start, Variable start, Procedure, Variable procedure, Create request, Alternative, Return, Decision 1, Message from user, Primitive from call control, Decision 2, Message to user, Primitive to call control, Save, Off-page reference, On-page reference, Multi document, Document, Disk storage, Divided process, Divided event, Terminator, Line-curve connector
Symbols.vss	Yen, Pound, U.S. dollar, Euro, Zone, "NO" sign, No smoking, Warning sign, Men, Women, Handicap, Coffee, Dining, Drinks, Fragile, Telephone, Bicycle, Airport, Rail transportation, Bus station, Lodging, Post, Park, Service station, Information, Radioactive, Biohazard, First aid, Square box, Sunny, Partly cloudy, Rain, Lightning, Storm, Recycle 1, Recycle 2
Timeline Shapes.vss	Divided timeline, Cylindrical timeline, Chiseled timeline, Diamond milestone, Circle milestone, X milestone, Triangle milestone, 2 triangle milestone, Dagger milestone, Line milestone, Cylindrical milestone, Block interval, Bracket interval, Square bracket, Cylindrical interval, Chiseled interval, Today marker, Elapsed time, Block timeline, 1-D timeline, Ruler timeline
TQM Diagram Shapes.vss	Transportation, Inbound goods, Storage, Procedure, Operation, Operation / inspection, Issue, Organization function, 2-part function, Decision 1 (TQM), Decision 2 (TQM), Multi in/out decision, External organization, External process, Inspection/ measurement, Metric, 2-part metric, System database, System support, System function, Delay, On-page reference, Off-page reference, Connected issues, Fabrication, Move, Store, Inspection, Selectable process, Work flow loop 1, Work flow loop 2, Feedback arrow, X-function - vert, X-function - horiz, Force-field analysis, Cause 1, Cause 2, Cause 3, Category, Effect, Fish frame, Dynamic connector, Line connector, Line-curve connector, Result, No result, Branch: return, Branch: no return, Interrupt, External control, Refinement, Text block 8pt
Transportation Shapes.vss	Stop light, Stop, Yield, No entry, No parking, One way, Street, Speed limit, HOV, Airport, Bus stop, Freeway exit, Train station, Information, Construction, Pedestrian crossing, School zone, Railroad crossing, Truck, Car, Rest area, Sanitation dump, Parking

TABLE A-2   Visio 2000 Standard Edition Stencils and Shapes *(continued)*

Name	Shapes
US Canada and Mexico.vss	Alabama, Alaska, Arizona, Arkansas, California, Colorado, Connecticut, District of Columbia, Delaware, Florida, Georgia, Hawaii, Idaho, Illinois, Indiana, Iowa, Kansas, Kentucky, Louisiana, Montana, Maine, Massachusetts, Maryland, Michigan, Minnesota, Missouri, Mississippi, Nebraska, Nevada, New Hampshire, New Jersey, New Mexico, New York, North Carolina, North Dakota, Ohio, Oklahoma, Oregon, Pennsylvania, Rhode Island, South Carolina, South Dakota, Tennessee, Texas, Utah, Vermont, Virginia, Wisconsin, Wyoming, Washington, West Virginia, Alberta, British Columbia, Manitoba, New Brunswick, Newfoundland and Labrador, Northwest Territories, Nova Scotia, Ontario, Prince Edward Island, Quebec, Saskatchewan, Yukon Territory, Aguascalientes, Baja California Norte, Baja California Sur, Campeche, Chiapas, Chihuahua, Coahuila De Zaragoza, Colima, Distrito Federal, Durango, Guanajuato, Guerrero, Hidalgo, Jalisco, Mexico, Michoacan de Ocampo, Morelos, Nayarit, Nuevo Leon, Oaxaca, Puebla, Queretaro de Arteaga, Quintana Roo, San Luis Potosi, Sinaloa, Sonora, Tabasco, Tamaulipas, Tlaxcala, Veracruz-Llave, Yucatan, Zacatecas
Work Flow Diagram Shapes.vss	Accounting, Accounts payable, Accounts receivable, Bank, Board of directors, Copy center, Customer service, Distribution, Finance, Information systems, International division, International marketing, International sales, Inventory, Legal department, Mailroom 1, Mailroom 2, Management, Manufacturing, Marketing, Motorpool, Packaging, Payroll, Person 1, Person 2, Personnel / Staff, Publications, Purchasing, Quality Assurance, Receiving, Reception, Research & Development, Sales/PR, Shipping, Suppliers, Telecom, Treasurer, Warehouse
World.vss	World 1, World 2, Africa, Asia, Europe, Greenland.194, Middle-East, North America, South America, Antarctica, Antarctica - Mercator

TABLE A-2   Visio 2000 Standard Edition Stencils and Shapes *(continued)*

A

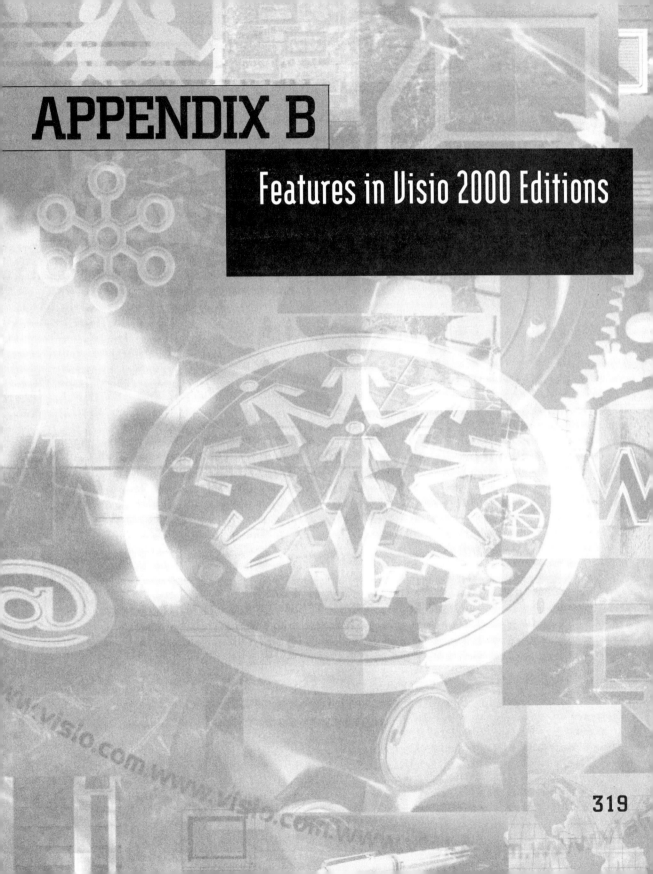

APPENDIX B

Features in Visio 2000 Editions

319

Appendix B will help you understand which of the four editions of Visio 2000 you need and give you ten reasons to upgrade to each one.

Visio 2000 Standard Edition

Visio 2000 Standard Edition takes the worldwide standard in business diagramming tools to the next level. Using Visio 2000's seamless Microsoft integration, you can drag and drop flowcharts, organization charts and other business diagrams into PowerPoint, Excel, and Word documents. You can add brilliant new backgrounds, borders, and color schemes, then leverage Visio 2000 Standard Edition's advanced Internet functionality to create, store, and exchange drawings via your corporate intranet or the Web.

Top Ten Reasons to Upgrade to Visio 2000 Standard Edition

1. The powerful new Visio 2000 engine, reengineered from the ground up, is faster, supports larger drawings, and is more scalable than ever before.

2. Richer Internet support allows you to instantly publish your business diagrams in a variety of Web-ready formats and embed hyperlinks to relevant external information.

3. The new dynamic grid saves you time by automatically aligning and evenly distributing shapes in your diagrams for you—making professional-looking layouts a snap.

4. New anchored windows elevate powerful features such as pan and zoom controls, custom properties data, and size and position details and place them at your fingertips.

5. The redesigned Organization Chart Wizard takes the frustration out of creating complex organization charts by instantly building them for you based on information that is stored in a database, or that you enter yourself.

6. A streamlined work environment includes page tabs for easy document navigation, consolidated toolbars, pop-up shape tips, automatic shape numbering, and real-time editing feedback.

7. Deeper Microsoft Office integration means Visio 2000 looks and works just like the desktop tools you use every day, while enhanced Microsoft PowerPoint compatibility lets you create more polished presentations in half the time.

8. Create stunning, full-color diagrams with ease using the new single-click color schemes, backgrounds, and borders.

9. Deployment and management of Visio technology is simplified thanks to support for Microsoft's new Windows Installer technology.

10. Personalize Visio 2000 just for you by assembling a toolbar of your frequently used tools, or create your own stencils with drag-and-drop ease.

Visio 2000 Professional Edition

Visio 2000 Professional Edition is the worldwide leader for fast and efficient IT diagrams.

Visio 2000 Professional Edition is the market leader in IT diagramming software, delivering acclaimed, industry-standard content and tools for rapidly producing network, database, and software diagrams. Professional Edition is designed for IT professionals who need fast, efficient solutions for:

- Designing high-level LAN/WAN network topologies and directory service hierarchies

- Visualizing proposed and existing database structures

- Documenting software projects with UML diagrams

- Creating instant diagrams of Web sites

With Professional Edition, users can easily create detailed IT diagrams and integrate them into documents, presentations, e-mail messages, and Web pages—making it ideal for anyone who needs to plan, manage, and document information systems.

Visio 2000 Professional Edition is designed for:

- Network/LAN/WAN managers

- Network engineers

- Database developers

B

- Software developers
- Webmasters
- IT project managers
- System integrators
- VARs and consultants
- Business analysts

Top Ten Reasons to Upgrade to Visio 2000 Professional Edition

1. New network-specific custom property fields let you define, store, and report on thousands of attributes for each network equipment shape.

2. New directory services diagramming tools help you visualize the structures of the leading network directory services.

3. Enhanced tools for database reverse engineering provide more detailed documentation of existing databases from leading vendors.

4. UML reverse engineering capabilities help you visualize class structures of code from all Visual Studio languages.

5. Advanced data flow diagramming solution lets you easily define process details through decomposition.

6. Improved Web site mapping tools discover a greater number of links for more complete Web site documentation.

7. Support for larger diagrams lets you document IT systems with thousands of nodes, tables, or classes.

8. Integration with Microsoft Office 2000 and Windows 2000 improves administration and lowers total cost of ownership.

9. Dynamic Web publishing tools let you produce high-fidelity graphics that users can pan and zoom using Microsoft Internet Explorer 5.0.

10. Streamlined work environment reduces screen clutter and lets you personalize your workspace.

Key New Product Features in Visio 2000 Professional Edition

This section describes some of the key features of Visio 2000 Professional Edition.

Latest Network Shapes with More Custom Property Fields

Users can keep their network diagrams completely up-to-date by working with new network shapes that represent the latest networking technologies, including network equipment and directory services structures. New network-specific custom property fields enable users to define, store, and report on thousands of attributes for each network equipment shape.

New Directory Services Diagramming

New directory services tools provide a graphical, hierarchical approach to diagramming and communicating the structure of the leading network directory services, including Microsoft Active Directory, Novell Directory Services, and LDAP-based vendors.

More Detailed Database Information

Now users can reverse-engineer databases from IBM, Informix, Microsoft, Oracle, and others to code-level detail, displaying views and checking clauses, triggers, and stored procedures. With this new functionality, users can quickly gain a more complete understanding of their existing database structures and produce more detailed documentation of it.

B

Expanded UML Software Design

The enhanced Unified Modeling Language (UML) solution supports all UML 1.2 diagram types and allows users to reverse-engineer Microsoft Visual Basic, Visual C++, and Java code to view the class structures in existing applications. Users can also exchange software models with other applications through the Microsoft Repository.

Advanced Data Flow Diagramming

The new advanced data flow diagramming solution provides automated support for defining process details. The Model Navigator enables users to reuse diagram components, while error-checking lets them verify semantic correctness.

Improved Web Site Mapping

Users can now discover and map Web sites in greater detail, including support for Java, ASP, and HTML tags. Users can quickly identify broken links. They can also take advantage of improved layout options, such as collapsible branches, to enable more customizable Web-site mapping and conceptual Web design.

Support for Larger Diagrams

The redesigned Visio 2000 platform supports thousands of shapes per page, including diagrams of large IT systems with thousands of nodes (networks), tables (databases), or classes (software designs). Users can zoom in and out or pan around larger diagrams more easily using the new Pan & Zoom window. Or they can browse the contents of any diagram in the Drawing Explorer window. For more details, see the "Streamlined Work Environment" next.

Streamlined Work Environment

Professional Edition provides numerous enhancements to help users work more efficiently, including four new auto-hide windows that put key functionality at users' fingertips:

- The Custom Properties window displays the data stored in selected shapes, such as part numbers, asset tags, and more. With this window, users can view, access, and edit the data more directly than before. They can also add new custom data types more easily.

- The Drawing Explorer window, similar to Windows Explorer, lists the contents of a diagram in a tree that can be browsed.

- The Pan & Zoom window provides a bird's-eye view of a diagram, no matter how much a user has zoomed in on the page. Users can access this window to quickly navigate diagrams of any size.

- The Size & Position window makes it easy to resize, reposition, or rotate a selected object.

Users can set the auto-hide windows to stay open as they work, or to pop up as needed whenever the user moves the cursor over a window's edge (thus reducing onscreen clutter).

In addition, users can customize toolbars to suit their needs, navigate multipage drawings by clicking on page tabs (like those in Microsoft Excel), and more.

Dynamic Web Publishing

Users can publish and share diagrams more easily on any intranet or Internet site. This built-in support for Web publishing now includes:

- Robust support for VML (Vector Markup Language), an emerging standard for exchanging, editing, and delivering drawings on the Internet (also supported by Microsoft Word 2000 and other Office 2000 programs). Users can pan, zoom, and navigate through multiple-page drawings in the Microsoft Internet Explorer browser with no additional software. VML-based graphics also download more quickly and provide higher fidelity than conventional raster-based Web graphics.

- Support for multiple embedded hyperlinks for any SmartShapes symbol. Users can now link a shape to multiple pages on the Web, to specific shapes or locations within a Visio diagram, or to external documents, such as Microsoft Word or Excel documents.

Reduction in Total Cost of Ownership

Visio 2000 Professional Edition is designed for easy, cost-effective deployment across large enterprises. It is:

- Delivered with the latest Microsoft Installer technology, supporting network installation, desktop profiles, automatic recovery, and installation on demand.

- Completely compatible with existing Visio drawings and applications, so users can maintain their investment in legacy drawings and tools.

- Compatible with Microsoft Office 2000, as well as with Office 97/98, Windows 95/98, and Windows NT 4.0.

- Integrated seamlessly with Microsoft BackOffice applications, delivering intelligent drawings that can link dynamically to corporate data.

- Year 2000-compliant and Euro currency-ready.

- Available through volume licensing at a lower cost per seat.

- Easy to learn and use—IT professionals can begin planning an IT project or documenting existing systems with little or no training.

Visio 2000 Enterprise Edition

Visio 2000 Enterprise Edition is the complete solution for automated IT design and documentation.

Visio 2000 Enterprise Edition is for information technology (IT) specialists who design, develop, document, and maintain networks, databases, and software applications. Using the in-depth, integrated solutions in Enterprise Edition, IT specialists can create conceptual, logical, and physical views of their information systems. In particular, they can:

- Produce detailed network documentation using AutoDiscovery technology, more than 18,000 vendor-specific Visio Network Equipment device shapes, and more than 20 network reports.

- Import schema from the leading directory services vendors to graphically represent and understand existing directory structures.

- Design, generate, and modify database schema via native drivers.

- Document and generate software code using the Unified Modeling Language (UML).

Enterprise Edition offers broad compatibility with other IT tools, so users can leverage existing files. For example, Enterprise Edition enables users to design and document directory services from Microsoft, Novell, and LDAP-based vendors; exchange database and software schema through Microsoft Repository; forward engineer code to and reverse-engineer it from Microsoft Visual Studio; and design and document database systems from IBM, Informix, Microsoft, Oracle, and others. In addition, users can integrate Enterprise Edition diagrams into Microsoft Office documents and presentations, e-mail messages, and Web pages for clear communication across an organization. Enterprise Edition delivers a powerful, all-in-one IT design and documentation solution that is cost-effective for any organization.

Visio 2000 Enterprise Edition is designed for:

- Network/LAN/WAN managers

- Network analysts

- Systems analysts

- VARs and consultants

- Database developers

- Software developers

- System integrators

Top Ten Reasons to Upgrade to Visio 2000 Enterprise Edition

1. Expanded network AutoDiscovery technology supports layer 2 and frame relay for more extensive network documentation.

2. More than 20 customizable reports help you create robust network documentation in presentation-quality format.

3. Enhanced importing features for directory services provide a customizable view of the hierarchy of existing directory services structures.

4. Collaborative database design tools facilitate the merging of individual database diagrams into a single model.

5. UML code generation to Microsoft Visual Basic, Visual C++, and Java helps you jump-start your development project.

6. Business rules-based database design solution facilitates collaboration with end users through support for natural-language business rules.

7. Support for larger diagrams lets you document IT systems with thousands of nodes, tables, or classes.

8. Integration with Microsoft Office 2000 and Windows 2000 improves administration and lowers total cost of ownership.

B

9. Dynamic Web publishing tools let you produce high-fidelity graphics that users can pan and zoom using Microsoft Internet Explorer 5.0.

10. Streamlined work environment reduces screen clutter and lets you personalize your workspace.

Key New Product Features in Visio 2000 Enterprise Edition

This section describes some of the key features of Visio 2000 Enterprise Edition.

Expanded Network AutoDiscovery Technology

Enterprise Edition provides enhanced network AutoDiscovery technology with new support for layer 3 (IP network) and frame relay network environments. New auto-layout technology makes it simple for users to generate network diagrams from the discovered devices. Plus, users can create a variety of reports about their network discoveries.

New Visio Network Equipment Shapes and Network Reports

Enterprise Edition now includes more than 18,000 manufacturer-specific network shapes, including more than 4,000 new shapes, so users can keep their network documentation completely up to date. What's more, users can automatically create robust, presentation-quality network documentation using more than 20 network reports.

Enhanced Directory Services Diagramming and Import

Users can import existing directory structures from Microsoft Active Directory, Novell Directory Services, and LDAP-based vendors to graphically represent and understand those structures. With the new import filter, users can specify which objects to import. The new Directory Navigator provides a high-level view of the directory structures, while offering greater control over the layout of diagrams.

Collaborative Database Design

Now database designers can produce collaborative database designs with team members working on individual database models and then merging them into a single project model. The database design team can make further refinements to the project model and migrate those changes back to the source models. Individual source models can be used in multiple database projects.

UML Code Generation and Reporting

With the enhanced UML solution in Enterprise Edition, users can generate Microsoft Visual Basic, Visual C++, and Java code headers from UML class diagrams to jumpstart development projects. In addition, users can reverse-engineer existing Microsoft Visual Studio code into UML 1.2 models. They can also produce detailed reports for static structure, deployment, and activity diagrams.

Business Rules-Based Database Design

Enterprise Edition provides integrated support for Object Role Modeling (ORM), which allows users to enter business rules in natural language and then automatically generate entity-relationship database models, DBMS-specific database schema, and data dictionary reports. This conceptual database design approach facilitates collaboration among a wider variety of contributors.

Support for Larger Diagrams

The redesigned Visio 2000 platform supports thousands of shapes per page, including diagrams of large IT systems with thousands of nodes (networks), tables (databases), or classes (software designs). Users can zoom in and out or pan around larger diagrams more quickly using the new Pan & Zoom window. Or they can browse the contents of any diagram in the Drawing Explorer window. For more details, see "Streamlined Work Environment" next.

Streamlined Work Environment

Enterprise Edition provides numerous enhancements to help users work more efficiently, including four new auto-hide windows that put key functionality at users' fingertips:

- The Custom Properties window displays the data stored in selected shapes, such as part numbers, asset tags, and more. With this window, users can view, access, and edit the data more directly than before. They can also add custom data types more easily.

- The Drawing Explorer window, similar to Windows Explorer, lists the contents of a diagram in a tree that can be browsed.

- The Pan & Zoom window provides a bird's-eye view of a diagram, no matter how much a user has zoomed in on the page. Users can access this window to quickly navigate diagrams of any size.

- The Size & Position window makes it easy to resize, reposition, or rotate a selected object.

Users can set the auto-hide windows to stay open as they work, or to pop up as needed whenever the user moves the cursor over a window's edge (thus reducing on-screen clutter).

In addition, users can customize toolbars to suit their needs, navigate multipage drawings by clicking on page tabs (like those in Microsoft Excel), and more.

Dynamic Web Publishing

Users can publish and share diagrams more easily on any intranet or Internet site. This built-in support for Web publishing now includes:

- Robust support for VML (Vector Markup Language), an emerging standard for exchanging, editing, and delivering drawings on the Internet (also supported by Microsoft Word 2000 and other Office 2000 programs). Users can pan, zoom, and navigate through multiple-page drawings in the Microsoft Internet Explorer browser with no additional software. VML-based graphics also download more quickly than conventional raster-based Web graphics.

- Support for multiple embedded hyperlinks for any SmartShapes symbol. Users can now link a shape to multiple pages on the Web, to specific shapes or locations within a Visio diagram, or to external documents, such as Microsoft Word or Excel documents.

Reduction in Total Cost of Ownership

Visio 2000 Enterprise Edition is designed for easy, cost-effective deployment across large enterprises. It is:

- Delivered with the latest Microsoft Installer technology, supporting network installation, desktop profiles, automatic recovery, and installation on demand.

- Completely compatible with existing Visio drawings and applications, so users can maintain their investment in legacy drawings and tools.

- Compatible with Microsoft Office 2000, as well as with Office 97/98, Windows 95/98, and Windows NT 4.0.

- Integrated seamlessly with Microsoft BackOffice applications, delivering intelligent drawings that can link dynamically to corporate data.

- Year 2000-compliant and Euro currency–ready.

- Available through volume licensing at a lower cost per seat.

- Easy to learn and use—IT professionals can begin planning an IT project or documenting existing systems with little or no training.

Visio 2000 Technical Edition

Visio 2000 Technical Edition is the leading tool for creating precise 2-D technical diagrams and drawings. Unlike CAD, it's fast and easy to use—just assemble drawings intuitively using more than 4,000 intelligent, industry-specific SmartShapes symbols. Technical Edition delivers powerful drawing solutions for process engineering, facilities management, AEC, electrical engineering, and more.

For years, engineers have had to rely on drafting experts to transform their design ideas into finished drawings. Now more than half a million engineers are proving that they don't need to be CAD experts to produce professional technical drawings. Instead, they're working with Visio 2000 Technical Edition—the fastest, most efficient tool for technical drawing and diagramming.

The key is Technical Edition's SmartShapes technology—more than 4,000 intelligent shapes designed to behave like walls, pipes, valves, pumps, and other real-world objects. With little or no training, engineers can assemble drawings by dragging and dropping these industry-standard shapes onto a page. They can even store data in shapes, or link them to databases or spreadsheets, and automatically generate detailed reports.

Even non-CAD users need to work with CAD drawings. That's why Technical Edition reads and writes DWG files from Autodesk AutoCAD (v2.5–R14 and AutoCAD 2000) and IntelliCAD, as well as Bentley Systems MicroStation (DGN) files. If a user inserts DWG drawings as backgrounds, Visio shapes snap automatically to the underlying geometry—for example, a door or window shape will rotate and snap to a wall.

Technical Edition delivers a wide range of industry-specific drawing solutions: engineers can create HVAC or fire and security diagrams; develop circuit layouts

B

and wiring diagrams; produce P&IDs, PFDs, and datasheets; and plan office layouts and manage assets. Technical Edition is also fully customizable using standard programming tools such as built-in Microsoft Visual Basic for Applications 6.0.

Visio 2000 Technical Edition is faster than CAD for anyone who needs to:

■ Create and share 2-D technical drawings and diagrams, including HVAC designs, electrical schematics, process plant layouts, and other 2-D diagrams that incorporate large numbers of predefined, connected symbols.

■ Work with Autodesk AutoCAD drawing files, including viewing, redlining, and annotating them; assembling SmartShapes symbols on top of inserted DWG backgrounds; or incorporating DWG drawings into technical documentation, presentations, and proposals.

Visio 2000 Technical Edition is invaluable for:

■ Facilities Management

■ Process Plant Design

■ Industrial and Building Controls

■ Electrical Engineering

■ Manufacturing and Assembly

Top Ten Reasons to Upgrade to Visio 2000 Technical Edition

1. **Faster navigation of larger drawings**   Move around and zoom in and out of large drawings with extraordinary speed using the new Pan & Zoom window. Maintain bird's-eye views of your drawing no matter how closely zoomed in you are.

2. **Support for CAD drawings**   Import and export DWG files from Autodesk AutoCAD (v2.5-R14 and AutoCAD 2000) and IntelliCAD, as well as Bentley Systems MicroStation (DGN) files. Snap shapes automatically to the underlying geometry in background DWG drawings.

3. **Streamlined work environment**   Work more efficiently with consolidated toolbars, page tabs for easy navigation in multipage drawings, pop-up shape

tips that help you browse and select shapes more quickly, automatic shape numbering, and real-time editing feedback. Even customize toolbars for a workspace that suits your requirements.

4. **Auto-alignment of shapes** Position shapes instantly with smart new snapping and aligning features. For example, when you drop HVAC shapes or electrical outlets on a background DWG file, they automatically rotate and snap into place.

5. **New auto-hide windows** Keep powerful tools at your fingertips with the new auto-hide windows: Quickly add or edit custom data for selected shapes; size, position, and rotate shapes; browse a drawing's contents; and more. Best of all, these windows appear when you want them and tuck out of the way when you need space on your screen.

6. **Powerful industry-specific technical solutions** Create HVAC or fire and security diagrams. Produce P&IDs, PFDs and datasheets. Plan office layouts and manage assets. And that's just the start when you're working with the broad range of industry-specific drawing solutions in Visio 2000 Technical Edition.

7. **Instant space plans** Move from a rough space plan to a fully dimensioned floor plan in a few quick steps. Drag door and window shapes onto walls and watch them automatically rotate and snap into place. When you adjust the placement of individual walls, doors, and windows, dimension lines move with them. Even calculate the square footage of your floor plan instantly with the auto-sizing space shape.

8. **Precision drawing tools** Draw shapes with pinpoint accuracy using shape extension lines. Snap to geometric points, such as endpoints, tangents, and intersections for precise results. Position and align shapes more quickly and accurately than ever with new dynamic grid and the Size and Position window.

9. **Enhanced Internet support** Publish and share drawings easily on any intranet or Internet site. Add multiple hyperlinks to any object to connect drawings to relevant information. Save drawings as HTML pages in GIF, JPEG, PNG, or VML graphics format.

10. **Customizable drawing platform** Create custom drawing solutions using Microsoft Visual Basic for Applications 6.0, Visual Basic, C, or C++.

B

Key Product Features in Visio 2000 Technical Edition

This section describes some of the key features of Visio 2000 Technical Edition.

Faster Navigation of Large Drawings

With Visio 2000 Technical Edition, users can work significantly faster with larger drawings. They can:

- Build 2-D technical drawings that contain thousands of shapes.

- Zoom in and out of large drawings or pan around them with lightning speed using the new Pan & Zoom window.

- Easily navigate between pages using new tabbed pages (similar to the ones in Microsoft Excel).

In addition, they can perform many common technical drawing tasks in fewer steps for enhanced productivity.

Streamlined Work Environment

Technical Edition puts key functionality at users' fingertips with four new auto-hide windows:

- The Custom Properties window displays data stored in selected shapes, such as part numbers, asset tags, and more. With this window, users can view, access, and edit the data associated with selected shapes more directly. They can also add new data types more easily.

- The Size & Position window makes it easy to resize, reposition, or rotate a selected object with numerical precision.

- The Drawing Explorer window, similar to Windows Explorer, displays the contents of a technical drawing in a tree that can be browsed.

- The Pan & Zoom window provides a bird's-eye view of a drawing, no matter what the actual zoom level of the drawing page is. The user can then use this window to zoom in and out or move around the drawing with extraordinary speed.

Users can set the auto-hide windows to stay open onscreen, or to pop up as needed when the cursor is placed over a window's edge.

Enhanced DWG and DGN Compatibility

Technical Edition delivers superb CAD compatibility for users who need to work with DWG and DGN drawings:

- Technical Edition reads and writes Autodesk AutoCAD files (v2.5–R14 and AutoCAD 2000). It also reads and writes Bentley System Microstation DGN files.

- It includes a revised DWG converter, which will help users insert or convert DWG and DGN files more easily. Users can explicitly set the drawing scale for an inserted or converted drawing—and even set it separately from the Technical Edition page.

- When users insert DWG files as backgrounds, shapes will automatically snap to the underlying DWG geometry for faster and more accurate placement. For example, electrical outlets, HVAC ducts, and furniture shapes automatically rotate and snap into place.

- Users can pan and zoom drawings with background DWG and DGN files as quickly as they can move their mouse.

Precision Drawing Tools

Technical Edition delivers new drawing tools for creating precise designs and custom shapes. Users can:

- Draw shapes with exacting precision using the new shape extension lines, which provide visual feedback about shape angles, tangents, and other useful geometric relationships.

- Position and align shapes instantly with the dynamic grid, which provides visual cues onscreen and intelligent object snapping to automatically place shapes in an evenly distributed and aligned order.

- Snap to geometric points, such as endpoints, tangents, and intersections for more accurate designs.

- Use the new Size & Position auto-hide window (described earlier) to precisely position, rotate, and resize shapes.

B

Built-In Microsoft Visual Basic for Applications 6.0

Visio products have long enjoyed a reputation as a world-class platform for in-house and third-party developers who need to create vertical drawing solutions for corporations or markets. Now Visio 2000 is joining Microsoft Office 2000 as the first program on the market to provide built-in support for Microsoft Visual Basic for Applications 6.0—the latest version of this popular programming environment.

Expanded Internet Support

Once users develop 2-D technical drawings, they can publish and share them easily on any intranet or Internet site. This built-in support for publishing on the Web now includes:

- Advanced support for VML, the new standard for creating, storing, and exchanging drawings on the Internet (also supported by Microsoft Word 2000 and other Office 2000 programs). With VML support, users can pan, zoom, and navigate through multiple-page drawings in their Microsoft Internet Explorer browser with no additional software. VML-based graphics also download much more quickly than conventional raster-based Web graphics.

- Support for multiple embedded hyperlinks for any shape. Users can now link a shape to multiple places, including other pages, drawings, and Web sites—and even to specific shapes or locations. The links appear on the right-click menu. If a user links one shape to another shape in a different drawing, Technical Edition automatically opens that drawing and zooms to the appropriate level for the shape.

Enhanced Industry-Specific Technical Solutions

Visio Technical 5.0 Plus introduced a number of powerful industry-specific drawing solutions for facilities management, process engineering, and more. Technical Edition builds on this legacy with a number of enhancements that streamline and enrich these and other built-in drawing solutions:

- **Walls, doors, and windows**   Users can move from a rough concept for a space to a fully dimensioned floor plan in a few quick steps. They simply drag and drop space shapes onto the drawing page or sketch out areas freehand using any of the built-in drawing tools. Technical Edition automatically displays the square footage for each space shape. As users join overlapping areas together using the Union command, Technical Edition instantly recalculates the square footage for the unified space. After roughing out a space, users can choose the Convert to Walls command from the right-click menu to instantly build a fully dimensioned measured drawing. Technical Edition cleans up wall corners and adds guides and dimension lines. When users drop doors, windows, furniture, and other shapes on the finished floor plan, these items automatically orient themselves and snap to the walls. If users edit their measured drawings by dragging or rotating the guidelines, they can direct Technical Edition to recalculate the size and dimensions.

■ **Facilities management**   Users can now link to and work with the data from any SQL-compliant database for which they have 32-bit ODBC drivers, such as Oracle, SQL Server, dBase, and Access. In addition, the CAFM Explorer—first introduced in Visio Technical 5.0 Plus to help users track and manage complex facilities data—is now a dockable auto-hide window, so users can view the data and their facilities drawings at the same time.

■ **Process engineering**   Datasheets—detailed specification documents for process equipment—now appear in a dockable auto-hide window for easier viewing and access. Users can modify the data specifications for multiple shapes as easily as they can edit custom properties. Users can also print multiple datasheets at once. In addition, the new dynamic grid and grouping features help users work with process engineering drawings: users can position and align objects more quickly with the dynamic grid, and they can subselect and resize or reposition a group member without undoing a group.

■ **HVAC diagrams**   HVAC ductwork shapes automatically rotate, align, and snap to each other intelligently for faster creation of HVAC layouts.

■ **Office layouts**   Furniture shapes automatically rotate, align, and snap into place intelligently for faster layout (regardless of whether a DWG file is inserted as a background).

Dramatic Reduction in Total Cost of Ownership

Visio 2000 Technical Edition is designed for easy, cost-effective deployment across large enterprises. Technical Edition:

■ Includes the latest Microsoft Installer technology, which supports network installation, desktop profiles, automatic recovery, and installation on demand.

■ Is completely compatible with existing Visio drawings and applications, so users can maintain their investment in legacy drawings and tools.

■ Is compatible with Office 2000 and Windows 2000, as well as with Office 97/98, Windows 95/98, and Windows NT 4.0.

■ Integrates seamlessly with Microsoft BackOffice applications, delivering intelligent drawings that can link dynamically to corporate data.

■ Is Y2K and Euro currency-ready.

■ Is available through volume licensing at a low cost per seat, making it easy to deploy throughout the organization.

■ Is exceptionally easy to learn and use: users can start assembling drawings with little or no training.

APPENDIX C

Resources

This appendix contains a selection of online and printed resources, including Web sites, addresses, and periodicals.

Visio Address and Phone Number

Corporate Headquarters
Visio Corporation
2211 Elliott Avenue
Seattle, WA 98121-1691

Customer Service
800-24-VISIO (800-248-4746)
Fax: 425-895-8496

Printed Resources

- The main printed resource for Visio 2000 is the *SmartPages* magazine. Subscriptions are free and delivery is print (quarterly) and online (monthly).

- Subscribe to *Visio SmartPages* via the Web at www.visio.com/smartpages.

- Get more information or submit articles, drawing samples, comments, and suggestions to *Visio SmartPages*; e-mail smartpages@visio.com.

- Or mail in subscription information to:

    Visio SmartPages
    Visio Corporation
    2211 Elliott Avenue
    Seattle, WA 98121-1691
    USA

Online Resources

- Resource information for Visio Corporation can be reached at: http://www.visio.com.

- Visio Training can be reached at: http://www.visio.com/support/training/index.html.

- To be matched up with a Visio Corporate Sales Executive, go to www.visio.com/sales and follow the links to your region, or call 800.VISIO.07 (800-847-4607) to talk directly with Visio Corporate Sales.

- To contact Visio Consulting Services for a project or question, go to www.visio.com/vdn/consulting.html, or call 800-24-VISIO (800-248-4746) and ask for information about Visio Consulting Services.

- For developer-level information relating to Microsoft and Visio products, go to www.visio.com/vdn.

- To find international Visio offices, go to www.visio.com/company/offices/.

- To check out a Visio product or developer forum, go to www.visio.com/support/forums/index.html.

Developer Resources

- An online version of the book *Developing Visio Solutions* is available at: http://www.visio.com/vdn/default.asp?content=dvs.asp.

- A diagram of the Visio Object Model is available at: http://www.visio.com/vdn/default.asp?content=ch11.asp.

- The latest articles and white papers are available at: http://www.visio.com/vdn/default.asp?content=allarticles.asp.

- Solutions Patterns are available at: http://www.visio.com/vdn/default.asp?content=patterns.asp. Patterns communicates knowledge gained by experts about how to solve common problems encountered while implementing Visio solutions.

- Links to the Visio Knowledge Base are available at: http://www.visio.com/tskb/index.html. You can search for all the articles available on a given subject from a topic list provided.

- Online Developer Training modules (two hours) on ShapeSheet Environment Development and ActiveX Automation are available at: http://www.visio.com/vdn/default.asp?content=audiovideo.asp.

C

- Sample code and applications are available at:
  http://www.visio.com/vdn/default.asp?content=devtrain.asp. You can
  download samples to help you create custom solutions.

- Visio Consulting Services are available at:
  http://www.visio.com/vdn/default.asp?content=ConsultingServices.asp for
  those who need help developing a custom Visio solution.

- Sample code and application are available at:
  http://www.visio.com/support/downloads.

- The Visio Developer's Forum is available at:
  http://www.visio.com/support/forums. This is for Visio developers to share
  their experiences with other developers. Visio staff occasionally
  participates, but the primary participants are developers.

- Visio Developer Support is available at:
  http://www.visio.com/support/contact/uscan.html.

- Visio offers one-to-one support with a Visio developer support engineer.
  You can purchase a support contract from customer service at
  800-248-4746.

HTML Resources

- http://www.ncsa.uiuc.edu/Indices/Resources/html-resources.html.
  National Center for Supercomputing Applications page for HTML
  Resources. A great site for those new to HTML.

- http://www.w3.org/MarkUp/. The World Wide Web consortium home
  page for HTML. You can find links to specifications, pointers, tutorials,
  bulletin boards, mailing lists, and more at this site.

Index

M

When you think of communicating visually...
Do you feel like a stranger

in a **strange** land?

www.visio.com/smartpages

You don't have to! You already have the guide to all things officially Visio. Now it's time for a look behind the scenes, with Visio SmartPages. Find out who uses Visio software. Browse the tips, tricks, and shortcuts the experts and our readers have uncovered the hard way. Learn what Visio Corp. is planning for the future. And here's the best part: it's absolutely free, online or in print. Simply fill out the online form at **www.visio.com/smartpages** to be placed on our mailing list.